AF540494

SOCIO-ECONOMIC PROFILE OF RURAL INDIA (SERIES II)

Volume Two
NORTH-EAST INDIA

ABOUT THE CENTRE FOR RURAL STUDIES

The Centre for Rural Studies (formerly Land Reforms Unit) of the Lal Bahadur Shastri National Academy of Administration was set up in the year 1989 by the Ministry of Rural Development, Government of India, with a multifaceted agenda that included among others, the concurrent evaluation of the ever-unfolding ground realities pertaining to the implementation of the Land Reforms and Poverty Alleviation Programmes in India. Sensitizing the officer trainees of the Indian Administrative Service in the process of evaluating of land reforms and poverty alleviation programmes by exposing them to the ground realities; setting up a forum for regular exchange of views on land reforms and poverty alleviation between academicians, administrators, activists and concerned citizens and creating awareness amongst the public about the various programmes initiated by the Government of India through non-governmental organisations are also important objectives of the Centre for Rural Studies. A large number of books, reports related to land reforms, poverty alleviation programmes, rural socio-economic problems etc. published both externally and internally bear testimony to the excellent research quality of the Centre.

About the Editors

S.C. Patra is presently Professor, Water Resources Engineering in North Eastern Regional Institute of Water and Land Management, Tezpur. He is associated in conducting training programmes and undertaking various studies in rural areas of North Eastern India. Prof. S.C. Patra is one of the editors of two books (i) *Characterization of Land Resources and Agro-eco-Zone in India* and (ii) *Renewable Energy and Energy Management.* Many papers are contributed by Prof. Patra in journals and seminar proceedings.

Ashish Vachhani, Deputy Director, Lal Bahadur Shastri National Academy of Administration, Mussoorie. (IAS: 1997, Tamil Nadu).

He completed M.Phil (International Organizations), School of International Studies, Jawaharlal Nehru University, New Delhi, before joining the Indian Administrative Service. He joined as Sub-Collector, Sivakasi, Virudhunagar District, in 1999 before moving over to the Finance Department in Government of Tamil Nadu as Under Secretary/Deputy Secretary (Budget)/Joint Secretary. While in Finance Department as the State Budget Officer, he was responsible for preparing the Annual Budget of the State Government, piloting it through the Legislature for approval and overseeing its implementation. He was closely associated with revenue collection, Plan formulation, scheme expenditure, preparation and posing of development projects for external funding from multilateral institutions etc. He has worked as District Collector of Dharmapuri District and Tiruchirappalli District. He joined the Academy in March 2008 and has keen interest in riding and hiking.

SOCIO-ECONOMIC PROFILE OF RURAL INDIA (SERIES II)

VOLUME TWO

NORTH-EAST INDIA

(Assam, Nagaland, Manipur and Tripura)

Edited by

S.C. PATRA

ASHISH VACHHANI, I.A.S.

Published for

Centre for Rural Studies

L.B.S. National Academy of Administration, Mussoorie

By

CONCEPT PUBLISHING COMPANY PVT. LTD.

NEW DELHI-110059

ISBN-13: 978-81-8069-721-0 (Series)
ISBN-13: 978-81-8069-724-1 (Vol. 2)

First Published 2012

Published and Printed by

Concept Publishing Company Pvt. Ltd.
Regd. Office:
A/15-16, Commercial Block, Mohan Garden
New Delhi-110059 (India)
Phones : 25351460, 25351794, *Fax* : 091-11-25357109
Email : publishing@conceptpub.com,
Website: www.conceptpub.com

Editorial Office:
H-13, Bali Nagar, New Delhi-110 015, India.

Cataloging in Publication Data--Courtesy: D.K. Agencies (P) Ltd. <docinfo@dkagencies.com>

Socio-economic profile of rural India (series II).
v. 2 cm.
Contributed articles.
Includes bibliographical references and index.

Contents: v. 2. North-East India (Assam, Nagaland, Manipur and Tripura) / editedby S.C. Patra, Ashis Vachhani.
ISBN 9788180697210 (set)
ISBN 9788180697241 (v. 2)

1. India--Rural conditions. 2. India--Economic conditions. I. Lal Bahadur Shastri National Academy of Administration. Centre for Rural Studies.

DDC 307.720954 22

Lal Bahadur Shastri
National Academy of Administration
Mussoorie - 248179 (Uttarakhand) INDIA

Padamvir Singh, IAS
Director & Chairman
Centre for Rural Studies

Foreword

Inclusive growth is a well accepted policy of the Government of India. Since independence, the nation has witnessed multifaceted development with the annual growth rate rising in the last decade. However, persistence of abject poverty, unemployment, lack of basic amenities in many rural areas, even in the face of increasing rate of growth, remains a cause of concern. The recent efforts of the Ministry of Panchayati Raj to focus on the backward districts of the country is a welcome step. The Mahatma Gandhi National Rural Employment Guarantee Act (MGNREGA), Bharat Nirman and Right to Information Act (RTI) are strong initiatives taken by the Government of India to accelerate development and empower people in rural areas. It is generally felt that the impact of Rural Development initiatives is not balanced and falls short of expectations in many parts of the country, especially in the North-East.

This book is the second volume of the series "Socio-Economic Profile of Rural India (Series II): North-East India". It is mainly based on the village study assignments of the IAS Officer Trainees carried out during their district training. This book covers the states of Assam, Nagaland, Manipur and Tripura.

I hope this book will provide useful insights into the socio-economic scenario in rural areas of the North-Eastern region of the country.

Padamvir Singh, IAS, Director,
LBS National Academy of Administration, Mussoorie

Tel. : (0135) 2632727 (O)
EPABX : (0135) 26332374, 2632489, 2632405, 2632236, 2632367 Fax: (0135) 2632350, 2632720
Website : www.lbsnaa.ernet.in

Socio-Economic Profile of Rural India (Series - I)

Vol. I : SOUTH INDIA
(Andhra Pradesh, Karnataka, Kerala, Tamil Nadu)
Edited by **V.K. Agnihotri** IAS

Vol. II : NORTH-EAST INDIA
(Assam, Manipur, Tripura, Nagaland)
Edited by **C. Ashokvardhan** IAS

Vol. III : NORTH-CENTRAL & WESTERN INDIA
(Himachal Pradesh, Punjab, Haryana, Gujarat, Maharashtra) *Edited by* **Rajendra Vora**

Vol. IV : EASTERN INDIA
(Bihar, West Bengal, Orissa and Uttar Pradesh)
Edited by **C. Ashokvardhan** IAS

Socio-Economic Profile of Rural India (Series - II)

Vol. I : SOUTH INDIA
(Andhra Pradesh, Karnataka, Kerala, Tamil Nadu)

Vol. II : NORTH-EAST INDIA
(Assam, Manipur, Tripura, Nagaland)
Edited by **S.C. Patra** & **Ashish Vachhani** IAS

Vol. III : WESTERN INDIA
(Gujarat, Maharashtra, Rajasthan)

Vol. IV : EASTERN INDIA
(Orissa, Jharkhand, West Bengal, Bihar and Uttar Pradesh)
Edited by **C. Ashokvardhan,** IAS &
Ashish Vachhani IAS

Vol. V : NORTH & CENTRAL INDIA
(Punjab, Haryana, Himachal Pradesh and Madhya Pradesh)
Edited by **Raj Mohini Sethi**

Preface

LBS National Academy of Administration, Mussoorie has entrusted me the responsibility of editing the Book, *Socio-Economic Profile of Rural India, Vol. II North Eastern Region.* This volume will give a general idea about the North Eastern Region which is connected to the main land of the county through the Siliguri corridor of West Bengal called as chicken neck by some people. Four states, namely *Assam, Manipur, Nagaland and Tripura* are covered in this volume with some important facts related to socio-economic profile and village level data collected by IAS probationers during village assignments and their interpretations.

The economy and environment in rural areas of many parts of the region are still influenced by shifting cultivation, a primitive practice of slash and burn system adopted for cultivation of agricultural crops. This system of forest and agriculture management and earning livelihoods is having its own impact on the traditions, cultures, land tenure system, community living, conflict management and socio-economic scenario. The 1950 earthquake that affected mainly Assam inflicting much damage, floods almost recurrent as an annual phenomenon, mountainous and hilly terrain, lack of infrastructure have come on the way of bringing the states of the North Eastern Region at par with other states of India.

The North Eastern Region (NER) of India comprises of eight states, namely *Arunachal Pradesh, Assam, Manipur, Meghalaya, Mizoram, Nagaland, Sikkim and Tripura.* There is a body unique to the region called North Eastern Council created by an Act in the Parliament in 1971 which looks after planning and development of the region. By an amendment to this Act in 2002, *Sikkim* was included under the purview of North Eastern Council thereby making the NER states as eight which was previously seven and was called as seven sister states by some people.

The states of North Eastern Region are geo-politically significant as it has large international borders with *Bhutan, China, Myanmar* and *Bangladesh.* The demography of many of these states have witnessed change due to partition of India and consequent influx of refugees. The economy of states were influenced after Independence due to hindrance of trading in the trade routes and trading points near the border.

The introduction part of the book contains an overview on the entire region. Economic development indicator of the four states focused in the book are furnished and salient details about *Manipur* and *Tripura* are covered. Sector specific discussions aimed at developments and certain national policies has been provided.

The portion of the book on *Assam* has touched upon history, economic profile, geographical information, demography, language, climate, art and handicrafts, administrative setup, educational infrastructure, *Panchayti Raj* system, rural development schemes, results of socio-economic studies conducted in 18 villages covering 8 districts and a SWOT analysis.

Demography, salient information at a glance, decadal growth, workforce, tribes and festivals, history, political process, progress made during 40 years (1962-63 to 2002-03) of statehood, land use pattern, status of agriculture, industrial development, mineral wealth, infrastructure development, transportation, power, water supply, health, education are briefly covered in the portion on *Nagaland.* Compilation of socio-economic status papers of 5 villages, prepared by IAS officer trainees covering 3 districts of the states are covered in this portion.

The portion on *Manipur* and *Tripura* include summary of socio-economic village assignment reports of 8 villages covering 5 districts of *Manipur* prepared by IAS Probationers. Also a compilation on socio-economic village assignment reports of 12 villages prepared by IAS Probationers covering 3 districts of *Tripura* are incorporated in this portion.

The IAS Probationers as part of their training are attached to districts. An officer trainee as part of the district training undertakes socio-economic survey/study to understand more about the people, their socio-economic conditions, psychology of farmers and learn about the village as a unit. It also helps the trainee to get examined, evaluate or assess the developmental schemes as they are undertaken at the grassroots level and the government people interaction at the lowest level. Understanding of the prevalent social-dynamics of the area automatically takes place through the process of the study.

Parts of the book on *Assam* and *Nagaland* has narrative reports on village studies covering village profile, compiled data on household survey, village infrastructure, basic amenities, types of houses in the village, status of electrification, customs and festivals, health facilities, educational scenario, land and agriculture, occupational pattern and income, non-farm activities, local governance structure and poverty alleviation programmes. The compilation of village assignment reports are divided with contents on Demography, Land, Irrigation, Agriculture and Allied Activities, Rural Industries and poverty alleviation programmes in the *Manipur* and *Tripura* part.

The editors wish to put on record their appreciation and thanks to Sri Padamvir Singh, IAS, Director, LBS National Academy of Administration, Mussoorie to complete the book in the present form and getting it published. The book is content rich and informative because of secondary and primary data as well as state-district profiles and grassroots level compilations of village specific studies. The book will provide an insight to the readers about the North Eastern Region which is tribal dominated, backward and details of which are less known throughout India.

S. C. Patra
Ashish Vachhani

Contents

List of Tables

List of Contributors

Prof. S.C. Patra, Ph.D, Professor, Water Resources Engineering, North Eastern Regional Institute of Water and Land Management, Tezpur, Assam.

Dr. C. Ashokvardhan, ***IAS,*** Principal Secretary, Departmentt of Revenue & Land Reforms, Government of Bihar, Main Secretariat, Patna.

Ashish Vachhani, ***IAS,*** Deputy Director and Coordinator, Centre for Rural Studies, Lal Bahadur Shastri National Academy of Administration, Mussoorie, Uttarakhand.

Jai Singh Shekhawat State Programme Manager, National Rural Health Mission, Department of Medical, Health and Family Welfare, Government of Rajasthan

Dr. Varunendra Vikram Singh, Faculty, Centre for Rural Studies, Lal Bahadur Shastri National Academy of Administration, Mussoorie, Uttarakhand.

Introduction

S.C. PATRA

Rural India is unique in the world because of the rich heritage, strong traditions, indigenous way of management of water, land and other natural resources, past practices in conflict resolution and local leadership. The villages are units which have existence over thousands of years and are engaged in managing their own affairs, utilizing individual resources, community resources and financial resources available from schemes of Central Government, State Government, local governance institutions. Understanding the socio-economic profiles and needs and aspirations of the rural populations in different States is very vital in planning of development and adjusting national policies to the local situations. The problems of villages and villagers require adequate attentions and proper redressal mechanism which falls under the rubric of the mandate of the District Administrations and State Governments besides Central Ministries.

India's North-Eastern Region consists of 8 States. Assam and Manipur has considerable plain lands whereas the other six States are hilly and mountainous. The region has large international borders and is surrounded by Bangladesh, Bhutan, China, Nepal and Myanmar. The region is rich in water resources and has the highest rainfall in the country with large and small river systems. The region is also marked with presence of bio-diversity hot spots, diversity of customs, cultures, traditions and languages and is home to around 200 tribal/subtribal groups and linguistic, ethnic groups.

Due to geo-political reasons and the historical background, the North-East region has remained as a backward region of the country.

Poor infrastructure, frequent damage to the infrastructure due to recurring floods particularly in Assam, low productivity puts the region into disadvantages position to achieve faster development. Social conflicts, insurgencies, different kinds of political movements are further impediments to the process of development and often slows down the implementation of developmental activities and brings in inefficiency in service delivery.

The eight States of North-East India has a geographical area of 2,62,179 sq. km which accounts for 7.9 percent of the country's geographical area. About 3.8 percent of the nation's population which comes to 39 million people (2001 Census) live in the region. Indicators normally used to depict the status of development of any State are compiled for the four North-Eastern States covered in this book is given in Table 1.

Table 1 : Socio-Economic Profile—NE Region

Sl. No.	Item	Assam	Manipur	Nagaland	Tripura
1.	Area ('000 sq. km)	78.44	22.33	16.58	10.49
2.	Population (lakh)	266.56	23.89	19.89	31.99
3.	Rural Population (lakh)	232.16	18.18	16.36	26.53
4.	Average exponential growth rate (percent) per annum	1.73	2.63	4.97	1.46
5.	Density of population (Person/sq km)	340	107	120	304
6.	Sex Ratio (Female per thousand males)	932	972	909	950
7.	Percent of Forest area to geographical Area	34.45	78.01	52.05	60.01
8.	Reporting area for land utilization ('000 ha)	7,850	2,211	1,560	1049
9.	Proudction of total grains ('000 MT)	3,895	392	389	558
10.	Per capita consumption of electricity (KWH)	105.5	72.9	61.4	111.3
11.	Road length per 100 sq km of Area (km)	114.09	51.21	126.79	155.41
12.	Road length per 1000 population (km)	3.29	4.76	10.51	5.09
13	Average population	21,906	31,021	28,821	17,928
14.	Credit deposit ratio (percent)	30.77	29.06	16.93	25.36
15.	Number of Health Centres functioning	5819	508	502	621

(Contd.)

Table 1 (*Contd.*)

Sl. No.	*Item*	*Assam*	*Manipur*	*Nagaland*	*Tripura*
16.	Persons served per PHC	274765	125307	91553	336098
17.	Birth rate (per thousand)	27	17	NA	15
18.	Infant Mortality Rate/'000	70	14	NA	34
19.	Literacy Rate percent	53.79	59.85	57.65	63.81
20.	Student-teachers Ratio				
21.	(a) Hr Secondary Schools	21	20	27	23
22.	(b) High Schools	18	19	20	23
23.	Population per post office	6,672	3,444	6,142	4,468
24.	Area served by a post office	19.63	32.13	50.93	14.57
25.	Population BPL (percent)	36.09	28.54	32.67	34.44
26.	Per capita NSDP (State income) current price (Rs.)	11,755	12,230	17,629 (00-01)	17,459 (01-02)
27.	Tenth Plan outlay/capita (Rs.)	3,119	11,737	11,200	13270

Agriculture in the region is still subsistence agriculture and commercialization is in nascent stage. The irrigation development is lagging behind thereby the yield level of most the crops grown in the region is far below the potential. The population in the hilly areas of Nagaland, Manipur and Tripura obtain their need of agricultural produces from a primitive practice of shifting cultivation (Locally known as *jhuming*) which is a kind of management of land-use in forested areas. The reduction in *jhum* cycles due to increase in population has endangered this practice and the amount of produces harvested by the *jhumia* farmers from *jhuming* earlier is no longer becoming possible due to decreased fertility and other types of degradation. The productivity of principal crops in Assam, Manipur, Nagaland and Tripura (Table 2) indicates scope for enhancing productivity.

The local governance in many parts of the North-Eastern Region are as per parts IX and IX-A of the Constitution or under the Sixth Schedule. The Nagaland has its own traditional system. Village development boards are functioning at the village level in Nagaland and there are 1286 village development boards in the entire State. Communitisation of the village bodies have been undertaken by the State Government which was found to be useful capacity building for discharging the responsibility of service delivery and planning for development of villages.

In Assam, there are two autonomous District Council, namely Karbi-Anglong Autonomous Council and NC-Hills Autonomous Council governed under the Sixth Schedule. The Boroland Territorial Council has recently been constituted. In Tripura, there is a autonomous council catering to the tribal inhabited villages.

Table 2 : Relative Productivity of Principal Crops in the NER in 2003-04

(*quintals per hectare*)

Crop	*Assam*	*Manipur*	*Nagaland*	*Tripura*
Rice	0.74	1.13	0.66	1.04
Maize	0.35	1.13	0.73	0.44
Small millet	1.06	—	1.94	0.00
Wheat	0.39	—	0.86	1.57
Total cereals	0.76	1.18	0.70	1.09
Total pulses	0.86	0.81	1.30	0.95
Total foodgrains	0.85	1.32	0.77	1.23
Sesamum	1.22	1.11	1.67	1.04
Rapeseed & mustard	0.45	0.39	0.89	0.70
Total oilseeds	0.49	0.44	1.00	0.67
Tea	0.96	0.13	0.07	0.52
Coffee	—	—	—	—
Natural rubber	0.61	—	—	0.61
Banana	0.54	0.50	0.71	0.50
Sugarcane	0.66	—	0.81	0.73
Potatoes	0.39	—	0.24	0.00
Chillies	0.61	0.56	9.15	1.33
Ginger	—	0.48	3.85	0.25
Coconut	1.21	—	0.42	0.33
Turmeric	0.19	—	1.39	0.77
Pineapple	0.96	0.54	0.93	1.30

Note: Figures are calculated.

Source: *Statistical Abstracts of India, 2003-04.*

There is a great need for capacity building of these village level institutions and Gram Panchayats to enable the people to have the right perspective. Autonomous district councils are facing many inherent problems due to the hilly and inassessible terrain. Development of village plans by the Gram Panchayats and municipal plans by the urban local bodies must properly be done and these plans must be incorporated into district plans. Proper planning is the key for holistic development in the rural areas of the North-Eastern States.

Getting insight to socio-economic profile of the villages and rural areas of the States of North-East India is very important for improving governance. Better governance, reaching out to the entire population by Government machinery and capacity building of the existing institutions and new institutions being created is very vital and should receive priority in the coming years.

1

Assam

ASHISH VACHHANI, JAI SINGH SHEKHAWAT
and VARUNENDRA VIKRAM SINGH

INTRODUCTION

Speak of a land of wooded hills and valleys with a wide river, of sprawling tea gardens, of enticing songs and dances, of fine silks, and you are already able to hazard a good enough guess. Add to that, the one-horned rhinoceros, the oldest refinery in India, a people made all the more colourful by a sizeable population of tribals and one of the most venerated Sakti temples in the country, and you know it is **Assam**—the land of the Red River, the Brahmaputra, and the Blue Hills flanking it.

For Assam is identified no better than by its **Bihu songs and dances**, the **Kaziranga Wild Life Sanctuary** where the rare **one-horned rhinoceros** roam at will, silks such as ***paat*** and ***muga*** which rank amongst the finest in the world, the State's tea which finds its way to millions of homes all over the globe, and the **Shrine of Kamakhya** which draws thousands of devotees every year.

WHAT IS IN THE NAME ?

In ancient times Assam constituted a part of the land known successively as **Pragjyotisha** or **Pragjyotishpura**, and **Kamarupa**. **Asom (Axom)** or its anglicized version **Assam** is a comparatively modern name. Opinions on the root of the name vary with one view ascribing its origin to the Bodo word ***Ha-Cham*** which means "low or level country" and a second view ascribing it to the word ***Asama***, meaning "unequalled", and used to denote the ***Ahoms***, a Shan tribe which ruled the land for six centuries from the 13th Century A.D.

The word 'Assam' is derived from the Sanskrit word 'Asoma', meaning peerless. The land of Assam is in fact, peerless, judging by her exquisite natural beauty, cultural richness and human wealth. Assam has a rich legacy of culture and civilisation behind her. Home to different races of men—Austric, Mongolian, Dravidian, and Aryan, who came to dwell in these hills at different points of time. Assam has developed a composite culture of variegated colour.

Assam, which is situated in the north-east corner of India is surrounded by Bhutan and Arunachal Pradesh on the north, Nagaland and Manipur on the east, Meghalaya and Mizoram on the south and Bangladesh, Tripura and West Bengal on the west. A narrow strip of sub-mountainous region of the Himalayas, connects Assam to the Indian mainland. The State is dominated by the river Brahmaputra, whose lush 700 kilometre valley is sandwiched between the Himalayan foothills to the north, and the hills and plateau of Meghalaya to the south.

Important tourist centres of the State around Guwahati are Kamakhya Temple, Umananda (Peacock Island), Navagraha (Temple of nine planets), Gandhi Mandap, State Zoo, State Museum, Sukreswar Temple, Geeta Mandir, Madan-Kamdev Temple and Saraighat Bridge. In the rest of the State the places of tourist interest are Kaziranga Park (famous for one horned rhinos), Sib Sagar (Shiv Temple), Majuli (largest river island in the world), Chandubi lake, Batadrava (Birthplace of great Vaishnav Saint Sankardev), and Saulkuchi (renowned for its silk industry).

HISTORY

Much of the ancient past of Assam still lies buried deep beneath its soil. Lack of proper and systematic archaeological research has resulted in a dearth of archaeological material, and though evidence of human habitation in the land has been traced back to the Early Stone Age, the overall picture remains vague and indistinct. That Assam, by whatever name, was known in other parts of the world as far back as in 100 BC is nevertheless clear from the records of the

Chinese explorer, Chang Kien, who traced his country's trade with Assam during that period. The *Periplus of the Erythrean* sea depicts how Chinese silk from Assam reached Egypt and Rome before the advent of Christianity. Ptolemy's geography also acknowledges the existence of Assam.

The earliest inhabitants of Assam can be safely said to be the Australoids or the pre-Dravidians. It was, however, the Mongoloids who entered the land through the eastern mountainous passes who were to almost overrun the land long before the time of the compilation of the Hindu religious literature known as the **Vedas** around the 10th Century BC. The Vedas called the Mongoloids *Kiratas*, and the present-day tribes of the North-East are all considered to be the descendants of the *Kiratas*. **Pragjyotishpura**—*the City of Eastern Lights*—was deemed to be the capital of the *Kiratas*, and the epics define a land of the *Kiratas* stretching from the foothills of the Himalayas in the north to the Bay of Bengal in the south. The *Kirata* King Narakasura is said to be the founder of Pragjyotishpura. The *Kalika Purana* and the *Vishnu Purana* identifies this land as **Kamarupa** saying that it extended for 450 miles in all directions from the shrine of Kamakhya atop the Nilachal Hills in modern Guwahati. Narakasua's successor, Bhagadatta finds mention in the epic *Mahabharata*, leading a huge *Kirata* army with a large number of elephants in the war between the Pandavas and the Kauravas against the former.

The records of the Chinese traveller Hiuen Tsang shed light on the area in the Seventh Century. Pragjyotishpura came to be known as **Kamarupa** in the medieval period. Hiuen Tsang speaks of a powerful and prestigious Kamarupa under King Bhaskaravarman. Kamarupa had perhaps achieved the zenith of its power during the time, for subsequent centuries were witness to repeated onslaughts by aboriginals, which reduced the power of the kingdom and led to its fragmentation.

Between the heydays of the Kamarupa kingdom and the coming of the **Ahoms** in the thirteenth century, the land experienced a spell of turmoil in which no single power could hold sway. Thus, when the Ahoms entered Assam through the eastern hills in 1228, they chanced upon a period in its history when it was at its most susceptible. Among the local tribes, only the **Chutias** and the **Kacharis** could offer a semblance of resistance.

Thereafter, the next six centuries belonged to the Ahoms who founded a powerful dynastic rule with their capital in Sibsagar of Upper Assam. It was after the Ahoms that the land was named ***Asom*** or its more anglicized version **Assam**. The advent of the Ahoms marked the beginning of a new era in the history of Assam.

The centre of power was thus shifted from Kamarupa in Lower Assam to Upper Assam, and the importance of Lower Assam declined sharply save for an intervening short period in the early sixteenth century when the western limits of the kingdom of the **Koch**, one of the Kirata tribes, increased considerably under their illustrious King Naranarayana.

Meanwhile, the unprecedented rise in power of the Ahoms was taken as a challenge by the **Mughal** emperors in Delhi who sent seventeen military expeditions to shackle the Ahoms, but all in vein. The last of these expeditions resulted in a long-drawn see-saw battle between the Mughals and the Ahoms at **Saraighat**—the present site of the first bridge over the Brahmaputra—near Guwahati, which climaxed in a resounding victory for the Ahom forces under its general **Lachit Barphukan.**

Lachit Barphukan achieved immortal fame and his heroism together with the battle and its many annecdotes—one of which relates the interesting incident of Lachit beheading his own uncle for slight of duty, as an example of his patriotism—are now integral part of the history and folk culture of Assam.

The victory at Saraighat was followed by a spell of treacherous court intrigues that threatened the very existence of the Ahom kingdom until **Rudra Sinha** assumed power and took the Ahom Kingdom from strength to strength. From this zenith however it was a plunge straight down, starting with the uprising of the **Vaisnavite Moamoria Mahantas** in protest against the religious harassment meted out to them at the instigation of the Sakta Ahom queen **Phuleswari**, in the eighties of the eighteenth century. It was during the troubled times of the uprising and many court intrigues and dissension sapping the strength of the Ahom rulers that the **Burmese** invaded Assam through its eastern borders.

It was history repeating itself, and just as the Ahoms themselves had overran the land six centuries before, so also were they themselves humiliated by the Burmese who were to be the rulers of the land till the **British** appeared on the scene in 1826 and forced them to cede Assam by the ***Treaty of Yandabu***.

The British soon realized that their latest acquisition was by no means a land of docile inhabitants when within four years of their conquest they had to face a joint resistance by the people of Assam. The bid was abortive but marked the beginning of the confrontation between the nationalists and the imperialist that was to end with the country achieving her independence in 1947.

The years in between, as in rest of the country, witnessed the saga of the **Indian Independence Movement** marked by ungrudging sacrifices and unbreakable determination. Maniram Dewan, Piyoli Phukan and Piyali Barua were hanged in connection with the Sepoy Mutiny. Martyrs like Kanak Lata, Kushal Konwar and Bhogeswari Phukanani gave their lives for the Mahatma's cause. Their sacrifices were not in vain.

The **Chinese aggression of 1962** was to pose a real enough threat to the independence of this particular part of the country and was thankfully averted by a strong military response and last-minute political understandings. But what was Assam back in 1947 constituted all the States of the present-day North-East except Manipur and Tripura. However, regional cultural variations were too distinct for the entire land to stay clubbed under a single political administration. Hence, we have the phenomenon of new States being carved out from erstwhile Assam one after the other. It started with the creation of Nagaland in 1963, followed by the separation of Meghalaya and Mizoram in 1971, and ended with the formation of Arunachal Pradesh in 1972. The part that remained as a single entity is the Assam of today.

And cultural identity has always featured prominently in the socio-economic and political scenario of the State. Thus we have the unprecedented **Assam Movement** of the 1980s, which is largely deemed to be an endeavour to preserve the cultural identity of the State endengered by large-scale infiltration of illegal immigrants from across the border from Bangladesh. In recent times, the State has also been ranckled by the terrorism propagated by some extremist elements.

AN ECONOMIC PROFILE

Nature has been bountiful in Assam. The State possesses an estimated 320 million tonnes of coal reserves, oil and natural gas reserves sufficient to sustain current production levels for at least another fifty years, and a vast, though largely untapped potential for power generation. Locationally there are several positive attributes. Guwahati is the communications and transportation hub for much of the North-East. The State's waterways can transport goods cheaply and efficiently. There is an extensive and growing railway network, one that is being converted in substantial part to broad gauge. The State is well placed to service the needs and markets of other States of the North-East. A modicum of incremental investment would allow access to other countries, in particular to the growing economies of South East Asia.

A nascent industrial infrastructure, capable of being built upon, already exists in Assam. There are four oil refineries, several large and medium sector manufacturing industries, including sugar mills, textile spinning units and processing houses, cement plants and fertiliser units. All of this is in addition to the traditional strengths in tea and jute. There is potential to set up industries in the hydrocarbon sector—gas cracker plants, aromatic complexes and downstream and ancillary industries.

Despite this, Assam's economic development is lagging behind that of the rest of the country—and the gap is increasing. At Independence, Assam's per capita income was only marginally less (a difference of 4 percent) than that of the average for the country. In 1998, the average per capita income for the country was over 1.8 times that of Assam. The relative stagnancy in the growth of income is attributable in turn to the inability of each of the component sectors to grow at rates that would allow the State to reach the levels attained by the rest of the country.

Industrial diversification and growth has been constrained by the inadequacy and quality of complementary infrastructure, the geographical isolation of the region, and the lack of well developed markets. There are few traditions of indigenous entrepreneurship, and the tentativeness of private investment from outside the State has necessitated a major, if not always efficient, role for the State.

In the agriculture sector, the overall growth rates since the 1980s has been a little over 2 percent, rates not sufficient to generate surpluses for investment, or create-purchasing power in the rural sector to provide a market for local industries. Cropping intensities and crop productivities remain low, and crop diversification is, at best, nascent. Fragmentations of holdings, low irrigation coverage and the limited adoption of new technologies and practices are some of the constraining factors. The regular occurrence and increasing intensity of floods is detrimental to the advancement of the sector. Not only do floods wreak annual havoc, but the accompanying uncertainty prevents farmers from taking risks and making investments in land improvement, and in higher cost, albeit high yielding, technologies and practices.

The inability to build on the promise afforded by the horticulture sector is largely attributable to the deficiencies in complementary investments, in storage, rural transportation networks and in market facilities. For the same reasons, fisheries, poultry farming and dairy are yet to acquire the momentum required to raise incomes substantially and sustainably.

There are 848 tea gardens, accounting for about 11 percent of the State's income, producing approximately 400 million kg of tea, including 160 million kg for export suffered setbacks, and consequent economic activity, income and employment are at levels much lower than even a decade ago.

In absolute terms, the number of poor people in the State increased from 7.8 million in 1983 to 9.5 million in 1999-2000. In 1999-2000, 36.09 percent of the State's population continued to live below the poverty line, a figure appreciably above the national average (26.1 percent). Only four States had a higher proportion of their population below the poverty line—Bihar, Madhya Pradesh, Orissa and Rajasthan.

GEOGRAPHICAL INFORMATION

Assam, known during epic period as Pragjyotisha or the place of eastern astronomy is strategically located and has international border with as many as four countries, namely China, Myanmar, Bhutan, and Bangladesh. It is surrounded on all other sides by predominantly hilly or mountainous tracts—Bhutan and Arunachal Pradesh on the north, Manipur, Nagaland and Arunachal Pradesh on the east and Meghalaya Mizoram and Tripura on the south.

Bordering States/Countries	
East	Arunachal Pradesh, Nagaland, Manipur and Myanmar
West	West Bengal, Meghalaya, Bangladesh
North	Arunachal Pradesh, Bhutan
South	Nagaland, Manipur, Mizoram, Meghalaya, Tripura
Longitude	89° 42′ E to 96° E
Latitude	24° 5′ to 28° N
Major Towns	Guwahati, Dhubri, Goalpara, Barpeta, Dibrugarh, North Lakhimpur, Golaghat, Diphu, Tinsukia, Jorhat, Tezpur, Nagaon, Sivasagar, Silchar.
Area (in sq. km)	78,523
Percentage of forest cover (1995-96)	27.41
Languages	Assamese, Bengali, Hindi, English

DEMOGRAPHY

Population			*Literacy %*			*Density*
Total	*Male*	*Female*	*Total*	*Male*	*Female*	
26,638,407	13,787,799	12,850,608	64.28	71.93	56.03	340

Source: http://www.indiainbusiness.nic.in/indian-states/assam/general.htm

RELIGION

As Assam is a State of many ethnic groups of people, it is also a State of many religions. It represents in full the religious diversity of the country. Besides the major religions, some of the tribes also follow animism, and worship nature in its various manifestations. Worship of trees, mountains and rocks are common among tribes such as the Dimasas of North Cachar Hills in the south.

The Vaisnava revival of the Middle Ages brought to the limelight the great Vaisnavite saint *Srimanta* Sankardeva (1449-1568) who developed and propagated *Eka-sarana-namadharma* (*a faith of allegiance to one God*) which was part of the neo-Vaisnavite movement of India and is characterized by absence of the rituals practised by the Saktas and the principle of equality which annulled all caste barriers.

Mahapurush Sri Sri Sankaradeva, as he is known in the State, composed hymns (*borgeet*), dance-dramas (*ankianaat*) and recitals, and with the help of his disciples, set up *sattras* (monasteries) and *namghars* (community prayer halls) for the propagation of the new faith that soon gained large-scale acceptance. Thus, Assam developed its own form of Vaisnavism, which is today the predominant faith among the Hindus. So much so that *borgeets*, *ankianaats* and many other Vaisnavite art forms and social norms are now considered to be integral parts of the Assamese culture.

Saivaism, which holds the procreative energy of males in reverence and is related to the worship of God Shiva as well as Saktaism are other forms of Hinduism still practised in the State.

The reformation movement of the Muslim saint and missionary Shah Miran, popularly known as Ajan Fakir, deserves special mention in this context. Ajan Fakir came to Assam from the Middle East about two hundred years after Shankardeva and found that the Muslims who had come and settled in the land as early as in the 13th century A.D. were practising a form of Islam somewhat distorted by elements of the local Hindu religion. He set out to reinforce Islamic ideals and religious practices, and composed religious songs (known as *Jikirs* and *Jaris*) in the spoken language much in the same style as the Borgeets of Sankardeva. Very soon he gained popularity and gathered a large following, and *Zikirs* and *Jaris* remain unique elements of Islam in Assam.

There are scattered populations of Buddhists, Sikhs and Jains in different parts of the State notable among which are the Buddhists among the Khamti tribes and the Assamese Sikhs of Borkhola in the district of Nagaon.

PEOPLE

You find traces of them all there: the **Australoids** who were perhaps the first to come to the land; the **Mongoloids** who came to the North-East in a series of migrations from the north, north-east and south-east; and the **Caucasoids** who came from the west by the valley formed by the Ganges and the Brahmaputra. Today, the people of the State can be broadly classified as the **Non-Tribals** or **Plains People** who generally live in the plains and the **Tribals** who have mainly been living in the hills. However, there is a substantial tribal population in the plains too.

ROOTS

At present, though there is no Australoid population as such in any part of Assam, but recent anthropological researches support that Australoid elements are discernible not only among many tribes but also in certain caste groups of Assam. Most of the ancient Australoid traits were absorbed by the Mongoloids and the Caucasoids in due course of time. It is very difficult to say who came first between the Mongoloid and the Caucasoid but by physical appearance they have both retained their identities as separate groups though it is very difficult, if not impossible to distinguish them on the basis of individuals. The Ahoms who figure so prominently in the history of the State were a Mongoloid people so are the small Buddhist populations of Khamti, Tai Phake, Khamyang, Aiton and Turung in Upper Assam. Among the Assamese castes, the Brahmans and the Kshatriyas find mention in the records of Hiuen Tsang and are considered to be people of Caucasoid origin.

A MEETING GROUND

Since time immemorial, Assam has been the happy meeting ground of people belonging to different ethnic groups, communities and cultural entities. For example, even the Brahmaputra Valley is an area rich with the contribution of such different groups most of whom got assimilated in the composite Assamese identity. To the south, in the Barak valley, Bengali-speaking people along with tribal communities have been making similar contributions to the emergence of a distinct identity of Assam.

Another group that deserves special mention is the tea garden community. During the second half of the nineteenth century, when the British started tea cultivation on a large scale in Assam, they were faced with the problem of dearth of labourers. Hence, they brought in people from other parts of the country—from Orissa and Bihar and from as far as Tamil Nadu and Kerala.

These people ultimately settled down in the State, and successive generations not only intermingled among themselves but also assimilated much of the Assamese culture to develop a life style of their own. Some of them left the tea estates and found other occupations. Today, with their attractive dances (*Jhumur*) and songs, and their close rapport with the tea plant, they have a distinct culture of their own and are called Bagania.

CENSUS FIGURES

The 1991 Census puts the population of Assam at 2,24,14,322 with a **sex ratio** of 896 females per 1,000 males and a **growth rate** of +53.26 per cent in the two decades from 1971 to 1991. There are 16 Scheduled Castes and 23 Scheduled Tribes constituting 7.40 and 12.82 per cent respectively of the State's population.

THE ASSAMESE

What we call the Assamese people of today is in fact the result of assimilation and integration of people of different racial stocks who migrated to Assam down the ages. The Assamese population can be divided into two broad groups: the **non-tribal people** who constitute the majority and the **tribals**.

THE NON-TRIBALS

The entire non-tribal population of the State can be said to be concentrated in the Brahmaputra and the Barak Valleys. Constituting the majority in the State and the dominant populace in almost all the urban areas, their lifestyle is considerably modern and closer to what is dubbed the "mainstream" of the nation. They are the people who speak the Assamese language. In terms of religion, the Hindus who are a majority among the non-tribals are divided into castes and sub-castes along the same lines as in the rest of the country though caste barriers are not as pronounced here. Thus we have the Brahmins and the Kshatriyas, and the Vaishyas and the Sudras. We have to however bear in mind that a majority of the non-tribal population of today were tribals of yesterdays, who underwent the transformation by adopting Hinduism and its way of life gradually rising in status in the Hindu caste system in a process which is termed by anthropologists as Sanskritization. The Ahoms themselves were absorbed into their Hinduized or Hindu Assamese-speaking subjects towards the end of their long reign.

The non-tribals can again be divided on the basis of religion amongst whom the Muslims constitute the second largest group followed by the Christians, Sikhs and the Buddhists.

EXQUISITE AND EXOTIC TRIBAL PEOPLE

The tribals on their part have been divided into the hill tribes and the plain tribes according to geography of their location. A majority of the tribals practise what has been dubbed *tribal religion* is very close to animism but with ingredients of Hinduism. A considerable part of the tribal population has also adopted Christianity and on the rare occasion, Islam.

Each of its 23 different tribes exhibits distinct and exquisite ways of life. There are tribes like the **Bodo Kacharis, Karbis** and **Lalungs** which are purely patriarchal, and the **Khasis, Jaintias** and **Garos** which are strictly matriarchal. Then there are the **Dimasas** who while having a patriarchal system of family structure also have a system of almost parallel male and female clans which accords exclusive rights to women.

A number of tribes such as the **Hmars, Rengma Nagas** and **Garos** have a social institution called the Youth Dormitory in which the young males live away from their families and undergo education and training. Dormitories also serve as centres of social work and are in some cases entrusted with the security of the village. The **Zeme Nagas** has dormitories both for males and females.

The term **Assamese** could thus very well be misleading. For when we talk of the Assamese People we do not restrict ourselves to the Assamese-speaking majority but all the tribes, sub-tribes and clans, the various religious groups and the castes and sub-castes which inhabit the land and come together to form a single entity called the **Assamese.**

LANGUAGE

With a majority of the total population using the tongue, **Assamese** is the major language of the State. Besides English, Assamese was accorded the status of the official language of the Brahmaputra Valley by the Official Language Act of 1960. However, Bengali and English were also simultaneously accorded the status of official language for the Barak Valley and the two Hill Districts by the same Act. The earliest specimen of the Assamese script is to be found in copper plates and inscriptions discovered in different parts of the region.

Scholars opine that the origin of Assamese goes back to the Magadhan-Prakrit script. By all standards it is a composite language into which words of Indo-Aryan and Indo-Chinese origins have made their way. Pre-Aryan and non-Aryan influences are also discernible not only in loan words but also in its grammar, syntax and pronunciation.

Speeches of the **Tibeto-Burman, Austro-Asiatic** and **Tibeto-Chinese** families abound among the tribal population. The widest variety of language found in the tribal popluation can, however, be attributed to the Tibeto-Burman family. The Bodo language group with its **Kachari, Lalung, Rabha, Moran** and even **Chutia** variations, in turn dominate the Tibeto-Burman family.

Other recognized Indian languages spoken in the State include **Bengali, Hindi** and **Oriya. Oriya, Mundari, Santhal, Tamil** and **Telegu** are mostly spoken by the tea garden labourers.

CLIMATE

Pleasant sub-alpine climate prevails in the hills. The plains however experience tropical climate making them uncomfortably humid especially during the rainy seasons. Winter sets in from around the end of the month of October and lasts till the end of February. The temperature drops to a minimum of 6° to 8° Celcius, the nights and early mornings are foggy, and rain is scanty. Summer arrives in the middle of May accompanied by high humidity and rainfall. The temperature reaches a maximum of 35° to 38° Celcius. The frequent rains however serve to push the mercury down. The monsoons blow full blast during the month of June. Thunderstorms known as ***Bordoichilla*** are a frequent occurrence during the afternoons. Spring and Autumn with moderate temperatures and modest rainfall are the best seasons.

Assam falls in a zone prone to earthquakes. Though mild tremors are familiar to the region, high-intensity earthquakes are rather infrequent. However, they do occur as in 1869 when the bank of the Barak sank by 15 ft in 1897, and again in 1950 when a large part of the State was ravaged by an earthquake of unprecedented intensity

ART AND HANDICRAFT

Handloom Weaving is a way of life in Assam. The number of looms in the State stands at around eight lakh, which works out to around 16 per cent of the looms in the entire country. More than thirty thousand looms operate exclusively in silk. Cotton, *muga*, *paat* (mulberry silk) and *endi* are the basic raw materials for hand-woven fabrics in Assam. Sualkuchi is the biggest centre of silk production and weaving in the State. There are more than 3,000 weavers in and around the township. Sualkuchi is known as the Manchester of Assam.

Muga silk has a natural golden colour and rare sheen that becomes more lustrous with every wash. *Eri* is a warm silk suitable for the winter. The designs used in Assam are mostly stylised symbols of animals, human figures, creepers, flowers, birds, channels, cross borders and the galaxy. Each ethnic group of the State has its own distinctive design and style. Assamese weavers produce beautiful designs on the borders of traditional garments such as the *mekhela-chaddar* and *riha* and on the *gamosa* (towel). The *Laichangphi*, produced traditionally by the weavers of Cachar district, is a popular quilt sought after because of its warmth and softness. The tribals make beautiful shawls.

Jewellery has been a tradition in Assam. Gold was available in many of the rivers flowing down from the Himalayas. In fact, a particular tribe of people, the Sonowal Kacharis, was engaged only in gold washing in these rivers. The Assamese jewellers (*sonaris*) make exquisite lockets (*doog-doogi, bana*, *jon-biri*, *dhol-biri*), earrings (*thuriya*, *loka-paro*, *keru*), bracelets (*gaam-kharu*), necklaces (*gal-pata*), etc.

Cane and Bamboo being quite common all over are used to make a variety of products. Cane furniture of Assam is much sought after both in the national and international markets. Bamboo is used mostly to make domestic products such as *chalani* (sieve), *kula* (winnowing pan), *khorahi* (small basket), etc. The fancy bamboo *japi* (hat) with its colourful design and motif is worn by the Assamese peasant while working in the field.

The Tradition of Painting in Assam can be traced back to several centuries in the past. The gifts presented to Hiuen Tsang and Harshavardhana by Kumar Bhaskara, the King of Kamrupa, included a number of paintings and painted objects, some done on exclusive Assam silk. Assamese literature of the medieval period abounds in references to *chitrakars* and *patuas* who were expert painters. Locally available material such as *hebgool* and *haital* were used for painting. Ahom palaces and *sattras* and *naamghars* are replete with brightly coloured paintings depicting various stories and events from history and mythology.

Sitalpati or mats made from the *patidai* or *mohtra* reed is a traditional craft of Cachar.

Brass and Bell Metal products of Assam are also famous for their beauty and strength of form and utility. Brass is an important cottage industry with highest concentration in Hajo of Kamrup district. The Sarthebari area of the same district is well known for its bell metal craft. The principal items of brass are the *kalah* (water pot), *sarai* (a platter or tray mounted on a base), *kahi* (dish), *bati* (bowl), *lota* (water pot with a long neck) and *tal* (cymbals). Gold, silver and copper too have formed part of traditional metalcraft in Assam, and the State Museum in Guwahati has a rich collection of items made of these metals. Gold, however, is now used only for ornaments.

Ivory Products such as combs, bangles, walking sticks and smoking pipes were made in the district of Barpeta. Their production has, however, been stopped since a ban was imposed on making and selling of ivory products as a conservation measure. Combs made of the horn of oxes are also a speciality.

Pottery is practised by two communities of artisans in Assam—the Hira and the Kumar. The Hiras make household articles using the compression method. The Kumars use their potter's wheel to make images for worship and clay dolls and toys. West Assam has long been proficient in the craft of terracotta. Asharkandi, a village in Goalpara district is famous for its graceful clay dolls.

Woodwork is an ancient Assamese craft. Exquisite wood carvings are seen mostly on doors, walls, beams, ceilings and the splendid carved *sinhasans* used in prayer houses. Decorative panels in the royal Ahom palaces of the past and the 600 years old *sattras* or Vaisnavite monasteries are intricately carved in wood.

A special class of people who excelled in wood carving came to be known as *Khanikar*. The painted woodwork of Golaghat is a folk art. Modern day *khanikars* have taken to producing articles of commercial value, including figure of one-horned rhino and replicas of the world-famous Kamakhya temple—two items heading the list of demands from visitors.

Kuhila Koth or fibre weaving is a famed handicraft of the Batadrava area of Nagaon district. *Kuhila* is woven on a simple loom-like gadget made of wood and bamboo poles to produce seats, mats and cushions. *Kuhila* craft is also an important cottage industry in the Gauripur area of Dhubri district in Lower Assam. Pith or Indian cork has also been used for toy-making since centuries in Assam. Such toys are chiefly made in the Goalpara region and they include figures of gods, animals and birds.

BASIC STATISTICS OF ASSAM

1. Geographical Area

78,438 sq. km. (of this 20% are hilly)

2. Administrative Division

(a) Districts: 23.
(b) Blocks: 219.
(c) Mahakuma Parishad: 43
(d) Gaon Panchayat: 2,489.
(e) Total villages: 25,590.

3. Population

(2001 Census Provisional as per Census of India)

(a) Total: 2,66,38,407.
(b) Male: 1,37,87,799.
(c) Female: 1,28,50,608.

(d) Rural population (1991 census): 1,99,26,527 (88.90%)

(e) Urban population (1991 census): 24,87,759 (11.10%)

(f) Decadal growth rate: 53.26 per cent of population (1991-2001)

(g) Density of population: 340 per sq. km. (India 324 per sq. km.)

4. Literacy Rate

(a) Total percentage: 64.28 per cent

(b) Rural percentage: 49.32 per cent (1991 census)

Rural Poverty (as per BPL Census 1998)

(i) Total rural families: 34,12,506

(ii) Total BPL families in rural areas: 20,28,058—SC: 2,59,316 and ST: 4,28,337

(iii) Percentage of BPL families in rural areas: 59.43 per cent

(iv) Geographical distribution of poverty

1. Highest PC of BPL families in the State: Goalpara (75.25%)
2. Next Highest: Dhubri (75.03%)
3. Lowest PC of BPL families in the State: Jorhat (41.00%) and Tinsukia (41.31%)

Agriculture Statistics (1998-99)—Land Utilisation in Hectares

(a) Total geographical Area: 78,43,800

(b) Total cropped Area: 39,88,600

(c) Cultivable wasteland: 80,194*

(d) Area under Forest: 2,35,798

(e) Land put to Non-agriculture: 10,30,378 uses

(f) Grazing land: 1,58,480

(g) Net Area sown: 27,01,053 (35.40% of geographical area)

---

*Excluding Karbi Anglong and N.C. Hills

(h) Area sowed more than once: 12,15,195

Educational Infrastructure in Assam

Assam State has enough pool of skilled and educated manpower. There is 53 percent literacy rate in the State. Assam has four universities, one Agricultural University, three Medical colleges, four engineering colleges, 23 vocational training institutes and eight polytechnics (Tablc 1.1). Tea gardens, oil refineries, organised big industries and small-scale industry employs skilled manpower with cheap rate.

Table 1.1: Educational Institutes

Type	*Nos.*
University	5
IIT	1
Engineering College	3
Medical College	3
General College	226
Junior College	76
Agriculture College	2
Law College	9
Veterinary College	2
Higher Secondary School	599
High School	3915
Middle School	8019
Primary School	31888
Pre-primary School	482
Industrial &Technical School	32
Polytechnic	8

Source: http://www.indiainbusiness.nic.in/indian-states/assam/socialinfra-assam.htm

PANCHAYATIRAJ SYSTEM

The System

Panchayati Raj Institutions—the grassroots units of self-government—have been proclaimed as the vehicles of socio-economic transformation in rural India. Effective and meaningful functioning of these bodies would depend on active involvement, contribution and participation of its citizens both male and female. Gandhiji's dream of every village being a republic and Panchayats having powers has been translated into reality with the introduction of the three-tier Panchayati Raj system to enlist people's participation in rural reconstruction. April 24, 1993 is a landmark day in the history of Panchayati Raj in India as on this day the Constitution (73rd Amendment) Act, 1992 came into force to provide constitutional status to the Panchayati Raj Institutions.

Evolution of Panchayati Raj System in Assam

The Rural Panchayat Act, 1948: Under this system there were two tiers of Panchayats—Primary Panchayats at village level and Rural Panchayats at Mouza level.

Assam Panchayati Raj Act, 1959: Under this Act a three-tier system was introduced which are Gaon Panchayat, Anchalik Panchayat and Mohokuma Parishad.

Assam Panchayati Raj Act, 1972: Under this system again a two-tier system was introduced which are Gaon Panchayat and Mohokuma Parishad.

Assam Panchayati Raj Act, 1986: Under this Act again a three-tier system is introduced—Gaon Panchayat, Anchalik Panchayat and Mohokuma Parishad.

Assam Panchayat Act, 1994: A three-tier system with Zilla Parishad has been introduced—Gaon Panchayat, Anchalik Panchayat and Zilla Parishad.

73rd Amendment Act, 1992

The Salient Features of the Act are:

(a) To provide 3 tier system of Panchayati Raj for all the States having population of over 20 lakh.

(b) To hold Panchayat Elections regularly every 5 years.

(c) To provide reservation of seats for Scheduled Castes, Scheduled Tribes and Women (not less than 33%).

(d) To appoint State Finance Commission to make recommendations as regards the financial powers of the Panchayats.

(e) To constitute District Planning Committee to prepare draft development plan for the district as a whole.

Powers and Responsibilities

According to the Constitution, Panchayats shall be given powers and authority to function as institutions of self-government. The following powers and responsibilities are to be delegated to Panchayats at the appropriate level :

(a) Preparation of Plan for economic development and social justice.

(b) Implementation of schemes for economic development and social justice in relation to 29 subjects given in Eleventh Schedule of the Constitution.

(c) To levy, collect and appropriate taxes, duties, tolls and fees.

Structure of the Panchayati Raj System in Assam

Gaon Panchayats

(a) President—directly elected by people.

(b) One Vice President—to be elected from among the members of Gaon Panchayat.

(c) Ten members—directly elected by people.

Anchalik Panchayats

(a) President—to be elected by the elected members of the Anchalik Panchayats.

(b) Vice President—to be elected by the elected members of the Anchalik Panchayats.

(c) Members—

1. One member from each Gaon Panchayat area to be directly elected by people.
2. President of the Gaon Panchayats falling within the jurisdiction of the Anchalik Panchayat.
3. Members of Parliament and Legislative Assembly.

Zilla Parishad

(a) President—elected from among the directly elected members of Zilla Parishad.

(b) Vice President—elected from among the directly elected members of Zilla Parishad.

(c) Members—

1. Members directly elected from the Zilla Parishad constituencies of the district.
2. Presidents of the Anchalik Panchayats.
3. Members of House of People and Member of Legislative Assembly.

Functions of the Panchayati Raj Bodies

Gaon Panchayat

1. Preparation of Annual Plans for the development of the Gaon Panchayat area.
2. Preparation Annual Budget of Gaon Panchayat.
3. Mobilisation of reliefs in natural calamities.
4. Removal of encroachments on public properties.
5. Organising voluntary labours and contribution for community works.
6. Maintenance of essential statistics of villages.
7. Such other development works as may be entrusted.

Anchalik Panchayat

1. Preparation of Annual Plan in respect of the schemes entrusted to it by virtue of the Act and those assigned to it by the Government or the Zilla Parishad and submission thereof to the Zilla Parishad within the prescribed time for integration with the District Plan.
2. Consideration and consolidation of the Annual Plans of all Gaon Panchayats under the Anchalik Panchayat and submission of consolidated plan to the Zilla Parishad.
3. Preparation of Annual Budget of the Anchalik Panchayat

and submission to Zilla Parishad for approval within the prescribed time.

4. Performing such functions and executing such works as may be entrusted to it by government or the Zilla Parishad.
5. To assist the government in relief operation in natural calamities.
6. Such other development works as may be entrusted.

Zilla Parishad

It should be the function of a Zilla Parishad to prepare plans for economic development and social justice of the district and ensure the co-ordinated implementation of such plan.

Standing Committees

Gaon Panchayat

There are three Standing Committees, which are:

(a) Development Committee.
(b) Social Justice Committee.
(c) Social Welfare Committee.

Members

Each committee shall consist of not less than three or more than four members elected from among the elected members of the Gaon Panchayats.

Functions

The Standing Committee shall perform the functions which are relating to the development of the rural areas and its people to the extent powers are delegated from the Gaon Panchayat.

Anchalik Panchayat

Three committees, they are

(a) General Standing Committee.
(b) Finance, Audit and Planning Committee.

(c) Social Justice Committee.

Members

Each Standing Committee shall consists of such number of members not exceeding six including the Chairman, as may be specified by the Anchalik Panchayat and chosen by the Anchalik Panchayat from amongst its members.

Functions

The Standing Committee shall perform the functions which are relating to the development of the rural areas and its people to the extent powers are delegated from the Anchalik Panchayat.

Zilla Parishad

There are four committees, which are:

(a) General Standing Committee.
(b) Finance and Audit Committee.
(c) Social Justice Committee.
(d) Planning and Development Committee.

Members

Each Standing Committee shall consist of such number of members not exceeding five including the Chairman as specified by the Zilla Parishad from amongst its members whose terms will be one year at a time.

Functions

Standing Committees shall perform functions to the extent, powers are delegated to them by the Zilla Parishad.

Gram Sabha

"Gram Sabha" means a body consisting of persons registered in the electoral rolls relating to a village comprised within the area of "Gaon Panchayat". The Gram Sabha has been designed to be the place where villagers will discuss development issues, plan accordingly, initiate development programmes and select beneficiaries for the schemes.

Functions of Gram Sabha under Assam Panchayat Act, 1994: Gram Sabha shall consider the following matters and may make recommendations and suggestions to the Gaon Panchayats:

1. The report in respect of development programme of the Gaon Panchayat relating to the preceding year and development programme proposed to be undertaken during the current year;
2. The promotion of unity and harmony among all sections of society in the villages; and
3. Such other matters as may be prescribed.

Functions

- Mobilising voluntary labour and contribution in kind and cash for the community welfare programmes.
- Identification of beneficiaries for the implementation of development schemes pertaining to the villages.
- Gram Sabha shall meet from time to time but a period of three months shall not intervene between any two meetings.

Sources of Income for Panchayats

(a) Share in land revenue.
(b) Local rates.
(c) Revenue earned from the settlement of hatt, fisheries, etc.
(d) House taxes and other taxes as specified in Assam Panchayati Raj Act.
(e) Fees for providing amenities, cess and tolls.
(f) Contribution and grants.
(g) Fine and penalties.

Rural people has got a noble duty to ensure that the Panchayati Raj bodies can mobilize resources from the above sources so that these bodies can work for the socio-economic development of the areas.

Reservations for Women

73rd Amendment of the Constitution in the year 1992 reserved 33 per cent seats for women in Panchayats. Accordingly, the provision has been incorporated under Assam Panchayati Raj Act. This provision is a major move towards strengthening the position of rural women. The introduction of women in sizable numbers into the new Panchayat could bring significant changes in the functioning of these grassroots level institutions. Involvement of women in the Panchayati Raj Institutions is expected to bring qualitative change in the matters relating to health nutrition, children welfare, family care, drinking water, etc.

Reservations for SC/ST

There is a mandatory provision for reservation of seats for SC/ST in every tier of Panchayati Raj System. The reservation for SC/ST is an another significant aspect for development of disadvantaged groups in the rural areas.

ROLE OF PANCHAYATS IN HUMAN RESOURCE DEVELOPMENT

(a) Panchayati Raj Institution should ensure development of human resources by providing weak and underprivileged opportunities like education, training, basic health services necessary for their growth and development.

(b) Panchayati Raj Institutes should ensure that all the sections of the society particularly weaker section including women and girl child get adequate opportunity for developing human resource potential.

(c) Panchayat can play a major role in development of human resource for weaker section by disseminating information on special development programmes for them.

(d) PRIs should encourage voluntary groups and local agencies in effective implementation of human resource development programmes.

Role of Panchayats in Social Mobilization and Participation for Development

Panchayati Raj system has provided avenues for facilitating people's participation at the grassroots level in the following ways :

(a) Gram Sabha will provide an open forum for discussion on various village level development activities thereby ensuring people's participation.

(b) Representation of weaker sections in the decision making process.

(c) Empowering rural women through an induction of one-third reservation in the Panchayati Raj bodies.

Panchayati Raj System and Micro Level Planning

Planned development being an essential feature of Indian economy, Panchayati Raj Institutions have to play an effective role in the preparation of planning for socio-economic development of the rural areas. Each tier has got responsibilities to plan for the socio-economic development of the rural people as per their felt need.

Ongoing Rural Development Schemes

1. Swarnajayanti Gram Swarozgar Yojana

Notwithstanding the impressive progress that has been by the country on different fronts, poverty continues to be a matter of serious concern. The effect of large percentage of the poor on the country's development is obvious. The situation needs to be redressed quickly. It is in this context that the self-employment programmes acquire significance. Swarnajayanti Gram Swarozgar Yojana (SGSY) is the single self-employment programme for the rural poor. Launched on April 1, 1999 the programme replaces the earlier self-employment and allied programmes—IRDP, TRYSEM, DWCRA, SITRA, GKY and MWS, which are no longer in operation. SGSY is an innovative and carefully thought-out Yojana. It takes into account all the strengths and weaknesses of the earlier self-employment programmes. It offers the perfect balance of credit and subsidy.

SGSY aims at establishing a large number of micro-enterprises in the rural areas, building upon the potential of the rural poor. It is rooted in the belief that the rural poor in India have competencies and given the right support can be successful producers of valuable goods/services. Persons assisted under this programme will be known as Swarozgaris and not beneficiaries. A significant aspect of SGSY is that every family assisted under this programme will be brought above the poverty line in three years and, therefore, the programme aims at creating substantial additional incomes for the rural poor. Subject to availability of funds, it is proposed to cover 30 per cent of the rural poor in each block in the next five years.

2. Pradhan Mantri Gram Sadak Yojana

Rural Road Connectivity is not only a key component of Rural Development in India, it is also recognized as an effective poverty reduction programme. Notwithstanding the efforts made over the year, at the State and Central levels, through different programmes, about 40 per cent of the Habitations in the country are still connected by all-weather roads. It is well known that even where connectivity has been provided, the roads constructed are of such quality that they cannot be categorized as all-weather roads. The Prime Minister of India announced it on 15th August, 2000.

The objective of the Government is to provide road connectivity, through good all-weather roads, to all Rural Habitations with a population of more than 500 persons by the year 2007 (end of the 10th Five-Year Plan). The primary focus of the Programme will be on construction of new roads. However, upgradation (to prescribed standards) of existing roads will be permitted to be taken up under the programme so as to achieve connectivity through good all-weather roads. Extension of existing roads to the SC/ST Habitation in the village would also be covered under upgradation. Upgradation would, however, not cover repairs of existing roads.

The rural roads to be taken up will, by and large, be surfaced roads (black topped/cement concrete). However, depending upon the soil conditions, all-weather roads may also be gravel roads, but with all necessary cross-drainage structures.

3. Employment Assurance Scheme

Employment Assurance Scheme (EAS) was launched on 2nd October, 1993 for implementation in 1778 identified backward Blocks of different States. The Blocks selected were in the drought prone areas, desert areas, tribal areas and hilly areas. Later, the scheme was extended to the remaining Blocks of the country in phased manner. At present, the scheme is being implemented in all the rural Blocks of the country. The programme has been restructured from 1st April, 1999.

As its name suggests, the primary objective of the EAS is to provide gainful employment during the lean agricultural season in manual work to all able bodied adults in rural areas who are in need and desirous of work, but cannot find it. The work may be either on farm or on other allied operations or on the normal plan/no-plan works during such a period. The secondary objective is the creation of community, social and economic assets for sustained employment and development.

4. Rural Housing

Housing is vital for human survival and, therefore, essential for socio-economic development. The need for improved housing is most acutely felt among the rural poor. As part of the efforts to meet the housing needs of the rural poor, Indira Awaas Yojana was started in May 1985 as a sub-scheme of Jawahar Rozgar Yojana. From 1st January, 1996 it is being implemented as an independent scheme.

The objective of Indira Awaas Yojana is primarily to help construction of dwelling units and upgradation of existing unserviceable *kutcha* houses of members of SC/ST, freed bonded labourers and also non-SC/ST rural poor below poverty line by providing them with grant-in-aid.

5. Credit-cum-Subsidy Scheme for Rural Housing

The Credit-*cum*-Subsidy Scheme for Rural Housing has been conceived for rural households having annual income upto Rs. 32,000 to enable or facilitate construction of houses for all households who have some repayment capacity.

6. Jawahar Gram Samridhi Yojana

Jawahar Gram Samridhi Yojana (JGSY) is the restructured, streamlined and comprehensive version of the erstwhile Jawahar Rozgar Yojana (JRY). It has been launched on 1st April, 1999. It has been designed to improve the quality of life of the rural poor by providing them additional gainful employment. The primary objective of JGSY is the creation of demand-driven village infrastructure including durable assets to enable the rural poor to increase the opportunities for sustained employment. The secondary objective is the generation of supplementary employment for the unemployed poor in the rural areas.

7. Wastelands Development

The Wastelands Development Division of Department of Land Resources, Ministry of Rural Development is implementing a wide range scheme for checking and degradation, increasing bio-mass availability, specially fuel wood and fodder and putting such wastelands into sustainable use.

8. Project Golden Thread

The Project Golden Thread is conceived as a rural development project through sericulture activity. This special project aims to increase livelihood of the poor through improvement of traditional sericulture activity in the North-Eastern India. The project involves development of non-mulberry silk, namely Eri (Endi) and Muga. These silks are found only in the North-East India. The project is implemented by Department of Panchayat and Rural Development, Assam in collaboration with Central Silk Board and Department of Handloom Sericulture, Assam. The project is under the special SGSY of the Ministry of Rural Development, Government of India.

The Project Golden Thread is a holistic project covering all aspects from plantation to spinning with modern machines and market linkage. It is now going on in the eight districts of Assam, namely Dhemaji, Lakhimpur, Karbianglong, Goalpara, Dhubri, Golaghat, Kamrup and Kokrajhar.

SOCIO-ECONOMIC PROFILE OF VILLAGES

This State paper is based on the socio-economic village study assignments of IAS Officer Trainees. Reference from some books, Internet material and secondary data sources are used in between to make the State paper significant and relevant. The study attempts to bring out the trends and current status in the socio-economic scenario in the rural Assam, covering the last 8 years of study (1994-2002) solely depending on the micro-level socio-economic surveys conducted by the officer trainees.

The broad areas covered are:

- Rural Infrastructure,

- Health and Family welfare,
- Education,
- Agrarian Relations,
- Social Structure,
- Economic activities,
- Anti-poverty and other Rural Development Programmes, and
- Panchayati Raj System.

List of IAS officer trainees (1994-2002) whose assignments were available and used for socio-economic State paper of Assam is given in Table 1.2.

Table 1.2: Assignments of I.A.S. Trainees

Sl. No.	*Name of the Officer Trainees*	*Village*	*District*	*Year*
1.	Avinash Joshi	Niz Lahoal	Dibrugarh	1994
2.	Rajeev Chandra Joshi	Mohbandha Gaon	Jorhat	1994
3.	Sanjay Lohiya	Nargaon	Kamrup	1994
4.	L.S. Changsan	Naharani Grant	Sonitpur	1996
5.	Anurag Goel	Senchowa	Nagaon	1996
6.	Caralyn Khongwar	Kalitakuchi	Kamrup	1996
7.	Krishna Kumar Dwivedi	Pachim Matia	Goalpara	1996
8.	J. Syamala Rao	Hatkhula Gaon	Dibrugarh	1997
9.	Shakil Ahammed	Binoigutia	Dibrugarh	1997
10.	Mukesh Chandra Sahu	Hatkhula Gaon	Dibrugarh	1998
11.	P. Sampath Kumar	Reng Beng	Nagaon	1999
12.	Ashutosh Agnihotri	Deodhar	Nagaon	1999
13.	Gyanendra Dev Tripathi	Saptagram	Cachar	2000
14.	Frederick Roy	Bengenamatti	Nagaon	2000
15.	Milind S. Torawane	Kuwamara Handique	Sivasagar	2000
16.	Vijayalakshmi Bidari	Ghoramari	Sonitpur	2001
17.	Mebanshailang R. Synrem	Dighaligaon	Sonitpur	2002
18.	M. Angamuthu	Namani Borpomua	Jhorhat	2002

RURAL INFRASTRUCTURE, HEALTH, EDUCATION

Rural Infrastructure

The infrastructure development in the State has been slow. It has been lagging behind almost every State of the country except that of Orissa, Rajasthan, Madhya Pradesh, Himachal Pradesh, Jammu &

Kashmir and other North-Eastern States. Power generation and distribution is not adequate to support the growth of industry in the State. The conditions of roads and bridges are not at all conducive for promoting any worthwhile economic activity like tourism. These deficiencies in infrastructure have to be attended on priority if economic activities and services are to be supported and encouraged. The power and energy and the following linkages should be provided on the existing infrastructure in the State.

1. Improve rural roads and bridges vital for the marketing of agriculture products and transport of agriculture inputs.
2. Develop urban roads/State highways and National highways for the development of tourism, trade and commerce.
3. Increase power generation to sustain industrial and agricultural growth.
4. Maintenance and repairs of embankments to protect agricultural lands from the damaging effects of flood.
5. Develop facilities and amenities relating to railways, airlines, telephones and post and telegraph services in specified areas for the benefit of people.
6. Develop Inland Water Transport as an alternative means of transport of heavy cargo and as tourist attraction.

Roads in the rural areas, which cater to the needs of transportation of agriculture inputs, and the agriculture produce need to be developed to facilitate growth of agriculture. To improve communication between the district and sub-divisional headquarters and to the tourist destinations, other State roads need to be developed.

Mohbandha Gaon (Rajeev Chandra Joshi—1994) village is situated nearly 1 km inside of N.H. 37. It is more than 20 km away from the district headquarters and the Circle office. The Block office is at a distance of 18 km from this village. The village is connected to the national highway by a PWD road (Pamua Bhakat Road). This road divides the village into two parts. The national highway No. 37 passes near the village (1.5 km) and it is the most preferred route to the village. On this highway there are continuously running private or ASTC buses. A bus from Golaghat to Jorhat town passes twice through the village (once either way). The Mohbandha railway station is at a distance of 6-7 km from the village. Villagers also use it for movement outside. However, the buses are preferred. There is one post office (Satria) in the village that caters to the postal need of the people. The village was settled way back. In fact the last survey and settlement was done in the 1958-59. The village boasts of a small library constructed in 1945.

Niz Lahoal (Avinash Joshi—1994) village is situated in the Lahoal development Block of Dibrugarh district. This village is situated on the east direction of the district headquarters, 10 km away from the town. This is an old village and the total geographical area is 273.63 hectares out of which 198.70 hectares is cultivable land, which is totally unirrigated. Cultivable wasteland including grazing land *gauchers* and groves is 36.83 hectares and 37.10 hectares of area is not available for cultivation. Total number of holdings *Dags* is 653.

Nargaon (Sanjay Lohiya—1994) village is situated at a distance of 30 km from Guwahati. It is a small village of mixed tribal (Rabha) and non-tribal population. There are no scheduled castes or Muslims in the village. Recently a *pucca* road has been built with funds from North-Eastern Council connecting the village to National highway No. 37. But the road network within the village is *kutcha*. The village is 3 km from Rani Block office. It is about 20 km from circle office at Mirza. But the village has not benefited much from government development schemes. It is small village with hardly any political clout in the Gram Panchayat.

Naharani Grant (L.S. Changsan—1996) Village is situated 2 km north of Rangapara town, on the Balipara Tarajuli Road. It is 35 km away from Tezpur, the district headquarters and 20 km away from Ghoramari, the Block headquarters. It borders the foothills of Arunachal Pradesh. The village is a tea village. Naharani Grant land belonged to the Naharani Tea Estate. This portion was netted under the Assam Ceiling Surplus Act, 1951 and the ceiling surplus land was allotted to 46 beneficiaries. Each beneficiary was allotted 6.5 bighas, i.e. 2.15 acres of land. The nearest market is Rangapara, 2 km away. Rangapara town is an old settlement with a mixed population comprising Nepalis, Bengalis, Nishis and a minority of the indigenous Assamese population. It is well connected by a metre gauge railway line, which runs from Rangia in Kamrup district of Assam, to

Murgaonselek in Dhemaji district. A PWD road (kutcha) runs through the village. The village has two lower primary schools, the upper Kacharigaon L.P. School, and the Naharani L.P. School. There is one playground, actually a village grazing reserve (VGR). The gaon panchayat office is located near the VGR. There is a health sub-centre too in the village.

Senchowa (Anurag Goel—1996) village is quite near the town of Nagaon. The Block office is at a distance of 3 km from the village. The post office, the bank and the bus stop are within 2 km of this village while the railway station and the district headquarters is within 7 km of this village. The infrastructural facilities like bank, post office and the telephone are easily accessible. Most of the basic amenities like electricity, all-weather approach road, bus stop, primary and middle schools, PDS shop, veterinary dispensary, safe drinking water, etc. are there in the village.

Kalitakuchi (Caralyn Khongwar—1996) village lies about 35 km to the west of Guwahati, and lies on the banks of the river Brahmaputra. One of the main arterial roads connecting the Nalbari, Barpeta districts of Lower Assam with the Capital (which is also a State Highway) runs through the village. The main centre of the village is the crossroads at which the State highway crosses another road leading to other villages. The Block headquarters, which is Hajo, is just 3 km away. At the crossroads, there are many shops established by the village people, most of them catering to the bus passengers. Since the Block headquarters is only 3 km away, all the infrastructural facilities, i.e. PHC, Post Office, Bank, Grain Storage facility, Chemists, etc. The nearest Police Station is also located at the Block headquarters. The village is totally electrified with only a few houses not having electricity connection.

The village **Pachim Matia** (Krishna Kumar Dwivedi—1996) situated on the bank or river Dudhnoi in Matia development Block, about 23 km away from district headquarters, populated by 3,218 people of Hindu, Muslim and Christian communities which speak Assamese, Garo and Hazong languages and settled in 5 hamlets, namely Shantipur, Islampur, Garopara, Damani and Matia. Basic mode of transport is bus since nearest railway station is 140 km away from the village. Post office, PHC Bank and small market are next to the village.

Hatkhula Gaon (J. Syamala Rao—1997/Mukesh Chandra Sahu—1998) village consists of four numbers of hamlets, namely

Duttachuk, Chaporichuk, Koibortochuk and Moderkhatsatra. The Duttachuk is the biggest of all hamlets and accommodates almost 50 per cent of the whole population. The village is almost 15 km away from the district headquarters in Dibrugarh. It is almost 7 km away from the Block headquarters of Lahowal. From one side of the village passes a reasonably good road that connects it to the Block and district headquarters. Although there is no bus stop as such, but the buses stops on the road if asked to by the passengers. The rail line connecting Guwahati and Tinsukia passes very close to the village and there is a railway station also very near to the village. The name of the station is Lahowal town and is almost 5 km from the village. However, villagers have hardly ever used this railway station for catching any train. Only small passenger trains stop here and people here prefer bus as a mode of transport for nearby areas.

Reng Beng (P. Sampath Kumar—1999) is a village located in the Revenue Circle of Kampur and the Block of Kathiatoli of Nagaon district of Assam. It is about 23 km southwards from the district headquarters, Nagaon. The national highway No. 36 is passing near the village. The Block headquarters is at a distance of 1.5 km from the village. The services of bank, market, PHC, police station, post office and bus stop are available at Kathiatoli, which is situated at about 2.5 km from the village. There are no streetlights in the village. Though there are electric poles passing through the village, no one in the village is accessing the electricity facility. The village is connected with the National highway with an earthen road, which is constructed under JRY programme.

Deodhar (Ashutosh Agnihotri—1999) is just 6 km from the Nagaon town, the district headquarters. The Block headquarters is just one km away from the village. Located along the metalled road, the means of communication in this village are fairly good, and the village is well connected with the town. It is located along the metalled road. The nearest bus stop is hardly one km far from the village and the nearest railway station, Haiborgaon is 6 km far. Auto rickshaws ply between the village and the town, and people feel that they enjoy a reasonably good existence because of these advantages and facilities. Railway line is available with Nagaon, Phulaguri and Bebejia as the railway station.

Saptagram (Gyanendra Dev Tripathi—2000) village is connected by all-weather approach road and is electrified. There is one primary school, one Panchayat bhawan, and one ME school (Middle School). There is a bus stop on the National Highway just near the village. The Bank is also only 2 km away from the village. There are 2 Anganwadi Centres functional in the village. The telephone lines are there in the village but not utilized by most of the people. The basic problem of the village is that there is no source of safe drinking water. People use the water of river and ponds for drinking and washing. There are 4 PDS shops in the village because the population of the village is quite scattered. The village has a post office, which operates from a thatch shade on the Mizoram Road.

Bengenamatti (Frederick Roy—2000) village falls under the Kuwaritol Gram Panchayat, and within the Borbhogia Mouza, under the Uloni Revenue village of the Koliabor Revenue Circle of the northernmost sub-division of Nagaon district. It is located 45 km from the District Headquarters, and 10 km from the Block headquarters, Koliabor, and only 2 km from the SDO (Civil) office at Koliabor. Nearest bus stop is 1.5 km and the closest railway station is located 45 km away. The village is well connected, comparatively by a few all-weather roads. However, in many areas, metalled and black topped roads are non-existent, thus causing some difficulties to the inhabitants. The village has all the basic amenities, which includes post office, bank, primary school, PHC, dispensary, ICDS centre and a *haat* area as well. Telephone facilities are however lacking. The village has a 30 bedded hospital in Oluni, but at present it has been occupied by the CRPF, thus rendering its IPD unit non-functional.

Kuwamara Handique (Milind S. Torawane—2000) is a small village in Kheluwa Block of the district. It is situated at a distance of 26 km from the Block headquarters, Kheluwa. The district headquarters, Sivasagar is around 12 km from the village. Both the Block and District headquarters are connected with the village by all-weather approach road. The World Bank has recently completed black topping of the road upto 8 km from Sivasagar and gravelling for the rest part upto Kuwamara Handique, under the ARIASP programme. Villagers are using Betbari at 2.5 km as the nearest bus stop. Sivasagar town offers the facility of town market place, PHC, bank and railway station. The village settlement pattern is of scattered settlement type. The houses are scattered in an area of about 4-5 sq km. Villagers are living in a group of 6-7 houses, built near their agricultural holdings. These are *kutcha/pucca* houses built with the use of bamboo, wood and brick cement materials. Easily available local building materials like bamboo, wood etc. have been used upto 70-80 per cent in the house construction. Considering the availability of natural resources and the infrastructure, the village has remained more or less agriculture village. It is certainly facing some growth constraints as the infrastructural facilities are moderate and the village people with other professional skills and high aspirations are moving out. The village seems to be self-sufficient in its own but from the outsiders view it is very much behind in fulfilling the basic minimum needs of the community life.

Ghoramari (Vijayalakshmi Bidari—2001) village is located in Sonitpur district under the Balipara Development Block. It is at a distance of 16 km north of Tezpur, the headquarters of Sonitpur district. The area of the village is 499.10 acres. Ghoramari village has 2 hamlets—Ahom Chuburi (hamlet) and Adibasi Chuburi (hamlet). It has a all-weather approach road, a bus stop, a national highway connects it to the district headquarters, the nearest railway station (Balipara) is 8 km from it and the nearest airport, Tezpur is 16 km from Ghoramari.

Dighaligaon (Mebanshailang R. Synrem—2002) village is situated at a distance of about 27 km to the north of Tezpur. Falling under the Udmari Gram Panchayat, it covers an area of about 682 acres approximately with a population of approximately 3,100 people. To the east of Dighaligaon, there is the Balipara Tea Estate, to the west, there are two villages—Eragaon and Konarigaon, to the north there is Bharatgaon and to the south there is Bamgaon. The village is flood prone and huge tracts of land have been lost due to erosion. It is situated on the banks of the Jia Bharoli River that has its origin in Arunachal Pradesh. Because of this large-scale erosion a huge number of people have been left with almost no land for agricultural purposes. Infrastructure, in the strict sense of the term, is poor, to say the least. Electrification is partial, the roads are kutcha, and there are only two Lower Primary schools. The PHC, however, is situated very near and is easily accessible to the villagers. There are no major shop inside the village and no public phone facility. The only relief is that the main market is nearby (only 0.5 km) and people often go there for their various needs.

Namani Borpomua (Majuli) (M. Angamuthu—2002) a Miri or Mishing village is situated in the north-eastern part of Majuli sub-division in Jorhat district of Assam. The village is located at a distance of 75 km from Jorhat town. Distance from Garmur (Administrative Headquarters of the sub-division) to this village is 25 km. Another town Jengraimukh (Block Headquarters too) is situated around 2.5 km from this village. As such there is no direct approach road to this village. But a small dyke constructed by the villagers themselves through the village is used by the villagers to reach from one end to the another end of the village. The nearest PWD road of the village is Pohumora Garmur and Jengrai Haldibari road where private buses, taxis run between Haldibari and Kamalabari *via* Jengrai and Garmur frequently.

Health Facilities and Family Welfare

Most of the villages visited during socio-economic survey of IAS Probationers, it was found that the villagers have the health facility like sub-centres and Primary Health Centre in the village or nearby village. Avinash Joshi (1994) says, "Villagers of **Niz Lahoal** go to 3 km far away Block hospital for their medical needs. Sometimes villagers go to the tea garden hospital which is nearby. This hospital serves the needs of both the tea garden labourers as well as of the villagers." The **Naharani** Health Sub-Centre is located within the village in the home of Smt. Debashri Boro, an ANM of the Health Department. The doctors visit once or twice in a month, quite regularly. The nearest Primary Health Centre is at Rangapara, 2 km away. There is also a railway hospital and Naharani Tea Estate Hospital nearby village. According to Krishna Kumar Dwivedi (1996) Most of the people of **Pachim Matia** avail medical facilities from private practitioner and not willing to go to government hospital since infrastructure and proper caring are not available in that hospital. Vijayalakshmi Bidari (2001) reveals in her report of **Ghoramari** "The sub-PHC functions from 8 am to 12 noon. It provides for immunization, antenatal care, treatment for minor illness, paediatric case, contraceptives and IUD insertion. There is also ICDS centre (anganwadi) in the same premises of sub-PHC. The ANM goes to the houses for regular check ups. There is no MPW in the village. The survey also revealed that the first point of contact for 37/45 households is sub-PHC, which means that most of the people in the village access the sub-PHC."

Benganamatti village has a newly renovated European Commission funded PHC is located at the very heart of the village. One ANM services this centre, and prior to pulse polio campaign, one female child died. No midwives are present in the village. As regards, medicines, supply is highly irregular. Costly medicines are often prescribed which at most times are out of reach for the villagers. Infant mortality is low, and vaccination is undertaken regularly. However, childbirth is mostly performed at home, and for serious and complicated cases, the patients are taken to the neighbouring district capital at Tezpur. Birth and death in last one year are as follows :

No. of births in the last one year	26
Male births	12
Female births	14
No. of deaths	2 (both female)
No. of infant deaths	2

Antenatal care, treatment of minor illness, paediatric care, and availability of oral CC are the other highlights of this PHC. Family Planning and Maternity Care status in the village is as follows :

Total number of married couples	399
Eligible couples for family planning	131
Total number of males who have accepted family planning methods	50
Total number of females adopting family planning methods	121
No. of domestic deliveries	12

Population Control Measures: IUD is used, together with oral CC. No. of institutional deliveries are 6. ANM/MPW regularly visit the village. People usually seek services of government health functionaries and government provided health services.

In **Dighaligaon**, Mebanshailang R. Synrem (2002) mentioned that “there were 53 births in the village in the last year. Out of these, 27 were males and 26 females. Out of these, 27 were home deliveries while the rest were institutional deliveries. There were 4 deaths in the village in the past year. The total number of married couples is 310 and out of these, 160 couples are eligible for family planning.

Family planning is not very acceptable to the people and a total of only 9 persons have opted for family planning of any sort. An interesting piece of information is that all of them are women. It was highly heartening to learn that a majority named the PHC as the first point of contact in case of any illness. However, almost everyone had a common complaint of medicines are not available in the PHC. The PHC is fully functional." In **Saptagram**, health and family planning situation is not very good in village. Out of total twelve births in last year, only 3 deliveries were conducted in hospital by trained personnel, in remaining 75 per cent of cases child is delivered at home with the help of untrained personnel. Out of total 59 eligible couples, only twelve females have adopted permanent family planning methods. No male member in the village has adopted permanent family planning methods.

The above facts show that even though the villagers have reasonable health facility in the village and but home deliveries were still more than the institutional deliveries. There were some cases of infant mortality too. The reports also mention that the cases of male sterilisation are almost nil comparative to female sterilisation.

In some of the village study reports it was found that the villagers were not happy with the health facilities in the village. Such as J. Syamala Rao (1997) revealed that **"Hatkhula Gaon** sub-centre which caters to the village is facing so many problems. The ANM does not stay in the village because of the dilapidated condition of her quarters. The sub-centre does not have water supply, electricity, chair/table, medicines, kerosene, stove, etc. the ANM visits the village three days in a week. The PHC nearby is also in bad condition. The electricity has been disconnected because of non-payment of bill. Hence vaccine storing is becoming very difficult." In **Kalitakuchi** there is no PHC in the village, not even a sub-PHC. However, the main PHC is just 3 km away in the Block headquarters. In the area of family planning there is no awareness at all.

P. Sampath Kumar (1999) **Reng Beng** mentioned that "There is no primary health centre or sub-centre in the village but there is a PHC at Kathiatoli, which is located at a distance of 2 km from the village. Once in a week, one ANM from Kathiatoli PHC visits the village for providing health services to the villagers." The same situation found in **Kuwamara Handique** "The villagers do not have the facility of PHC or primary health sub-centre so they have to depend on the PHC at Sivasagar at 12 km from the village". And in **Mohbandha Gaon** "the village falls under Baghchung PHC but it is at a distance of 18 km from the village."

Most of the villages found very neat and clean and as such there is no problem as far as sanitation is concerned. Mosquito is a big problem in the villages. Health department gives DDT to fight this problem. People are generally healthy. There is not much prevalence of diseases. Common illnesses are gastroenteritis, malaria etc. Drinking water supply exists in the villages. Sanitary wet latrines do not exist in the villages. But most of the houses, especially those of the indigenous Assamese have proper toilets.

Family welfare programmes have been well accepted here. Oral contraceptives are distributed. Families are mostly planned and are limited to two or four children. Iron tablets are freely given to the pregnant women. Pregnant mothers have undergone antenatal care and were given TT immunization. But when it comes to childcare—there has been only partial immunization. The ICDS workers are also involved in the immunization programmes and pulse polio programme has been quite successful here. Even though the ANM is involved in house to house check-ups and in spite of the anganwadi workers also involved in immunization programme, there has been not much success. Most of the children are partially immunized as revealed by the survey. In the villages, there are considerable number of couples who have undergone laparoscopy or other family planning methods still there are about 8-10 couples who are willing to undergo this operation. There are very less number of males going for sterilization. Villagers seem to have lack of faith in the Block Health Centre and so they prefer medical college. Therefore, it is advisable to conduct a laparoscopy camp at the Block level with wide publicity. People are conscious of their health and hygiene. Medical facilities are reasonably good, and for serious illness, one can easily go to the nearby town.

Education

The education system in Assam is quite peculiar and follows 4+3+3 system whereas in other parts of the country it is 5+3+2+2 system. Education plays a very important role in the rural development. Even though most of the villages have primary or middle school. But for secondary and higher secondary education villagers have to go out of the village. Both secondary and higher secondary schools are 4-20 km away from the villages. Some of the facts that found during the socio-economic surveys are as follows :

In **Naharani Grant** village, Literacy rates are highest for the General category, and lowest for the OBC category. Out of a total sample population of 174, 100 persons are literate, i.e. a literacy rate of 57.47 per cent. It is interesting to note that there is no graduate amongst the sample population. There are 20 matriculates. A large majority of educates are mostly below matric. Village has two lower primary schools—Kacharigaon L. P. School and Naharani L.P. School. The nearest higher secondary school is one km away, i.e. the Rangapara High School. Don Bosco School run by the Catholic mission is also at nearby Rangapara. The Kacharigaon L.P. School was set up in 1984-85 under JRY scheme. It has 84 students and two teachers. Naharani L.P. School was constructed under the EAS. Children from the nearby Kulibari village came to attend school here. In **Pàchim Matia,** there are primary and high schools in the village. Only 33.64 per cent people are literate in which the numbers of the graduates are only 22. The data shows that the rate of dropouts after the primary level is very high. Overall environment as regards to education found to be dismal in the **Binoigutia** village. The villagers to look into the problem form an education awareness committee. They started free tuition in the village for the tenth standard students. There is a Middle English School consists of 5th, 6th, 7th and 8th class only, which started in 1989 under the help of TATA Tea Estate. A pucca building with furnitures are there for the school. Unfortunately the school is yet to get the recognition from the government. The villagers run it and they are finding it difficult to run the school.

In **Hatkola Gaon** the standard of children in the primary school is not up to the mark. The school has got two teachers who belong to adjoining village. Both passed SSC only. The school is facing so many problems. The mid-day meal scheme has come to a halt since last year because the food items are not supplied. There is shortage of desks and tables. There is only one room for all the four classes. The condition of school building is very bad. There is no equipment for playing. Attendance is around 85 per cent on the day of visit. The condition of anganwadi centre is very bad. Virtually nothing except teaching of alphabets to children takes place. No materials are received for nutritional programme. There is one government lower primary school and one government Middle English school in **Reng Beng** village.

These are located in the outskirts of the village catering the educational needs of two more adjacent villages. There is one private primary school within village. The percentage of literacy of the village is very low compared to the literacy of the State as a whole. It is only about 30 per cent compared to the literacy rate of State of 52.11 per cent. There is large number of dropouts at middle school level. In the age group below 14 years, 24.18 per cent of children were never enrolled, 13.19 per cent dropped out after enrollment, and 12.09 per cent are enrolled but irregular. Only 48.36 per cent of children go to school regularly. In **Saptagram** population set above 14 years age group, 42 per cent are illiterate, 9 per cent are matriculate, 18 per cent are higher secondary, 5.21 per cent have done diploma and 13 per cent are graduate and post graduate. Only one member had the technical degree. From the above statistic it is clear that literacy rate in this village is about 58 per cent which is much higher than State literacy rate in rural areas.

Ghoramari village has a lower primary school, middle school, high school, higher secondary school, and a vocational training institute all in a 1 km radius. It does not have an Adult Literacy Centre. The adult literacy rate is very poor, and no opportunities to pursue education in the non-formal way. The 1991 census figures say that the number of literates is 253/696 out of which 147 are males, 106 are females.

The Male Literacy is 147/353 × 100 = 41.64 per cent
The female literacy is 106/343 × 100 = 30.9 per cent
Total literacy figure is 253/696 × 100 = 36.35 per cent

The survey revealed that in the above 14-year population:

Illiterates	43
Upto primary	11
Upto Secondary	11
Above secondary	7
Total	**72**

The below 14-year population :

Never enrolled	18
Dropped out	01
Enrolled and goes to school	19
Total	**38**

The data shows that around 50 per cent of the below 14-year populations are in school. This is definitely not encouraging. The village has access to government L.P. School, Hem Baruah High School and Higher Secondary School, Vocational Training Institute. They are in good condition. The attendance of the teachers and students on the survey days was quite good. The L.P. School has 76 girls, 101 boys enrolled from classes I to V. The student-teacher ratio is 177/4 for the L.P. school.

Educational facilities up to college level are available in an around the **Namani Borpomua** village. There is one Junior Basic school within the village, which was established in 1933. Besides this a Junior Basic school in the village, there is one government aided H.S. school at Jengrai Mukh Tiniali, situated at a distance of 2.5 km from the village. Total enrollment in the year 2003 was 550, of whom 481 were Mishing and 69 were of Non-Mishing community. Distribution of population by sex and educational status of the village is given in Table 1.3.

Table 1.3 : Population by Sex and Educational Level

Educational Status	*Children below 15 years*		*Adults*		*Total*	*%*
	Male	*Female*	*Male*	*Female*		
Illiterate	78	102	128	109	457	39.53
Primary (dropped out)	53	81	66	98	298	25.73
ME Standard	58	72	40	45	218	18.85
Matric/HSLC	—	—	69	41	117	10.12
Graduate	—	—	35	12	47	4.06
PG	—	—	15	4	19	1.65
Total	**193**	**255**	**353**	**354**	**1156**	**100.00**

About 39.53 percent of the total population in the village are illiterate and the rest are literate and educated. The percentage of literacy of the village is equivalent to that of Assam as a whole, which is 62 per cent according to 2001 census.

There are two L.P. schools in the **Dighaligaon** village and compared to the total population in the village, the enrollment is quite poor. The number of children who have never enrolled is also alarmingly high in the age group 6-14 years. Infrastructure is bad, to say the least, and the schools desperately need a facelift in the shape of more classrooms as well as basic amenities like latrines and proper drinking water.

There are two primary, two middle and a high school in **Benganamatti** village. Annual enrollment is about 102/112 as per 2001 census. The educational infrastructure in the village is fairly adequate. The literacy rate of the village is as follows :

Male	661	60.5%
Female	555	52.6%

Teacher-student ratios: The middle school has 9 teachers, with the LP school having 5 teachers for 180 students. The Adarsha High School has an enrolled capacity of :

Total	257	ST	92
Male	134	SC	41
Female	123	Others	124
Teachers	15		

Kuwamara Handique has primary and middle school run by the Education Department of the Government. The village does not have any private school. Total number of students going in the primary school is 205, out of this 140 are boys, and the rest 65 are girls. The strength for middle school is 83 with 59 boys and 24 girls. Total teachers for primary school are 19 with 11 male and 8 female teachers. For middle school, these are 11, 7 male and 4 female teachers. The village is having a literacy of 63.9 per cent as per the revised records of the Zila Saksharata Samitee (ZSS). The ZSS runs an adult education centre in the village. Amongst the literates 709 (75.59%) are males and 463 (51.67%) are females. The literacy percentage amongst the tribal population is as little as 36.61 per cent with 44.44 per cent in males and only 26.53 per cent in females. The SC population has comparatively better literacy percentage as 53.85 per cent for total and 68.18 per cent and 35.29 per cent for male and female SC population respectively. With 19 teachers for primary school and 11 teachers for middle school; the teacher-student ratio comes out to be 11 and 8 respectively. It means for every 11 primary school students and 8 middle school students there is one teacher. This favourable teacher student is not indication of any progress in the field of education but it is due to the fact of far excess recruitment of teachers by the government during last 7-8 years. The dropout figure is upto average 7-8 per cent in each year for Class I to IV. It rises upto 15-20 per cent at the entry level of middle school, i.e. Class V. Large percentage of dropouts comprise the tribal students who do not want to continue education. Often they are engaged in household activities of pig rearing, fishery, poultry, etc. The village has benefited from the literacy campaigns. The literacy percentage was found to be 51.8 per cent in 1994 at the time of launching of total literacy campaign (TLC). ZSS surveyed 132 persons as targeted illiterates, out of which 98 (74.2%) passed all three primers and 63 (47.7%) achieved NLM norm. In the Post Literacy Programme (PLP) in 1997, 81 persons enrolled and 68 completed PL-I. 4 youths from the village got opportunity to participate in the skill development programme. Now, ZSS has planned to start Continuing Education Programme and it has identified Kuwamara Handique as one of its Continuing Education Centres (CEC) site. The literacy movements have delivered far more benefits than imparting literacy skills. These campaigns have tried to bring awareness amongst the illiterates and neo-literates about community participation, social and democratic rights, family welfare, health care, national integration and conservation of environment etc.

There are two primary schools in the **Mohbandha Grant** village. One of these is inside the tea garden. The high school and the higher secondary education are available at Pamua Bhakat village (at a distance of 1 km). There is one higher school proposed in the village but its building is yet to be completed. The primary school caters to the need of nearby villages. The school building is almost in a dilapidated status. It was constructed under NREP, 1989. Within six years of its construction, it is almost in dire state of affairs. The minimum furnitures, viz. 2 tables and 2 chairs for the two teachers who look after 787 children from first standard to fifth. The blackboards are not yet all black literally, as they were painted last at the time of school construction. There are cement boards on the walls itself. The attendance is quite poor and rate of dropout is very high. According to the study, the class-wise dropouts are 25, 92, 36, 84, 21, 43, 30 and 50 per cent in Class I, II, III, IV and V with an average rate of class-wise dropout of 32.84 per cent. But, if we compare with the enrollment at class I and the final students reach class V, the dropout rate is as high as 70.37 per cent indicating poor economic and illiterate background of the families. The teacher-taught ratio works out to be 39 since there are two teachers for all the 78 students enrolled. Both the teachers are lady teachers. They are permanent. But the general complaint from the villages, they do not take the teaching seriously and quite unpunctual.

Provision of better education and health facilities is necessary to strengthen the capabilities of the poor and vulnerable groups to earn income. Resource constraints make it imperative that poorer geographic regions need to be targeted first so that resources are not thinly spread and the quantum of subsidy is large enough to pull the poor out of poverty on a sustained basis. Resource constraints need to overcome through innovative means, e.g. use of health cards (similar to ration cards) to protect the poor and introduction of user charges for certain health services. Universal elementary education can be achieved by providing special incentives such as mid-day meals and special subsidies, for example to girl children to close gender gaps in education. Innovative measures can be used such as the Education Guarantee Scheme of the Madhya Pradesh government to reduce the costs of schooling and increase the accountability of teachers.

AGRARIAN RELATION

Assam is known primarily as a producer of tea and oil. But agriculture is the basic source of living of the majority of the population. The population of the State has been increasing at a faster rate than the rest of the country both due to natural growth and immigration. Agriculture production did not increase at an encouraging rate during the plan periods. Assam was self sufficient in respect of rice production till the Second Five-Year Plan period but became deficit in rice thereafter. Agricullture production in Assam is unstable because it depends almost entirely on rainfall. Although rainfall is heavy it does not help raising productivity of the main rice crop. It has now become apparent that the green revolution in India has taken place only in areas, which are endowed with irrigation, rural electification, roads and developed markets. Favourable institutional framework in these areas helped the farmers to take initiative.

Agriculture is a composite term and agricultural development is a difficult process. It is difficult to make a comprehensive study on agriculutral development in areas which are generally backward and indepth studies on development are either scanty or absent. This is particulary true in the case of Assam. Data on many aspects of the agricultural economy of the Assam are not available. However, these socio-economic reports of IAS officer trainess would help us to understand the nature of crop production in Assam and analyse the process of agricultural development for a period of eight years (1994-2002).

LANDHOLDING

Ownership of the land is well disbursed among all the sections of the village population. Almost all the households of the villages have got their own land, though the area of the holding varies from 2 bighas to 50 bighas. The people in Assam use Bigha, Katha and Lessa system for measuring landholding. Although, the survey booklet clearly asks for recording the data in acre, it could not be recorded like that because people were saying in BKL system only. While entering the data in the computer, however, the conversions were done to acre system. The conversion factor: 1 bigha = 5 katha, 1 katha = 20 less, 1 acre = 3.025 bigha. Agriculture is the mainstay of the people. Almost all the households have at least a small plot of land which they cultivate. Otherwise they work as agricultural labourers. As each household has got some amount of land, the landholdings are generally very small and not economically viable. Only the subsistence form of agriculture is followed. In **Naharani Grant** village the average land owned per head is 2.03 acres. Out of the total land owned by the sample population, viz. 60 acres, 35 acres fall under cropped area. 42.86 per cent of the total cropped area is cultivated by the persons belonging to the OBC, 32.86 by the ST, 5.71 per cent by SC and 21.43 per cent by those of the general category.

The total area of the **Pachim Matia** village is 1,657 acres out of which cultivable land is 554.77 acres, fallow land is 150.23 acres and land for homestead is 335 acres. Total land under cultivation is based upon rainfed. No irrigation project is taken up in the village. The village land can be divided into following classes Shali, Bari Lahitali Faringgatu and commercial land. There are 1,085 acre of government land (khas land) in the village and 10.6 acre of land has been taken out surplus from ceiling thus total surplus land is 1095.6 acres, out of which 5 acres have been distributed among 13 people.

Total area is divided in 1,247 plots (Dag). Total 496.77 acres area is under ownership cultivation while 58 acre is under tenancy. 202 out of total 535 households in the village have no land while 144 households have below 1 acre land holdings. No household has more than 10 acre of land. 294 operational holdings are below 1 acre while only 5 acre between 5-10 acre. Mostly one crop yielding is common in the village. Multi-crop cultivation is not prevalent since lack of proper irrigation facilities.

In **Kalitakuchi,** out of the 1744.55 acres or 3873.28 bighas of land, 2,258 bigha is under cultivation. Out of this, 21 bigha 4 katha is fallow land, 308 bigha is pasture or grazing land belonging to the community, 553 bigha is wasteland, 552 bigha is under homestead use, and the net sown area is 1310 bigha. The total area under irrigation is only 30 bigha 3 katha and 15 lessa. There are no government irrigation projects in the village.

Total area of the **Saptagram** village is 918.26 acre or 371.19 hectare. The distribution of land ownership is shown in following Table 1.4:

Table 1.4 : Landholding, Number of Households

Sl. No.	*Landholding (Acre)*	*No. of Household*
1.	Landless	201
2.	Less than one	98
3.	1-3	131
4.	3-5	26
5.	5-10	Nil
6.	More than 10	Nil

It is clear from above table that around 45 per cent of households are landless. About 30 per cent of the households fall in the category of marginal farmers and as it is clear from the table that there are only 26 families who have more than 3 acres of landholding. Thus in the village there is mostly marginal farmers and very few small farmer. In the last ten years, about 22 per cent of families have sold their land, and in all the cases the purchaser was general community member. In the same period, about 17 per cent families have purchased any kind of land. Here 70 per cent sellers were upper caste and remaining 30 per cent were SC. There are about 201 landless households in the village. Most of the landless fall in the Hindustani or Bengali Muslim community. Most of them are daily workers in the field or on the brickfield. Some of them are involved in some business or shop keeping others are practicing some form of the craftsmanship—carpentry, barber shop, tailoring etc.

Land use pattern In **Hatkola Gaon** (in hectares) :

Total area of the village	222.85
Land under cultivation	155.77
Land under forest cover	0
Fallow land	0
Grazing/pasture land	12.84
Cultivable waste land	0
Not available for cultivation	33.94
Land under miscellaneous tree and groves	20.068
Net sown area	155.77

The land is evenly distributed and the disparities are not much. Nobody has got land in excess of 4 ha. Only a tea garden possesses land in excess of 10 hectares. The distribution is shown below :

Class Size (ha)	*Number of Landholders*
<1	124
1-2	25
2-4	16
4-10	0
10+	1

The total area of the **Reng Beng** village at present is 39.18 ha. Out of this land for cultivation is 25.86 ha, fallow land is 1.47 ha, land under miscellaneous tree and groves is 1.23 ha, homestead land is 10.49 ha and land under Namghar and *mandirs* including small *beel* (pond) is 0.13 ha.

In **Ghoramari** village the survey shows that the size of the landholding is less than one acre for 24 households out of 45 surveyed. Types of land utilization :

Land for cultivation	377.73 acres
Pasture and grazing land	8.13 acres
Wasteland	6.74 acres

Land for homestead	69.51 acres
Community land	21.79 acres
Net sown area (land for cultivation + part of wasteland + part of land for homestead)	422.13 acres

There has been no irrigation project in the village (government or private). Hence it is mainly rain fed agriculture.

The total area of the **Senchowa** village at present is 262.5 acres out of which the categorization is as under (in acres) :

Land for cultivation	138.85 acres
Fallow land	50.00 acres
Pasture and grazing land	1.43 acres
Land for homestead	57.14 acres
Community land	5.43 acres
Miscellaneous	12.68 acres

The total land area irrigated is 98 acres. The sources of irrigation are river, water pumps and the rains. Most of the people own homestead land and not the cultivable land. Most of the people own landless than 1-2 bighas. There is a need for land consolidation.

The total area of the **Hatkhula Gaon** village is 550.59 acres of which 249.91 acres (45.39%) is under ownership cultivation. Out of the remaining 300.68 acres of land, a major chunk of 141.8 acres (25.75%) is wasteland, 98.79 acres (17.94%) is used for homestead while 58.36 acres (10.6%) of land is marked as pasture and grazing land. Only 1.73 acres (0.32%) of the land is being used as community land. There is no forest cover in the village and there is no fallow land either. 84 per cent of the population has land holding of less than 5 acres. From the field it was also seen that all the lands are fragmented in many parts. On an average, each plot must not be measuring more than one-third of an acre. On such small holdings, it becomes difficult for mechanization of the agriculture process. Only bullocks can plough these fields. Now-a-days power tillers are slowly being introduced for small plots.

In **Namani Borpomua** village, out of 109 households, only 6 households (5.50%) are landless. The landless households in the village belong to the non-Mishing community. Only 15 to 13.76 per cent of the total households have land below 2 hectares or 15 bighas and the total land possessed by these households is 24.93 hectares or 6.11 per cent of the total land in the village. These households are regarded as small farmers. Most of the households in the village (68.81%) possess land between 2 to 6 hectares and these households own 69.34 per cent of the total land. The rest of 13 households (11.93%) are considered as rich cultivators and the land possessed by the each of these households is above 6 hectares. Distribution of owned land according to size group of operational holdings of the village is as follows :

Size group	*No. of Households*	*Total Area Owned*	*%*
Landless	6	0.69	0.17
Below 1 ha	3	2.44	0.60
1-2 ha	12	22.49	5.51
2-4 ha	55	181.14	44.40
4-6 ha	20	101.75	24.94
6-8 ha	10	75.34	18.46
8-10 ha	2	12.30	3.01
10-12 ha	1	11.89	2.91
Total	**109**	**408.04**	**100.00**

Operational holdings here include the land owned by the villagers plus government lands cultivated by the villagers and land taken on lease minus land leased out to others. All the households in the village except the landless have operational holdings. About 55 per cent of the total households in the size group of 2-4 hectares have occupied 44.13 per cent of the total operational holdings in the village. The average size of the operational holding of the village as a whole is 3.50 hectares.

The total land in the **Dighaligaon** village is 681.16 acres of which 342.55 acres is for cultivation, 8.86 acres for pasture and grazing, 171.34 acres for homestead land and a further 159.11 acres for other miscellaneous uses. A majority of the households have land under one acre with a few between 1-3 acres. Between 3-5 acres, there are a negligible number of households. There are a few landless households and as per the SDCs records, the number is only 3. The entire land is low lying and used mainly for agriculture and backyard farming. Landholdings of a majority of the respondents are so meagre that any form of sustainable agriculture is not possible. They are thankful for the little piece of homestead land they possess but they are skeptical that they may lose even this in the near future if nothing concrete and substantial is done fast.

Land utilisation in **Deodhar** village:

	(*in acres*)
Land for cultivation	692.92
Land under forest cover	0
Fallow land	3.69
Pasture for grazing land	4.30
Wasteland	0
Land for homestead	93.23
Net sown area	589.55
Community land	2.15

Small size of agricultural holding is another obstacle in the path of modernization of agriculture. The average size of operational holding is only 1.37 hectares.

Distribution of land ownership :

Landless	0
< 1 acre	92
1-3 acres	107
3-5 acres	39
5-10 acres	0
10-20 acres	0
20 acres	0

Area under cultivation yielding :

One crop	423
Two crop	137
Multi crop	29

Land utilization in **Benganamatti Village :**

Land for cultivation	495.86
Land under forest cover	2.52
Fallow land	18.38
Pasture for grazing land	93.49
Wasteland	46.77
Land for homestead	37.26
Net sown area	453.54
Community land	25.33
Miscellaneous	19.08

Distribution of landownership :

Landless	35
< 1 acre	52
1-3 acres	47
3-5 acres	21
5-10 acres	10
10-20 acres	5
20 acres	Nil

The **Kuwamara Handique** village has total land area of 782.07 acres. Out of this, 692.96 acres (88.60%) is cultivable land. In the rest, the utilization is as 33.05 acres (4.23%) for homestead, 6.52 acres (0.83%) as pasture and grazing, 15.09 acres (1.93%) as community land, 22.15 acres (2.83%) as wasteland and 12.3 acres (1.57%) as miscellaneous. From the land utilization pattern it is very much clear that most of the land is under cultivation. Only a little portion (0.83%) is pasture and grazing, this may be the reason for very poor dairy activities in the village. The proportion of wasteland is also comparatively less, i.e. just 22.15 acres (2.83%). This wasteland is particularly the land which is near the river embankments.

AGRICULTURE, CROPS, SOIL AND IRRIGATION

The available cultivated land can be divided into 3 basic categories, viz. homestead land, highlands usually fallow or used for grazing purposes and low lands for paddy cultivation. There is no system of irrigation. Cultivation is totally rain dependent. The soil is quite fertile. Fertilizers are hardly used. There is no system of irrigation. Agriculture here is totally rainfed. Productivity is below average. Subsistence form of agriculture is practiced. Double or multiple cropping is unfamiliar to the villagers of Naharani Grant. Upon questioning, the villagers expressed their difficulty regarding infrastructural facilities. They do not have many implements and often they even have to borrow ploughs, hoes etc. They sow self-grown seeds, though a few families grow PUSA and JOYA variety of seeds. Only few farmers were found to use fertilizers and HYV seeds. There are very few institutional facilities for supply of inputs for agriculture and veterinary, such as seeds, fertilizers, pesticides, insecticides, medicines etc. The Block supplies seeds and fertilizers at subsidized rates upon linking up with certain schemes under the department of agriculture. Most of the bank loans are taken to invest in agriculture, land etc.

Salient Features of Agriculture in North-East

1. Peasant farming.
2. Small and tiny holding (as per this study in village holding size is 48 for operational holding).
3. Fragmentation (as family gets divided; the small holding further gets divided).
4. Predominantly rainfed.
5. Low investment.
6. Low application of inputs.
7. Large area under mono crop (in fact in present study whole agricultural households took one crop only) even in the whole village only 1.6 ha (15 bighas) of land is under double cropping.
8. Subsistence farming (as pointed out whole of the agricultural household, do agriculture for self-consumption. If some surplus is generated then it is sold but primarily the idea of agriculture is to grow as much so as to meet the yearly foodgrain demand).

The villagers sell a part of their produce in the nearby market. The principal crop is rice. For this, not much input is required as it is solely rain dependent, seeds are self-grown, fertilizers and pesticides are not used. The yield per acre is low and is about 780 to 800 kg per acre. This crop brings in an income of Rs. 4,000-5,000 at the rate of Rs. 5 a kilo. This meagre income is not enough to support a family and so alternative avenues are sought to gain supplementary income. Almost all the farmers have a garden in their homestead land where they grow fruit trees such as mango, jackfruit and citrus trees. Coconut and arecanut trees are also grown widely and they bring in a sizable income. Sale of agricultural produce is very limited as very little part of produced grain is sold in market. Some of the household sells vegetables as villages are close to town. Some households also sell flower, as consumption of flower is very high in Assam due to religious establishments.

As there is no irrigation facility, most of the crops are single crops. Ahu (kharif) and Sali (rabi) are the two seasons. As kharif crops, the paddy covers the total sown area. In Rabi season land is left unsowed except some land where mustard and two other varieties of the paddy is sown. Land of villages is of very fertile, therefore, the farmers do intensive cropping of paddy. The productivity level of the paddy achieved by a few farmers is quite impressive about 5 MT per hectare.

The main crop of the village is Sali (summer rice) which is sown somewhere around in the end of May and harvested in winters before the end of December. Similarly tea is also grown in the village but it is totally grown in the tea estate. Tea leaves are plucked from April till September/October. This is the time when the factor operates. From October onwards pruning operation starts. A cycle of three years is followed in it, that is, in one year 1/3 of the tea estate is pruned. Double cropping is negligible in the village. Total village area is 444.88 ha. Settled net crop area is 339.38 ha and unsettled net crop area is 67.40 ha. Total net crop area is 406.78 ha. Out of total net crop area of 406.78 ha only 1.61 ha (15 bighas) land is double cropped. The reason being lack of agricultural enterprise and technical know-how. The fruits and vegetables are generally grown in the homesteads. The productivity of Sali rice is 280 to 320 kg per bigha that is nearly 10 quintal per acre. As Sali paddy (summer rice) is the main crop of whole village. It is sown during summer season of June-July when rain are there. Most of the people interviewed told that they use the seeds saved from last cropping for growing of *dhan*.

Table 1.5(a) : Crops grown by the villagers and growing seasons

Sl. No.	*Crops*	*Months of sowing*	*Months of harvesting*
1.	Paddy	January-March & July-August	June & December
2.	Wheat	November-December	March (last week)
3.	Mustard	January	March
4.	Jute	March	July
5.	Lentils/pulses	December-January	March
6.	Peas	December-January	March

Table 1.5(b) : Agricultural productivity in **Ghoramari** village

Kharif crops	*Area under cultivation*
Sali paddy	62 ha
Ahu paddy	3 ha
Vegetables	3 ha
Rabi crops	Area under cultivation
Mustard	1 ha
Wheat	1 ha
Potato	4 ha
Other vegetables	4 ha

After harvest, one can see the whole dried paddy plant in the field minus the top portion. There are two losses in this method. First, they miss the straw and its various uses. Second, there is substantial loss to foodgrain. People in the village, however, give the counter argument that if the plant is left in the field, the fertility of the field remains intact. Other than paddy, few vegetables, like cauliflower etc. are also grown in the village during the kharif season. Villagers also grow banana, coconut, bitternut etc. But these are grown along the homesteads and not in the fields. However, the area involved in this cultivation is very small, something around 3 acres. Lack of proper irrigation facilities may be one of the reasons for this. During Rabi season, most of the fields remain empty, except for around 10-12 acres of field where vegetables like cabbage and brinjal are grown. Other than these seasonal crops, there are some perennial crops also grown in the village. Coconut is grown in around 2.5 acres of land. One of the main perennial crops of the village, and for that matter for the whole of Assam is *Tamul* (arecanut) and banana. These are, in fact, grown side by side in the same area of land. Around 75 acres of land must be under this kind of cultivation. Takul is in very great demand in the whole part of North-East. Tea has also made a good hold in the village. There is a sufficiently big Tea Garden in the village and couple of other small tea gardens have come up very recently. Considering irrigation as a major stumbling block for the development of agriculture, the district administration took up a big lift irrigation project in the village. It was proposed to lift the water from the Sessa River and to supply it through the whole village. The problem of soil erosion is acute since there are floods every year and huge amounts of earth get washed away.

Irrigation

There is virtually no irrigation in the village. The agriculture is rain dependent. Few irrigation canals has been constructed but no pump set or channels have been dug for drawing water. The canals are choked with weed and sand. After the canal has been constructed only once water has been released. As there is no irrigation facility available, only single crop cultivation, i.e. Sali or winter rice cultivation is there. Wheat cultivation is not taken up because there is no sufficient awareness among the farmers, and also because they are not enterprising.

Soil

The soil of the village is alluvial and composed of varying degrees of clay, loan and sand. Its soils are very fertile and suitable for cultivation of various field crops such as paddy, wheat, pulses, mustard and potato. The soil in the village is generally classified in six categories for the purpose of revenue assessment. These are as follows :

1. Sailora—cultivable land
2. Badi—homestead
3. Asrawa—low lying land
4. Char—tilla land
5. Patit—fallow land

Sailora and Asrawa are used for purchase of cultivation. In some areas above lands are also known as Faringati. In high land areas mostly tea is grown.

Due to deposition of alluvium every year by flood waters, the farmers grow their crops successfully with the use of manures and fertilizers. Paddy (Ahu, Bao and Sali) as food crop and mustard as cash crop are the main field crops of the village Namani Borpomua. Ahu paddy cultivation is generally done in a mixture with Bao paddy in the village but sometimes it is cultivated as mono crop. Mustard is usually cultivated as the second crop in the Sali paddy land by most of the villagers. Apart from paddy, the villagers produced some other field and garden crops such as black gram, tobacco, onion, garlic, etc. Input in agriculture means cost of seeds, fertilizers and manures, family labour and bullock labourers, hired human and bullock labour, charges of irrigation and hired agricultural tools and implements, etc. The rainfall varies from 50 cm in June to 5 cm in January. Almost all the districts of Assam are flood prone. The people have yet to develop any water harvesting technologies.

In **Mohbandha Gaon** the soil is quite fertile, rain is abundant and thus nature is there to meet the demand of food. However, it has led to lack of entrepreneurship in agricultural aspect. Since one crop of paddy is sufficient to provide foodgrains enough for the year thus double cropping is very less. In this village out of the total crop area of 414 acres only 5 acres is under double cropping. The fields are smaller in size and nearer to the basti areas. The homesteads are big in size compared to other parts of India. Generally the households have some sort of crop either of beatle nut or the vegetables grown in the homesteads to meet the demand of personal consumption. The whole tea plantation is rainfed. In fact, the area is under high rainfall zone, hence few occasions of drought with regard to tea plantations. During rainy season, paddy is grown. Only one crop a year is produced. No improved techniques of cultivation are followed. The tea management has given land to some labourers on the agreement that land revenue can be paid by the cultivators. The occupants are paying 'Tauzi Bahira' revenue to the Mauzadars of the revenue administration. Out of 33 ha of land which is not put to agricultural usage we have 1.6 ha for burial grounds, school buildings and roads, 4.15 ha of land as marshy lands and rest of the land is under homesteads or not put to any use.

Even though agriculture remains the major means of livelihood for the majority of people in the village, and in the State as a whole, it is a pity that neither the government has taken adequate steps to modernize agriculture and increase productivity, nor the villagers themselves have shown any keenness and interest to ensure that their means of livelihood provides them improved socio-economic status and better living conditions. Socio-economic factors like farmer's conservative outlook, ignorance, etc. stand in the way of adoption of modern techniques in the village. Further, the antiquate organization of agriculture run by illiterate, ignorant and ill equipped person cannot raise the agricultural productivity of the State. Adoption of progressive agricultural technique is to the extent impossible under the present position. Agriculture coupled with trade is most beneficial. Thus trade activities should be increased. For it, strengthening of market structure and providing adequate opportunity is must. Agriculture alone is not sufficient because of poor productivity. Emphasis should be placed increasingly on double cropping.

LAND REFORMS/TENANCY

The history of land reforms in Assam can be traced back to 1929 during the colonial rule. There was the Goalpara Tenancy Act, 1929, an Act extended to the Goalpara District alone, but which marked an important milestone in the history of land reforms in Assam. The Act was governing the relations between the landlord and the tenant in the permanently settled areas of the erstwhile Goalpara district. It aimed at improving the conditions of the tenant class by conferring upon the occupancy raiyats permanent, heritable and transferable rights. Further, to sub-tenants and under tenants it conferred the rights of use and occupancy. Under this act, protection was accorded to the tenants against illegal ejectment and enhancement of land rent. This act was in force even the abolition of the Zamindari system in 1955-57 and was amended in 1970 to include provisions of the Adhiar Tenant Protection Act, 1948. The Goalpara Tenancy Act was finally repealed in 1974 when the Assam (Temporarily Settled Areas) Tenancy Act, 1971 was extended to the hitherto permanently settled areas of the Goalpara district. In 1935 came the Assam (Temporarily Settled District) Tenancy Act which recognised 4 classes of Tenants—privileged raiyat, occupancy raiyat, non-occupancy raiyat and under raiyat. This Act was amended in 1953 giving permanent, heritable and transferable rights to the first-two classes of tenants, i.e. privileged raiyat and occupancy raiyat while conferring subordinate rights of use and occupancy with suitable protection against illegal ejectment upon the last two classes of tenants, i.e. non-occupancy and under raiyat.

Land reforms had taken place in the village in the 1960s, after the passing of the Assam Temporarily Settled Areas Act, 1959. The land reforms can be said to be fairly successful. As can be ascertained from the distribution of landholding, nobody has got land more than 4 ha. All the lands, which has been acquired or surrendered, to government has been distributed. There is no litigation. All the people have got some land.

In **Pachim Matia,** mostly the households have less than 3 acres of land. Only 2.97 per cent households have 5-10 acres of land. 1095 acres of land was declared surplus and was taken in possession but only 5 acres was distributed among the landless poor. In the beneficiaries 69.23 per cent were from downtrodden class. The total land declared surplus in the **Kalitakuchi** village is 406 bighas of which all were taken possession by the government. However, only 20 acres have been distributed to the landless. Most of the tenants cultivating the land pay in kind, mostly in the form of produce of agriculture, as rent to the landlord. Some of them do give in money as and when the landowners want. Mostly, the produce of the land is share between the tenant and the landowner on a 50 : 50 basis.

In **Hatkola Gaon,** there is an improvement in the status of people who have been given this ceiling surplus land. There is no tribal land in the village. Land records are not up-to-date and complete. The Lot Mandals do not write the change in the area cultivated in the records. There are a number of mutation cases pending. The details of tenancy are also not written. Most of the tenants are not aware of their rights. No land consolidation took place so far.

Ceiling Surplus land in the **Reng Beng** village : Originally 37.73 ha of the total 39.18 ha land of the village belong to Kandoli Tea Estate. A total land of 7300B-3K-4L of Kandoli Tea Estate was acquired under the Assam Fixation of Ceiling on Landholdings Act, 1956 (as amended) by the Order of the Collector and Director of Land Requisition, Acquisition and Reforms, dated 22.1.73. Then the acquired land was allotted to the landless people during the period of 1973-76. But in the revised Order of the Collector dated 7.6.76, the total excess surplus land from the Tea Estate was declared only 6275B-1K-0L (836.70 ha). The Tea Estate prayed for return of 139.3 ha. Of excess land, which was handed over to the government based on the previous Order. Reng Beng grant also comes under this excess land. The Commissioner and Secretary of Government of Assam, Revenue

Department by his order dated 21-9-98, decided to return back this land to the Tea Estate. Accordingly Land Records are being corrected at present. Only 18 original allottees are in the actual possession of this land. These allottees are paying Tauzi Bahira, a revenue fee for occupying the allotted government land. These 18 allottees will retain their possession. The rest of the allottees sold the land illegally to the present occupiers. These occupants are paying the Tauzi Bahira in the name of original allottees. As per Assam Land Revenue Regulation and the Land Policy of Assam these occupants are treated as encroachers. Government allotted land cannot be transferred. If any allottee transfers his land he/she will lose any rights over that government allotted land. Hence except the land possessed by the 18 original allottees the rest of the land will be transferred to the Tea Estate. All the landowners are small and marginal farmers and so there is no much tenancy in the village. Few farmers who are having a land of more than 7 bighas (0.9 ha) have given their land for tenancy to their relatives. This informal kind of tenancy is called *adhi* where all the input like seed, fertilizer, ploughing, sowing, labour in weeding and harvesting etc. is done by the tenant and 50 per cent of the output is given to the landowner. The owner pays the land revenue. Though the ceiling surplus land was allotted long back there is no effort on part of the Revenue Administration to settle the land permanently with the allottees. This is coming in the way of the spirit of the ceiling legislation.

The Assam Ceiling on Landholdings Act, 1976 puts a limit of 50 bighas on size of landholdings. But in **Nargaon** village even the biggest landowners do not own land more than 20 bighas. Out of 3,000 bighas of land in the village, over 300 bighas of land was declared ceiling surplus. Most of this land is now under possession of former tenants or other actual tillers, though most of them have not received pattas as yet.

In **Senchowa** village, the land distribution appears to be skewed. Some residents seem to have more than 50 bighas of land while most of them have land for only homestead purpose. A form of tenancy called *Adhiers* or sharecropping widely prevalent. The land is highly fertile and most of it yields two crops. The pasture and grazing land is slowly being encroached upon. No watershed programme has been taken up in this village. The land reforms have also been piecemeal in this village with only 5.39 acres of land declared surplus and only 3.93 acres of land actually distributed benefiting only 15 persons (12

SCs). Though there is no zamindari and problems of eviction, yet I feel that there is a need to educate the existing tenants of their rights. The landlords in this village are not absentee landlords as the village itself is very close to the town.

In **Hatkhula Gaon,** as far as the distribution of the land is concerned, it is found that there is no person who is landless in the strict sense of word. Everybody has got his own land for his own house. The Government of Assam has, therefore, defined any person having less than 3 acres of land as landless. From this definition there are 53 households which can be said to be landless (0-3 acres of land). They constitute around 35.57 per cent of the total households, which are 149.72 households (i.e. 48.32%) have land between 3-5 acres area, while 18 households (i.e. 12.08%) have between 5-10 acres of land. Only 5 households, which are 3.36 per cent of total, have large holdings of 10-20 acres. One tea company has land above 20 acres. **Kuwamara Handique** –About the land ceiling operation, only 2-3 cases were made and ceiling surplus land was acquisitioned. This land was later on distributed to landless workers. Except one other land receiving households have improved their condition. The allotted land was not a good quality land and lots of efforts were put by these households in earth filling and levelling. The government has not supported them with any kind of material or financial support, therefore, the income from the allotted land has remained modest.

No doubt there is a demand for the land in **Majuli**. But people are not crazy. Especially tribal people that too Mishings. They love to have a land in their possession, but not in excess. These Mishing community people knew the objectives of equity, productivity and stability. Because in whole Majuli :

- Absolutely there are no landlords;
- Absolutely no concept of zamindars. There are no zamindars only;
- Society is far away from the feudal setup;
- People are literate; and
- Society is absolutely egalitarian.

In the village **Namani Borpomua**, land is held under one system Khiraj-annual. Out of 405.28 hectares of total land owned by the villagers at the time of bench mark survey in May/June 1975, on the 1.14 hectares are of Khiraj-priodic lands and this land was converted from Khiraj-annual to Khiria periodic by the owner only facilities to himself to take loan from the bank of by mortgaging it besides the villagers have used some government lands for cultivation and these lands are classed as Torjubad land.

Land reforms in the **Dighaligaon** village are not very large in scale. As per data collected from the Circle Officer, ceiling land that has been declared surplus is to the tune of 1.74 ha and all this land is in actual possession of the beneficiaries. As regards tenancy, there are only three recorded tenants in the village cultivating a total area of 1.61 ha approximately. There is, however, a difference in the tenancy system in this case in that the entire produce is harvested and consumed by the tenant himself. Government land as on the date of survey stands at 10.4 ha approx. of which 2.4 ha is homestead, 6.7 ha cultivation and 1.3 ha used for other purposes. There are a total of four tribal households in the village owing a total of 0.4 ha approximately as on the date of survey. It was very strange to notice that, in spite of the fact of the land holdings being dispersed, there has been no effort at initiating the process of consolidation of landholdings. The maintenance of land records is also not very up-to-date and there is no clarity regarding the finer details of the actual landholdings. It was very interesting to note that the data supplied to me by the *Lat Mondal* was different to that given by the Circle Officer himself. It was only after proper verification of the records that the actual data could be retrieved. There is also an urgent need for computerization of land records not only in this particular area but also in the entire State. For this purpose, a pilot project, financed by the Department of Information and Technology, has already begun in the District and one hopes that its implementation brings about a sea change in the maintenance of land records.

Tenancy

Sharecropping is very common phenomena in the village, where the tenants are called Adhiyar. Sharecropping as a form of tenancy is a bottleneck but to remove it land should be settled with landless. Land settled should be sufficient to lift these families above the poverty line. Adhiary is a system of sharecropping in which landless peasant cultivates land belonging to a *mahajan* on the condition that half of the produce from the land is given to the landowner. Moreover the peasant gives another quantity of the paddy from his own share to the landowner if he borrows paddy from the latter. Thus whatever is produced by the poor peasant in a year is exhausted by the end of the year. To protect the right of the sharecroppers they are to be recognized and recorded in the Khatian register. However, this record is not maintained properly. At this point it is worth mentioning that sharecropping is one of the better methods of tenancy as the sharecropper and landowner both have a stake in the productivity.

In **Bengenematti,** of the total surveyed, there are 6 tenants, and they occupy around 13.88 acres. There were no unrecorded tenants. Area under self cultivation of landholder is 12.55 acres, and absentee landlords hold about 2.33 acres. Though Bengenematti village is largely tribal and chiefly populated by the Bodo tribal community, surprisingly in the land records there is no documented or recorded tribal land.

Kuwamara Handique The data collected from the tenant households shows following trends, in almost all the cases the tenant has his own land and is cultivating the neighbouring agricultural field. The landowner has moved out of the town for some occupation outside or for other reasons. As he is not a resident of the village, he is not offering any input share in cash or kind. Again it is convenient for him to take a fixed rent than to have share in output crops. In two cases the tenants have taken loan from the landowners. The tenant landowner relationship was also found to be stable and the main causes for termination of tenancy are end of the term and landowner came back to the village. **Mohbandha Gaon**—The ownership pattern along with operational holding then we can see that 35 per cent of families have less than 0.5 acre of land ownership but 80 per cent of families have more than 0.5 acre of operational holding. Thus it indicates that some form of tenancy exists in the village. Out of 21 cultivating families 6 are working on Adhiary basis (sharecropping). They have negligible ownership of land.

Poverty and landlessness forces individuals to become tenants in other's fields, with the hope of earning his livelihood. The main occupation of almost all tenants is agriculture. The tenants are mainly small farmers and marginal farmers. Many of the tenants (80%) are literate and educated. A number of tenants have received education up to higher secondary level, and a few are graduates even. This is a reflection on the absence of employment avenues in Assam, and the frustration it can breed in educated unemployed youths. The form of tenancy is basically '*adhi*' which implies that the landowner and the tenant would share the input price and the produce on 50 : 50 basis. In some cases the cost of seeds (the use of fertilizers is minimal and irrigation facilities are practically non-existent). Hence, the input price for these are negligible is borne by the landowner. A tenant can barely meet his needs. He borrows money, mainly from the landowner or from the affluent people of the village. The rate of interest is not fixed and is negotiable. The villagers feel shy to talk about these matters, and also feel that these things should not be disclosed in front of a government official.

Tenancy reform is another important step required for agricultural development in Assam. Despite the legal measures taken in the State since Independence against exploitative tenancy, as reported by NSSO in its 48th round, the proportion of tenanted land in total operated area in Assam had increased from 6.4 per cent in 1981-82 to 8.9 per cent in 1991-92. The rate of growth is high, and probably, it continues to grow at the same rate, if not more. With the present practices of tenancy where the costs are not shared proportionately, as indicated earlier, at least 10 per cent of the operational area of the State will continue have low productivity. Therefore, the existing tenancy reform programmes should be implemented in the State more vigorously. So far, the issue has eluded any action.

OTHER AGRICULTURAL PROBLEMS

There is problem of land erosion and water logging in the village. Every year there is a flood in the village and soil erosion is quite severe in the paddy fields but replenishment rate is also quite fast. The flood plays havoc in the life of the people and the problem of water logging is useful as well as injurious to the agriculture. Because of water logging the Boro crop is grown but the Sali crop of the paddy cannot be grown because the season for the Sali is peak rainy season.

The causes for backwardness in agriculture are :

1. Lack of irrigation facilities in dry season, either wells or tube wells or canals.

2. Lack of credit to buy power tillers or even bullocks.
3. HYV seeds are not used.
4. No encouragement has been given to promote crops other than rice.
5. Small holdings which do not generate enough reinvestible surplus.

Namani Borpomua—Jengraimukh Tiniali is the only nearest marketing place of the village. Besides one weekly market (*hat*) at Phuloni, used to gather at a distance of 5 km from the village offers some marketing facilities to the villagers. Paddy, mustard, vegetables, fish, milk and poultry birds, eggs, etc. are some of important products, which the villagers offer for sale.

STRATEGIES FOR AGRICULTURAL GROWTH

Agricultural growth can be stepped up by taking measures to improve cropping intensity. Since crop cultivation in the kharif season is faced with natural risks such as floods the use of HYV seeds and chemical fertilizers and pesticides has been low, resulting in lower yields. Therefore, Rabi season cultivation needs to be promoted with a continued emphasis on irrigation through shallow tube wells. Taking into account, the transport bottleneck and the perishability of the primary produce in the shortrun greater emphasis needs to be given to food processing industries. Cultivation of vegetables, fruits, and spices and commercialization of agriculture needs to be encouraged by investing in marketing and storage facilities. Institutional reforms are needed to ensure equitable distribution of benefits from the rich ground water resources of Assam. Effective participation of the poor farmers can be ensured through revitalizing the local bodies such as the Panchayats. Poor farmers also need to be provided adequate training and extension services.

Assam can produce enough agricultural surplus through appropriate technological intervention designed for increasing cropping intensity from its present level of about 146 per cent to at least 200 per cent, and evolving a cropping pattern consistent with its agro-climatic factors. A large part of the State gets severely affected by floods every year, nevertheless, as the technical experts have shown, at least 200 per cent of cropping intensity can be achieved even in the flood prone areas. This, however, requires assured irrigation. Assam is enormously rich in ground water resources on the basis of which, another 47 per cent of the net sown area of the State can be brought under assured irrigation.

SOCIAL STRUCTURE

Household Population and its Distribution

Table 1.6 : Sex-wise Household Population and Total Area of Land

Village	*District*	*Year*	*HH*	*Population*	*Male*	*Female*	*Sex Ratio*	*Total Area (acre)*
Niz Lahoal	Dibrugarh	1994	760	4076	—	—	—	675.86
Mohbandha Gaon	Jorhat	1994	458	2079	1034	1045	1011	1098.85
Nargaon	Kamrup	1994	129	793	411	382	929	600
Naharani Grant	Sonitpur	1996	323	1615	—	—	—	—
Senchowa	Nagaon	1996	—	1716	904	812	898	262.5
Kalitakuchi	Kamrup	1996	—	5150	—	—	—	1744.22
Pachim Matia	Goalpara	1996	535	2318	67.5	32.5	481	1657
Hatkola Gaon	Dibrugarh	1997	—	935	490	445	908	550.43
Reng Beng	Nagaon	1999	—	782	398	384	965	96.77
Deodhar	Nagaon	1999	409	1636	843	793	941	1385.84
Saptagram	Cachar	2000	—	4000	1950	2050	1051	918.26
Bengenamatti	Nagaon	2000	—	2146	1091	1055	967	1192.23
Kuwamara Handique	Sivasagar	2000	—	1834	938	896	955	782.07
Ghoramari	Sonitpur	2001	110	696	353	343	972	452.05
Dighaligaon	Sonitpur	2002	—	3031	1376	1655	1203	681.16
Namani Borpomua	Jhorhat	2002	109	1156	605	551	911	942.3

Niz Lahoal—Number of households is 760 with the population of 4,076. Population structure is quite heterogeneous. Majority of the villagers is Hindus and Muslims, Christians and Sikhs are very less in number. This village does not have any communal problems. Village has population of SCs, STs, and OBCs. Koiborta, Munda, Das, Chutia, Ahoms form the majority of the population of the village. Gaon Panchayat president is from the OBC community, which is the largest population segment of this village. Bokul tea estate is nearby this village. Most of the houses are kutcha.

The **Naharani Grant** village has 323 households. It has a total population of 1,615, comprising a majority of tea tribes (OBCs) and Boro tribes, as well as the Assamese, Nepalis, Biharis and Muslims. The main religions are Hinduism and Christianity. The language spoken is generally the 'cha-bagicha' language, which is a mixture of Assamese, Hindi, Bhojpuri, Oriya, etc. The culture is also of a mixed nature.

Total population of the **Pachim Matia** village is 2,318. Remarkably the ratio of male and female is very different from the National data. 67.5 per cent males and 32.5 per cent females during the 1991 census.

Kalitakuchi village is a village of 5,150 large population and it falls under Hajo circle (tehsil) of Kamrup district. The area of the village is 1744.22 acres and consists of 7 hamlets. In nearly all the households surveyed, except one, all the heads of households are male. In some cases, even when an elderly mother is there, the head of the household are usually the elder sons. This reveals the patriarchal/ paternalistic structure of the village society. 52 per cent of the households are nuclear and the rest joint. This presents a problem in the distribution of landholdings, leading to a fragmented land structure.

The total population of the **Saptagram** village is 4,000 out of which 1950 are males and 2,050 are females. Hence the sex ratio is favourable to the females and is much higher than most of the other places of the country. The household survey data reveals that about 50 per cent of household have pucca houses, 5 per cent have kutcha houses, 20 per cent have kutcha-pucca houses and 25 per cent of households are having straw thatched huts. Most of the houses are constructed on inherited own land. About 70 per cent of houses are electrified. Even in remaining 30 per cent most of them use katibijli though in survey due to fear they did not admit this. About 70 per cent of households use public hand pump for drinking water, 10 per cent use their own hand pump/tube well, 5 per cent use tap water and remaining households use own dug well or public dug well. Around 25 per cent of households use modern latrines for defecation and remaining 75 per cent goes to open field. Percentage of use of modern latrine increases in rainy season. About 50 per cent of families use wood as main sources of fuel, 10 per cent families use gobar gas, 2.5 per cent use LPG and remaining about 37.5 per cent of families use cow dung cake as main source of fuel.

The **Hatkola Gaon** village has a population of 935, out of which males are 490 and females are 445. Sex ratio is 908 females for every thousand males. Scheduled Caste population is 258 and the Scheduled Tribe population is nil. In terms of percentages SCs constitute 27.6 per cent and ST zero per cent. All the population belongs to Hindu religion.

Ghoramari—The different clusters in these 2 Chuburis are Ahom Chuburi: It consists of the Ahom clusters like Gogoi, Borah, Barua and also has Christian and Muslim population. It consists of the people of higher economic status in the village. The Adibasi Chuburi has Santhals, Mundas, Buala and other Tea Tribes, they also have Orang, Maji, Karmakar, Rajowar population. The Adibasi Chuburi consists of people who have come from outside the State to work in tea gardens a few generations back. The population of the village as per 1991 Census is 696, out of which 353 are males and 343 females.

Nargaon—Almost all 129 households have homestead land in their own names. Average size of a homestead plot is one bigha. In this plot of land there are one or two Assam type houses (kutcha or pucca). Each household has at least a wooden chair and a bench. None of the houses have sanitary latrines. There is some open space, which acts as living space and also used for spreading paddy for drying. Rest of land has mostly betelnut trees, papaya trees, some vegetables are also grown. Some people have small 'Pukhuri' for fish and ducks. There is also thatch for the livestock for people who have it.

The village **Senchowa** in the Khagorizan Development Block Nagaon (sadar) revenue circle has a total population of 1,716. The male population is 904 and the female population is 812. The SC population in the village is 986 and the STs are only 2. The people of different communities like upper castes, SCs etc. are living cohesively in the same locality. The decade growth rate of the population is 51 per cent, which is more than the growth rate of population in many parts of India. It is believed that a substantial portion of the increase in the population is due to immigration due to the nearness of the town to this village.

The sex ratio in **Namani Borpouma** is 91 females per 100 males, which is slightly higher than that of Jorhat district (89) and Assam (90) according to 1991 census and this ratio is normal. The number of females is higher than that of males in the age groups between 16 and 30 years, which is due to existence of large number unmarried girls in the village.

Dighaligaon—There was 1,376 males and 1,655 females making it a total of 3,031. SCs constituted a bulk of the population—about 65 per cent while the rest were distributed between general, OBC and STs.

The total population of the **Deodhar** village as per the 1991 census is 1,636, with 843 males and 793 females. The village has a sizeable SC population also, with 210 males and 196 females. The ST population is, however, insignificant, with just 5 non-descript male members of the community living in the village. The village has 238 households and all of them are occupied.

There are 3 major community clusters within the **Bengenamatti** village. They include Bodos, Nepali and Assamese. The dominant community is the Bodos which number around 300 households, followed by the Nepalis with 200 houses. The Assamese number about 40 families. Interestingly, there is no ghettoisation in the village, as various families, coexist alongside each other peacefully. There has never been a history of any community clash or friction amongst them as well.

Kuwamara Handique has a population of 1,834 as per the 2001 census. Amongst them 938 are males and 896 are females. Thus the sex ratio comes out to be as 955 females for 1000 males against the district figure of 926. SC and ST population figures are 78 (4.25%) and 112 (6.10%) respectively. The district has very low population of SCs and STs and the percentage figures of the district are as low as 3.34 and 3.68 respectively.

As per 1991 census the **Mohbandha Gaon** village has a total population of 2,079 with 458 households. On an interaction with the villagers the approximate break up (basti-wise) is as follows: Satria—73, Rabidas line—10, Muslim line—53 and Tea garden families—322. Since there are 458 households in the village so this amounts to average family size of 4 (actually it is 4.5).

CUSTOMS AND CULTURE

Social organizations consist of both caste Hindus and tribals. These villages do not have high tribal population. Social life in the village is generally centred around a family system which is paternal in character. Today we can see discernible trend of switching over from joint family to single family system, but still this village has not seen a major shift in this regard. Marriage is the most important occasion in the family. Infant marriage is unknown. Average age of marriage for both males and females is fairly high and dowry system is not prevalent among the people of this village.

Marriage

There is no hiatus between tribal and non-tribals. Castes within the general population are not strictly defined. Inter-caste and tribal non-tribal marriages are very common and are readily accepted by the society. In fact people here do not think on caste lines. Caste system is not rigid Inter-caste marriages are not prohibited. In **Binoigutia** village the villagers are not supposed to marry between them so all the village boys and girls consider each other brothers and sisters. So during last day of Bihu where dancing girl supposed to find there better halves. Young boys from the village are not supposed to go near the tree around which the girls dance for the whole day. The youngsters from other village can come and watch the dance and even find their matching one too.

Dowry System

Some of the traits of the social life of the village are really admirable. One of them is the absence of dowry system. Women enjoy better status in the society compared to other parts of India. Social differences are also not much. The status of women is better in the Assamese community as there is no dowry system. Women are participating in economic activities like handloom weaving in addition to household work.

Untouchability

The tradition of untouchability is very less in Assam and due to the city effect nearby, it is still less in this village. The scheduled castes enjoy equal footing in social matters. There is no practice of untouchability. Society is not so complicated and infested with evil ideas and belief like in North or South India. Social values with regard to the institution of marriage are also stronger. Social barriers are not ossified. Dalits live with dignity. They are not denied any access to things like water facility, temple entry, shop entry, services of barber, tailor, sitting arrangements in school/panchayats etc. Their houses are located amidst the houses of the others. Their custom, food habits and economic conditions do not differ much from the others. The Harijan of the village **Saptagram** are concentrated at one place. The basti was well organized and clean. They have separate water facility in terms of well and hand pump. The financial position of the Harijan people is also good because most of them are involved in some kind of economical activities or in government service. Untouchability could be seen in this village in its very diluted form. There is only one primary school in the village. The children of all castes including Harijan sit and play together but the caste tag is always there and hence, sometimes upper caste students and even teachers uses derogatory words to call them.

FESTIVALS

Agriculture is the main occupation of the Mishing and some of the various festivals celebrated by them are mainly related to agriculture. *Ali aye ligang* and *Porag* or a *Narasiga Bihu* are two important festivals of the Misahings and both are related to agriculture. They (*Mishing*) have the tradition of living in joint families, which are patrilineal and patrilocal. The eldest male member in the family becomes its head and takes the sole responsibility of smooth running of all domestic affairs. The Mishings practice both monogamy and polygamy but now-a-days monogamy is becoming more popular. There are 4 main systems of marriage among the Mishings including marriage by capture. The child marriage is not allowed. Widow marriage is also prevalent. Divorce is allowed but rare. The main cause that leads to divorce is adultery in case of both men and women. The system of bride price is also prevalent among the Mishing and, therefore, the question of compensation sometimes occurred at the time of divorce.

ECONOMIC ACTIVITIES

Employment

Occupations are broadly divided into two groups (a) Agricultural and (b) Non-Agricultural. Again, agricultural occupations are sub-divided into two occupations such as (a) Owner cultivator and (b) Agricultural labour. Non-agricultural occupation divided into sub-groups such as (a) Trade, Commerce and Transport and (b) salaried job. Agriculture is the main occupation of the villagers. Some of the villagers work in government departments also and many of them work in the nearby tea gardens. Habitations are concentrated on the basis of caste but as such there is no segregation. Outsiders are less in number but their economic condition is better as compared to the locals. Each household also has a supplementary sources of income from activities such as poultry, fishery, piggery, cows, and goats etc. Upon analysis, it is clear that maximum per capita income accrues to those in government service, and the minimum to the agricultural labourers.

The womenfolk of the village largely practice weaving. Items such as shawls, mekhala chader etc. are woven and they are sold in the nearby market. Designs are traditional and very attractive. Development of handloom industry has a large linkage in the form of the nearby market. Also, if some scheme is taken up under DWCRA or TRYSEM, the products can be marketed from the DRDA sale outlet at the Block Headquarters. On the whole, most of the workers are males. The women are usually found to be working with their homesteads. There are a few petty businessmen, such as grocery shopkeepers who were beneficiaries under the IRDP. People are generally content with the way they are, especially the self-cultivators who see no need to grow a second crop in one year. There is no incidence of bonded labour in the area. Agricultural labourers usually get paid in kind. The daily wage of construction workers, delivery boys etc. range from Rs. 27 to Rs. 33. Employer-employee relationships are not too clear, but it is reasonable enough to believe that there is not much tension between the two.

There is seasonal out-migration in the winter months due to lean agricultural season. However, the majority of the migrants migrate because of other reasons, as for example, there are a quite a few number of men from the village who are working as drivers either in Hajo, Guwahati or in other places. Some of them are working in the government and some of them as labourers.

Naharani Grant Village—The correlation between annual per capita income and literacy rate to be a positive correlation. The general category and the SC category have the highest per capita income of Rs. 3,800 and Rs. 5,000 respectively and their literacy rates are also the highest at 82.05 per cent and 81.82 per cent. At the same time, the OBCs have a per capita income of Rs. 1,084 and a literacy rate of 42.45 per cent. There are 7 out of 50 workers in government service. People here mostly go for the government jobs, as it offers maximum security of jobs, perks etc. They prefer it to starting their own petty business. In fact, marked lack of entrepreneurship and business sense is noticeable among the people.

In **Pachim Matia** village, employment opportunity is very less and many people are under-employed. Seasonal unemployment is also another problem. Mostly people (75%) are engaged in primary sector's activities and 16.82 per cent population is employed. No person is involved in the secondary sector while 7.67 per cent population gather livelihood through service and trade. There are 200 handloom units in the village and 400 persons are engaged with it and only one sericulture unit was found there.

Kalitakuchi—More than 70 per cent of the people are engaged in agriculture either as cultivators or as labourers. The wage rate is Rs. 40 per day, higher than the prescribed minimum wage rate of Rs. 33. However, women are paid less than men and are at the rate of Rs. 25 to Rs. 30. The agricultural labour is of course seasonal and the season of peak unemployment is winter. Under the JRY and EAS schemes, a number of villagers were benefited. Apart from the agriculture, the other economic activities going on in the village are fishery, grocery shop, stationery, poultry farming, weaving and miscellaneous trades like tea shops, etc. Weaving is also another activity, which, however, is not as big as in the neighbouring Block of Sualkuchi. Though Hajo (Block headquarters) is famous for brassware, where they make the traditional Horais, yet it is not to be found in Kalita Kuchi. There are quite a few independent businesses. There are around 9 trucks owned and operated by the owners themselves, 4 taxis and 16 rickshaws.

The **Binoigutia** village has got a rich tradition of weaving almost all the households except a few are involved in this. Some people are still making bed sheets with outdated loom, which requires strenuous. Recently a woman cooperative has been formed which is yet to be registered to procure improved looms. There are enough local buyers as Tea Gardens, hospitals, etc. who have already agreed.

Local employment condition is very good in **Saptagram** village. This is mainly due to three reasons: (i) Proximity with the Mizoram where labour rates are quite high—in the tune of 100 rupees per day.

(ii) Village Saptagram is very close to Silchar, therefore, large number of persons is engaged as casual industrial labour. (iii) During the survey it was found that many people have developed skill in hand pump boring works. Because of above three reasons, wage rate is quite high in this village. Government approved minimum wage rate is Rs. 47 per day, but local labour charges are more than Rs. 70 a day. Thus it becomes very difficult to get local labour for JRY schemes. Last year, village labourers were paid Rs. 60 a day for construction of road under JRY, which is not possible without manipulation of muster rolls. The above difference in minimum wages and local wages has resulted in entry of contractor in implementation of JRY schemes. The occupational structure, which reflects the nature and volume of employment in the village, is the basic foundation on which the edifice of the village economic system is laid. Only 6.62 per cent of the people are self-cultivator. About 23 per cent are student, about 10 per cent of population is self-employed in trade, traditional occupation etc. Women are mainly involved in traditional domestic work. About 2.5 per cent of population is engaged in tenancy. About 1.65 per cent of population is engaged in some sort of permanent job. If we see the data in aggregate, out of 302 people, 219 people are non-earning dependent.

The striking thing about the **Hatkola Gaon** village is its egalitarianism. There is not a single big farmer in the village. Economic disparity is also not so prominent. If some families have better standard of living it is because of the government service and those who are in agriculture hardly have any surplus to be reinvested elsewhere.

Ghoramari—The survey reveals that 59 people are self-cultivators, 2 tenants, 31 casual labourers, 1 casual rural non-farm labour and 79 unemployed among the households surveyed. It means that unemployment is exceptionally high. It is true about seasonal employment too because large chunk is casual agricultural labourers. There are no industries nearby or no avenues for people for self-employment.

Nargaon—Agriculture is the main source of livelihood. Most households also possess a handloom for weaving cloth for personal use. Some villagers get work in cutting and transporting wood from nearby forest in agriculturally lean season. Most tribal households brew rice beer for personal consumption and also for sale to non-tribals.

Senchowa—Maximum population depends on agriculture. The people are also involved in poultry, piggery and fishery as alternative occupations. Some villagers also do rickshaw pulling, thela pulling and vegetable vending in the nearby town area. During lean seasons, the JRY programme is run in this village. Due to town area being nearby, the people have also resorted to non-farm labour, rickshaw pulling, cart pulling, vegetable vending etc. Some of them also work in the Roller Flour Mills of Nagaon. A few are also doing carpentry and other skilled crafts. Most of the people are unaware of the economics of running a household enterprise.

The overall economic life of the people in the **Hatkhula Gaon** village cannot be said to be very bad. Every person in the village has some or other form of employment. Almost everybody has land for cultivation, although the holding is not very large. There are many persons from the village who are in service. In fact, the current Principal of the Lahowal College is from the village. A few educated people from the village are employed in the State government service also.

The occupation pattern of **Namani Borpomua** generally conforms to the general occupational pattern of a plain village of Assam, which is usually characterized by the dominance of agriculture. About 80 percent of the total population in the village are engaged directly or indirectly in agricultural occupations and rest is engaged in other occupations. Out of 96.80 per cent of the total population in the village, 95.94 per cent are owner cultivators, which signified dominance of agriculture in economic pursuits of the villagers. Only 10 persons in the village are agricultural labourers. All the persons in the occupation of Trade, Commerce and Transport belong to non-Mishing community and they are setting in the village only for the business of fish and fishing nets.

Dighaligaon—A majority of the people surveyed is employed in traditional occupations with a very low proportion engaged in agricultural activities either as self cultivator or even as casual labour in agriculture. There is also a significant proportion of the populace involved in works such as mechanic helpers, electricians and bus conductors. When agriculture ceases to be the main sources of income, people have to find other ways of earning their livelihood.

Bengenamatti—Weaving is a major activity in every household, especially in the Bodo households. Handicrafts and the making of traditional bamboo crafts and wares is another important activity. Many tribal youth of the village are enrolled and employed in the army and paramilitary forces. The Nepali community that resides in the village is, however, principally engaged in teaching and in the tending of cows. Most of the Nepalis, therefore, are in the milk supplying trade. The prevailing wage rate is Rs. 50, whereas the unemployment condition in the village is fairly poor. The major employment activities besides agriculture centre are piggery, poultry and weaving.

Main occupation of the **Kuwamara Handique** village is agriculture and agriculture allied activities. Nearly 75-80 per cent households are directly engaged in cultivation. Out of this nearly 60 per cent households own land and are working in their fields. 15-20 per cent are landless agricultural labourers. Others, particularly Missings do piggery along with other wage earning activities. Fishing, poultry and duckery are allied activities. Many households also have weaving and handloom activities but these are not commercialized. 5-6 households are engaged in retail trading activities and running grocery shops or stationary article shop. Few houses are in the transport business with 3 households having their own trucks; others are doing the jobs of driving. In 35-40 houses one or two members of the family are having government or public sector service jobs. The details of occupational pattern in Kuwamara Handique is given below.

Mohbandha Gaon

There are nearly 66 per cent cultivator families (21 families) out of which only 2 households are depending on agriculture solely. Incidentally as it will be pointed out later both these families belongs to lower strata of income. Similarly, nearly 66 per cent households are engaged as labours, here it is important to mention that out of total 21 households very few (only 4 or 5) are permanent labours. Rest all is daily labours or Hazira Workers known as locally. About 50 per cent of total worker consist of cultivators and agricultural labourers. However, it is noteworthy that agricultural labourers consist of 5.33 per cent of total workers because of two reasons. Firstly, the per cent of landless labourers are a very few. Secondly, the most of the area is under tea gardens and tea garden labourers are not classified as agricultural labourers. The tea garden labourers are here included under other workers, which consists of 50 per cent of total workers.

Livestock

Household poverty is very common in this village and almost 25 per cent of the households have got poultry, which satisfy their own need of eggs. No commercialization has taken place in all these areas and people are quite satisfied with whatever they have. For supplementary income, almost every family keeps livestock, such as draught and milch cattle, goats, fowls, pigs etc. Fishery is also taken up as a source of income. There is a lot of scope for the development of livestock and horticulture. The government through the veterinary and the horticulture departments must provide the necessary backward linkages such as good breed of animals, good quality seeds, fertilizers, pesticides, medicines etc. For the forward linkages, a new daily market complex is being constructed by the DRDA Sonitpur under the EAS just a few hundred metres away from the village. This will greatly facilitate the marketing of the produce especially since there is no proper means of communication to the present market except by foot, cycle or thela. Petty sellers should be able to benefit much from this.

Naharani Grant Village

The net annual income from land and livestock amongst the various categories is remarkable that while the general category persons derive as much as Rs. 6,200 from this source, the OBC persons make only 807.04 on the average from this source. **Pachim Matia**—16 households have milch cattle, 19 households have pet calves, 16 households have goats and 14 have fowls while 3 households have pet pigs. These are the simple activities, which generate some financial source for them.

Binoigutia Village

Binoigutia village has got a tradition of pisciculture with 7-8 ponds. It can be made much more profitable if some of them are developed scientifically and proper training is provided to them. In the **Saptagram** village economy, livestock is also considered as symbol of status. With inception of mechanized farming the strength of cattle are being reduced. Out of total 39 households, 26 households have reported to have milch cattle such as cows and buffaloes and 9 families have no livestock. Thus it can be inferred that still 80 per cent of households are keeping livestock for the livelihood.

Ghoramari

Most activities are farm based and the non-farm activities only include animal husbandry (piggery, goatery, and duckery) in small pockets. Employment is lowest in farm based activities in the rainy season. Women get some employment for sowing paddy in rainy season. Unemployment is quite high in the village. The survey also reveals that most people do not have permanent or continuous employment.

Namani Borpomua

The role of cattle and buffalo is quite important since this village economy is traditionally agriculture based. Cattle, buffalo and pigs are important livestock population of the village. As they do not take milk regularly, so the Mishings do not milk the cows. All the livestock animals in the village are of local breed and are small in size. The **Bengenamatti** village undertakes duck, goat, and buffalo farming to maintain livelihood. In **Mohbandha Gaon**—Position of livestock in rural household is not very promising. Out of 31 households only 16 households had one or the other livestock wealth.

Credit/Loan

Institutional loans from banks is not forthcoming, minimum standards of living is also poor, though efforts of NGOs like Prayash by organizing the people around economic and employment generating activities have been geared towards alleviating the economic condition of the village. Cooperative bank is functional in the village and United Bank of India is also operating in the village. But there are a very few bank accounts of villagers. As such there are no moneylenders in this village but during the time of crisis well to do people lend money to the villagers. No need to say that the interest rate is very exorbitant. The banks give hardly any credit for the agricultural purposes. Now-a-days farmers have started applying for the loan for the purchase of the power tiller. Those of the farmers, who have the surplus production, sell it in the local market.

All of the borrowings amongst the various sections of the sample population are from commercial banks. Apparently there are no moneylenders in the village. All of the borrowings are above Rs. 1,000 at least. As far as the credit details is concerned, very few people gave the total money that they owned to the banks or the moneylenders.

As per the annual target lead banks and its branches are allotted different Gram Panchayats and against each GP, physical as well as financial quota allocation is done. Then GPs are asked to submit list of beneficiaries in consultation with Gaon Sabha. The main criteria of selection are landless than 15 bighas, annual income less than rupees 11,000 and no costly movable assets. Other than this other regulatory criteria regarding number of SC and STs are maintained accordingly. Then finally the sponsoring bank screens the proposals.

Naharani Grant Village—Average debt of ST households is highest at Rs. 4,550 while it is lowest for SC households at Rs. 1500. The average debt per general and OBC households is Rs. 3,160 and Rs. 1984.61 respectively. The main sources as stated earlier is bank loan and sometimes relatives. The interest rate is 10 per cent to 12.5 per cent. The reasons cited for borrowing are mostly for investment in land, in agriculture etc. The maximum borrowings are in the range of Rs. 1,000-5,000.

Pachim Matia—Local moneylender and Pragjyotish Bank are sources of credit but people are scared about borrowing and have limited access to credit giving sources. **Binoigutia**—Overall repayment under IRDP and others are fair, with a few exceptional cases. **Ghoramari**—The credit facilities are not accessible and there is single cropping. Lack of irrigation has led to a limited rainfed agricultural season leading to seasonal unemployment.

ANTI-POVERTY AND OTHER RURAL DEVELOPMENT PROGRAMMES

Poverty

Most of the villagers live marginally above the poverty line and they at least enjoy their four square meals a day. These are the overall observations, which can be discerned from an analysis of the various anti-poverty schemes and their implementation in the village :

- Selection of beneficiaries is largely done on party lines;
- Disbursement of loans is not in time;
- There is delay in the execution of schemes;
- Over-stocking of foodgrains for JGSY and mid-day meal schemes;

- Politicization of various grassroots committees;
- Lack of awareness with regard to viable economic activities (everyone comes to the Block office only, for example for agricultural activities, they could be advised to approach the Block agricultural office);
- Sloth and dependency exists to a large extent, however, it was quite refreshing to notice self-sufficiency and independent mindsets especially in the tribal communities;
- JGSY funds were not released in time during the period of my stay in the village as a result, as previously mentioned, there was a problem of over stocking; and
- Village has not yet been covered under JRY, as a result progress and achievement of this scheme is yet to be ascertained.

The BPL list is a basic document prepared by the BDOs to plan their developmental schemes. It is an important database for surplus land distribution.

The tribal communities are mostly poor because of lack of employment opportunities. They get seasonal employment during the time of sowing and harvesting only. They have very meagre resources and therefore, face hardships during the lean agricultural season. Some EAS schemes provide them employment, which is not sufficient. They usually go to town area and undertake any labour activity available.

Indebtedness is not a problem in **Niz Lahoal** village. Workers get better wages as compared to their other parts of the country. We cannot see abject poverty in this village because everyone has got land. In **Pachim Matia,** 2.5 per cent households are BPL. 31 households have less than 1 acre of land and no household has more than 10 acres of lands. Muslim households have no land at all. Total 8 households sold their agro-produce. 87.5 per cent seller sold the produce in the nearest *hatt.* 12.5 per cent sold at doorstep. 50 per cent producers sold the produce just after the harvest. It shows that the farmers are forced to sell their produce on very low price to the traders probably to repay the loans and purchase the other domestic commodities.

In **Kalitakuchi,** most of the populations living below poverty line are from the STs, about 20 families. The fishermen community (halois) who are only 4 families also live below the poverty line. There are around twenty landless families in the **Binoigutia** village. Most of them have only homestead land and five to six of the households do not have homestead land even. Among them two are widows. They are doing daily labour in other households to meet their requirements.

The BPL population in the **Senchowa** village is 685 and normally, all are SCs. Nobody in the village appears to have taken loan to start a capitalistic enterprise. Loans appear to have been taken in lieu of PAPs only. The trend of a moneylender is not there in this village. In **Hatkhula Gaon,** there are 90 families who have been placed below the poverty line. They are the main targets in most of the government schemes. 50 out of the 90 BPL families are from the SC and the rest 40 arc OBC family.

The **Kuwamara Handique** village has around 42 per cent population below poverty line. But this BPL list has been prepared by the DRDA in 1995 and by this time some of the families have come above the poverty line. There is a need to revise the BPL list by conducting a fresh survey.

In **Mohbandha Gaon,** there is considerable number of the villagers in absolute poverty. Out of 32 households studied, 50 per cent of them are with an annual income of less than Rs. 15,000. The distribution of household studied according to annual income is given in Table 1.7.

Table 1.7 : Number of Households and Annual Income

Sl. No.	*Annual Income (Rs.)*	*No. of Households*
1.	Less than 15,000	15
2.	15000-20000	9
3.	20000-25000	4
4.	25000-50000	2
5.	More than 50000	2

The 15 households with annual income of less than Rs. 15000 are in absolute poverty and perhaps who come under the fully unemployed.

Development is incomplete without social development. The poor performance in terms of rural poverty is mainly due to the low productivity of non-skilled agricultural labour and low real wages. Assam ranks 12th among 16 States in terms of human and gender development indices. Poor indicators are not as much due to expenditure shortfall as they are due to inefficient expenditure management. Public expenditure on health and education as a percentage of SDP is higher than the average for all States and increasing. Per capita expenditure on education is higher than the average for all States and increasing. Large percentage of expenditure is, however, unproductive, going to wages and salaries. Gap between plan outlay and utilization exists possibly due to the inability in mobilizing resourcess to meet the matching fund requirements for centrally sponsored programmes. There is a need to recover costs of providing public services to the maximum extent possible, reduce establishment costs and administrative overheads and transfer expenditure authority to local bodies who are directly responsible and accountable to the local people.

POVERTY ALLEVIATION PROGRAMMES

The poverty alleviation programmes implemented in the State are SGSY, JGSY, EAS, IAY. The earthworks are more popular among the works taken up under JRY. This gives rise to the possibility of underutilizing the funds and using them for personal purposes by the stakeholders other than the public.

The state of IAY is also not very good. In this scheme Rs. 20,000 is provided to BPL family to construct a one room pucca house with 3 ft high wall and bamboo mat fencing with GCI sheet roof. The money is not given to beneficiary. The first stage in IAY is the selection of beneficiaries. According to the guidelines of government the beneficiaries must be selected by the process of Gram Sabha. Since the Panchayat is not functional in the village hence the selection process is nothing but a process to be implemented by the BDO and village secretary after taking some cut out of it. There are normally two lists are prepared—one is shown to be ratified by the Gram Sabha and another list is given by the local MLA after some consideration. The BDO now strikes a balance by accommodating some members from both the lists—mostly 50 : 50. The materials GCI sheets, cement and iron are provided by the DRDA directly. This purchase is done centrally at State government level and about rupees 900 are deducted against materials. The rest amount is released directly to the local contractor by the BDO. Another interesting feature of IAY is that because the financial limit for the difficult areas is rupees 22,000 and 20,000 for non-difficult areas.

In **Niz Lahoal,** most of them have got shops, cows and bullocks from the IRDP loan. Selection process is not very democratic and more or less it depends on the discretion of Anchlik Panchayat president. This president informally decides about the beneficiaries in consultation with the Gram Panchayat president. Almost in 75 per cent of the cases assets are found in the good condition. Some of the beneficiaries are earning regular income from their assets. Number of the beneficiaries under the IRDP is very small in this village. Still it has a positive impact on the villagers. In short we can say IRDP in this particular village is a marginal success.

There were six IAY beneficiaries in the **Naharani Grant** village in 1995-96. Each of them was given Rs. 14,500. All the houses are one room tenements with brick walls, earthen floor, wooden roof, trusses and tin roof are now completed. As far as the impact of JRY on the poverty situation of the village is concerned, there is not too much of visible impact. But the IAY has certainly benefited the homeless rural poor. But there are problems in identification of the beneficiaries, quality of construction materials, low unit cost, scattered location of the houses etc. No doubt, JRY provides employment to the rural poor of the village. But sometimes, labour, especially skilled labour has to be brought in. More of judiciously selected need-based schemes ought to be taken up, keeping in mind the sustainability such that they remain as permanent assets to the people.

In **Pachim Matia,** all the beneficiaries benefited by wage employment. 16.67 respondents told that females are paid less than males. Wage is paid weekly. 58.33 per cent labourers took cash, 25 per cent food and 16.67 per cent preferred both, as mode of payment. 21.05 per cent beneficiaries alleged corruption in the JRY yet another 44.44 per cent beneficiaries held the view that JRY improved their living condition.

75.96 per cent of the households are BPL in **Ghoramari** village. SGSY was implemented in the Balipara Block from May 2000. The key activities identified are: Farm based: Farm mechanization, duckery, piggery, poultry, goatery, mushroom cultivation, fishery, horticulture, dairy development. In the non-farm based activity are weaving, cane and bamboo furniture making. But in the village the main activities were piggery, goatery, duckery and weaving. The IAY programme also has been implemented in the village. The survey of 10 beneficiaries of IAY in the last few years revealed that the allotted funds (Rs. 20,000) has been released to the beneficiaries in most cases. But none of the houses had a IAY board displayed. They also do not have sanitary latrines, smokeless chulha and nearby drinking water facility. The money was said to be just sufficient for constructing the building but latrines and smokeless chulha could not be constructed. The Gram Sabha did the selection of the beneficiaries and the beneficiaries say that they have not given cuts to anybody but also state that the second installment was quite delayed.

No JRY work has been undertaken in the **Nargaon** village in past few years. Under the Employment Assurance Scheme (EAS) 1993-94 the primary school building was built at a cost of around rupees one lakh. But no local person found employment. Contractor who brought labourers from outside did the work.

Senchowa—In 1996-97, out of the total 7 IRDP beneficiaries, all belong to SC category, two are women and one is assignee of surplus land. The total credit disbursement was Rs. 64,000 out of which Rs. 17,000 was given to women and Rs. 9,000 to assignee of surplus land. Out of seven beneficiaries, three are marginal farmers, two are agri-labourers and one is a non-agri labourer. In the year 1996-97, five numbers of women were trained in the TRYSEM programme for the purpose of weaving. All of the women belonged to the SC category. Out of these women, four were self-employed and one was instructor at the Block centre. The works taken under JRY in 1996-97 were land development (levelling of school field), construction of two kutcha roads and construction of four numbers of houses under IAY. Under JRY, the works done were land development, road making and IAY houses. The quality of the works was also poor. There seemed to be a lot of corruption in the construction of IAY houses.

Dighaligaon Village—The sanction of IAY houses has come as a boon to all BPL families. However, people are so poor that almost each and every household is in dire need of a house under the IAY. I have also come to realize that local politics plays a vital role in the selection of IAY beneficiaries.

DWCRA is operational in the **Deodhar** village and six groups were initially formed under the scheme, of which only two are operational now. Total number of active members is thirty-three and the activities they are generally engaged in are weaving and the paddy business. The women are not aware of and neither they are educated about what other productive and profitable activities they can undertake under this scheme. The village was not covered under the JRY, and it is only recently that it has been covered under JGSY and 5.03 lakh have been allotted to the village. The progress and achievement of the scheme is yet to be seen.

Kuwamara Handique village has self-employment programmes as well as wage employment programmes. Previously as the panchayats were non-existent such activities were planned and implemented by DRDA only. Till this time, the implementing authorities at the office level have done selection of beneficiaries. Now as panchayats are the implementing agencies, they are expected to select the beneficiaries through Gram Sabhas. Swarnajayanti Swarojgar Yojana is being implemented through the BDO offices in the village. The scheme has 70 per cent loan component and 30 per cent subsidy component. Identifying productive activities is the most crucial part of the scheme. Some of the beneficiaries have just been included in order to complete the target on time.

At present in **Mohbandha Gaon** four houses are under construction, was provided the ceiling surplus land on which IAY house is constructed. This is a good example of linking more than one scheme or programmes for better and sustainable benefits. People do feel happier to have PDS since their hard-earned wages could be effectively used to get more foodgrains.

In the case of Rabina Begum Barbhuiya of **Saptagram** village, her husband died in 1994. She was selected as IRDP beneficiary on the compassionate ground after direct intervention of DC, Cachar. She was selected for a scheme to make the Cane and Bamboo furniture under the IRDP 1994-95. The total financial outlay of the scheme was Rs. 9,000 out of whom 3,000 was subsidy and 6,000 was loaning component. She was not provided any asset in the scheme. She had to give a cut of Rs. 1,200 to the supplier of the bank. She utilized the remaining amount to mortgage 1.5 bighas of land for cultivation. She utilized the remaining amount for personal consumption. Because of this compassionate ground she also got selected for IAY house which is under construction. Now she is willing to take another loan for poultry farming. In this case she never tried to repay the loan because she understood that this loan is part of the relief under National Family Benefit Scheme. She was not given any training in Cane and Bamboo furnitures and most of the officials are interested only in the release of money not in the true development of the beneficiary. In all the cases of IRDP loan distribution, middlemen apply same method to share the cut and no asset is provided to beneficiary. The beneficiary is also selected with the motive of getting cuts. The beneficiaries take the remaining amount in cash and use where they want. Some uses it for consumption purposes, some uses for house construction and some of them waste in drinking. Some of the beneficiaries show their old assets such as *hathkargha* to bank and get loan by paying cuts. Thus a very good scheme to help BPL families is being used as sources of income for person responsible for implementing it. The IRDP scheme have failed in this village because of nexus among Block, contractor, bank officials and supplier. The aim of JRY is to provide wage employment to poor people and at the same time create community assets. Involvement of contractor is banned in this scheme. The wages to be paid are determined by minimum wages. For unskilled labourer, the rate is Rs. 47 a day. But local wage, for unskilled labourer is Rs. 70 per day, is much higher than the minimum wages. Hence it was not possible to follow guidelines strictly. The works were done by contractors and which resulted in poor quality of work. This also defeated the very purpose of providing wage employment to BPL families. In some schemes the work is shown completed but no work has been done actually. In actual practice, the GP Secretary or village secretary hands over the cheque of Rs. 10,000 to beneficiary only when he gives Rs. 4,000 to GP secretary. The poor beneficiary starts construction of his house with the remaining amount. Somehow he completes the construction till roof level to get second installment. The second installment of Rs. 7,000 is given after this without any cut. If the beneficiary is very poor he does not use this money for completing house construction. He uses rupees seven thousand for consumption and put straw thatched roof on the walls. He does not bother about his third installment of Rs. 3,000, which is to be taken for construction of pit latrine. Pit latrine is neither very popular nor it can be properly constructed in Rs. 3,000 hence, the beneficiary normally does not bother about this money. In some cases it was found that money was not given even after constructing latrine. Though village secretary was suspended for not giving Rs. 3,000 to beneficiary as last installment, it has impact on others for not constructing the latrine. Those who are bit better financially have completed their houses by putting some own contribution but the poor have left it till the roof level.

POOREST PERSON

Case Study of the Poorest Person/Family

Duleswar Bora (Naharani Grant Village) is a man who has seen much travail in his 35 years. He originally hails from Goalpara district. He had come to Darrang district when he was a young boy, in search of livelihood. He has a wife called Mani, and a young son of three years. He has no land except for the small homestead land of about 0.33 acre, which he was allotted under the MNP house sites scheme. He has no permanent occupation and he works as a daily wage labourer in and around Rangapara town or as an agricultural labourer in and around Naharani village. He barely gets an income of Rs. 28-30 a day, and there are many days in the year when he cannot find any work. After much prodding, his wife broke down in tears as she narrated her tale of woe and poverty. She said that they barely got to eat one meal a day. Sometimes, they and their child would simply go hungry for want of anything to eat. A typical day in the life of this family would be of Duleswar going out in search of work, and Mani staying back with the child. The latter does not attend school. Their assets are few. They have a small thatched hovel. In the last year, 1995-96, they were granted a dwelling house under the Indira Awas Yojana. They have few utensils, steel plates, glasses etc. To add to their woes, Mani was kept in the mental asylum as she had some serious problems. Now they are trying to pull on the best they can. They both, except further assistance from the government, for they say that they have no one else to turn to. I urged the BDO that a DWCRA weaving cooperative be started so that Mani Bora should be a beneficiary of the Scheme.

INTEGRATED RURAL DEVELOPMENT PROGRAMMES

Some people of the village have received IRDP loans for various schemes over the years but none except one of them has been repaying the installments regularly and do not intend to do so. They see the process of securing an IRDP loan a tedious one. They had to give few hundred rupees as bribes. In spite of poor recovery and misutilization of funds, IRDP has made impact in improving the condition of the beneficiaries. But the schemes have not had any effect on general condition of village as a whole.

Niz Lahoal Gaon panchayat building was built under the JRY 3 to 4 years back. This village has two lower primary schools. There is no community centre in the village. Some work is done under the IAY in this village this year. 6 houses are built for the STs. 15 tube wells have been constructed under the MWS.

On the whole, the IRDP has been doing pretty well in the **Naharani Grant** village. All the beneficiaries reported that there quality of life have improved through enhancement of income and financial security. Also, four out of five say that they would like supplementary loans. But, there has not been too much impact on the overall poverty situation as the number of beneficiaries are limited, and also all are not so successful in handling their loan amounts.

Total 13 beneficiaries were surveyed in the **Pachim Matia** village out of which there were 30.77 per cent were women while 30.70 per cent were SC/ST. 50 per cent of the total money distributed was given for tertiary sector while agriculture, bee keeping, industry and animal husbandry were non-funded area. Handloom and irrigation were the area of the interest where maximum loans were distributed. At present 71.43 per cent IRDP schemes are continuing and 16.67 per cent schemes perished. 41.67 per cent women benefited under TRYSEM while the percentage of SC/ST beneficiaries were 33.33. The average income of the DWCRA members was Rs. 1,200.

The IRDP in the **Hatkola Gaon** village has forced the beneficiaries to become defaulters. The assets provided to them are of bad quality. For example, cattle supplied die within a year. The beneficiaries are not aware that the amount received is a loan and has to be repaid. Almost all of them have paid cuts to bank officials and Block officials. The IRDP in the village is a total failure.

Reng Beng—As most of the villagers are not having PP (permanent patta) land they could not able to avail any IRDP individual loan. There are 3 DWCRA groups in the village who got revolving fund for handloom weaving. Through these looms they are making gamoshas (towels) by which each member is earning approximately Rs. 600 per annum. Two persons of the village got training for self-employment under TRYSEM.

The programme of TRYSEM has been highly successful in the **Senchowa** village. There was no DWCRA scheme in this village. However, in view of the proximity of the town to this village, the DWCRA groups in this village can be given a trade for which there is a ready market in the town, e.g. making bamboo baskets, weaving etc.

Both the SGRY stream-I and the SGRY stream-II are operational in the **Dighaligaon** village and a lot of people have been benefited either through wage employment or in the form of individual beneficiaries (IBS). It is very interesting to note that while most of the beneficiaries had no idea of the wage rates as prescribed by the government, they were fully aware of the cash and foodgrain component given to them as wages during the course of their employment.

The IRDP has been functioning in the **Deodhar** village for quite some time, but again with very limited success. The beneficiaries have got money for individual activities, like opening a grocery or a stationary shop, or for tailoring and weaving. Even though the beneficiaries have been able to pay the loan back in most of the cases, they have not succeeded in creating lasting productive assets.

The IRDP has been functioning in the **Bengenamatti** village for quite some time, since it was introduced, but it has met with very little success. The beneficiaries have got money for individual activities like eri rearing, and muga rearing. JGSY schemes in the period 2001-02: Development of the Uloni market and construction of Agri Bunds at Bengenamatti crop field. Though SGSY commenced from April 1999, but in practice, it was implemented only from April 2001.

In **Kuwamara Handique,** the selection of JGSY community assets to be constructed was done at the office level with a view of fulfilling the scheme target. Therefore, the works completed were found not as per the requirement of the villagers. In other social welfare programmes, some beneficiaries have been identified under the National Social Assistance Programme (NSAP). Under National Old Age Pension Scheme (NOAP), 13 people are getting a sum of Rs. 75 per month. Under NMBS, 3 BPL women were given financial assistance of Rs. 500 after delivery in the last year. In Annapurna scheme 2 families are getting foodgrains at subsidized rates. Under the Antodaya Anna Yojana scheme 3 persons were selected.

As far as the IRDP projects are concerned, it was found that almost all the schemes have very meagre impact on the beneficiaries. Almost all the beneficiaries are defaulters now. There seems to be many causes for the failure, but we will discuss a few of them here :

1. There was no planning done for these projects. Many people were asked to take up poultry and duck vending scheme. To take up the scheme, they were provided a bicycle as the asset and were given some money. What people naturally did was to use the money for private purpose and use the cycle for general transport. The scheme never came up.
2. The scheme was thrust upon the people. They did not get the project they wanted to do, but they had to choose from a list of project that was supplied.
3. The schemes that were taken up had no demand in the village. For reaching to the urban market, these villagers have no infrastructure and facilities.
4. Corruption is very much there in IRDP projects. It was said that in some cases in the village, the bank manager paid Rs. 500 less to the beneficiaries.

CASE STUDY OF AN IRDP BENEFICIARY

Manisha Boro—The Weaver of Naharani

Manisha Boro is a typical artisan of Naharani Grant Village. She is 35 years old and a mother of three children. Her husband is a jawan in the Indian Army and is presently serving in Kashmir. As she has to make both ends meet to run the family. She keeps livestock like fowls, cows etc. and she weaves. Manisha purchased the weaving equipment for Rs. 1,000 many years ago. She had not taken any loan for it. She purchases the yarn from Rangapara, at the rate of Rs. 23 per bundle. It takes five bundles to make on 'juthi' from which 10 pieces of chadar can be woven. She takes the ready products to Rangapara every week, and sells them for Rs. 25 each to shopkeepers in Rangapara. Thus, she makes a profit of about Rs. 135 on the average per 10 pieces. The shops, however, sell each for Rs. 30 to Rs. 35. Manisha is also the beneficiary of an IRDP loan for cattle. An active lady, she was found to be perpetually bustling around the house or seated at her loom.

She and a few other women can be organized to set up a cooperative society to benefit them further.

Name of the Beneficiary—Shri Dulal Bora

Dulal Bora, 45 years of age, is an inhabitant of Naharani Grant Village. He originally hailed from Parbatia near Tezpur. He is the head of a family of five members. When he moved to Naharani Grant Village, his economic condition was very poor. He was living hand to mouth for survival. He was identified as a beneficiary for an IRDP scheme. In 1983, he was given a loan of Rs. 2,400 for setting up a grocery shop. With Rs. 2,300 from himself, he set up the shop. As his business progressed, he took another IRDP loan of Rs. 5,000 in 1984, and extended his shop. Today, Dular Bora's shop is estimated to have a value of at least Rs. 70,000. His annual income from the grocery shop is Rs. 3,500 and from the agricultural land, Rs. 3,000. A smiling Bora said that it was not easy to come up to this level. Starting from a modest hut, today he is the proud owner of a pucca house, and his grocery shop is doing very well—thanks to the IRDP.

PANCHAYATI RAJ SYSTEM

The panchayat plays a pivotal role in all the development as well as poverty alleviation programmes within its jurisdiction. The different ward members identify all the beneficiaries before they are finally selected in the Gaon Sabha meetings and recommended for the various poverty alleviation schemes. The Panchayat is the main implementing agency in all the developmental works. All developmental funds are channelized through the Panchayat down to the executing agencies. This has instilled a feeling of belongingness as well as a sense of ownership of all the community assets. In my interactions with the villagers regarding the allocation of developmental works as well as selection of beneficiaries, the one unanimous answer was that the panchayat had done everything.

Panchayats are not very powerful. It is generally personality based. Some influence of the Panchayat can be seen at Anchalik (intermediary) level but still Panchayats as an institution has to go a long way and people have to work hard to give roots to this local body government. Democratization of Panchayats has not taken place in this village.

There was no village Panchayat in the village between 1997-2002. The elections under new Assam Panchayat Act, 1994 have not taken place so far. The last elections took place in 1992 under old system of Mahakuma Parishad. The Panchayat lapsed in 1997 and now waiting for the fresh elections. The elections were likely to be held in the month of October 2000. Recently Panchayat elections were held in Assam in January 2002.

The Gaon Panchayat have three committees to look after specific functions. These are Development Committee, Social Justice Committee and Social Welfare Committee. As the elections are held just 3-4 months back these committees are yet to be formed and made operationalized. The Assam Panchayat Act, 1994 has specified some functions to be undertaken by the GPs. These functions are agriculture, animal husbandry, fisheries, social and farm forestry, village industries, rural housing, drinking water, means of communication like roads, bridges, waterways etc., rural electrification, poverty alleviation programmes, education, rural sanitation, public health, women and child welfare, social welfare and public distribution system etc. But so far, the State Government has not taken any step towards delegating powers to the newly constituted PRIs for execution of these functions.

Naharani Grant Village has a gaon panchayat called Naharani Gaon Panchayat. Women, SC, ST and minorities are fully represented in the membership of the panchayat. The Anchalik Panchayat (between GP and Mahakuma Parishad at district level), the GP and DRDA fund are executed through the GP president. Taxes, such as cycle, go-cart, building tax, etc. are collected by the Panchayat to maintain the village. The Panchayat is involved in Total Literacy Campaign, supply of essential commodities, and the identification of new development projects to be undertaken by the DRDA.

Saptagram—All households of village know the role and functions of village Panchayat very well. Many of them have approached to village Panchayat for one work or other and wherever possible have got the satisfactory result. Almost every one has voted in general election. This shows that village is politically aware and mature.

The **Ghoramari Gaon** Panchayat has 415 voters. The Gram Panchayat has one elected member from each Ward of the Gaon Panchayat (i.e. 10 members). The Gram Sabha last held was in June 2003. **Senchowa**—Though the people know that the panchayat exists yet most of them are unaware of its functions. Most of them do not know that the panchayat is supposed to ameliorate their problems of unemployment etc. Upper castes people dominate the Panchayat in this village. However, the women have got proper representation.

Bengenamatti—It only in December 27-31, 2001 that Panchayat elections were held, the last elections were held only in 1994. As such though elections were held, however, the elected members have not been administered oaths. In a significant development, Panchayat elections were held on December 27-31 in the entire State of Assam after a gap of nearly a decade, to three levels GP (Gaon Panchayat), AP (Anchalik Panchayat), Block level and ZP (Zila Parishad) district level.

SWOT ANALYSIS

Strengths

The strength of the village lies in their people and resourcess. Most of the land in Brahmaputra Valley is very fertile. Fertility of the land is so strong that multiple cropping may easily be made possible. The tea estate, which created this village over a period of time, is a major strength of the village, which can provide greater employment to the village.

- Natural resourcess particularly land;
- Proximity to the national highway;
- Peace, communal harmony and spirit of accommodation among the villagers;
- No labour problem;
- Absence of abject poverty and exploitation; and
- All households having land.

The democratic bodies such as the Panchayat are doing their fair share of development work along with ensuring that people too participate in the selection as well as implementation of the schemes. This is a step in decentralization and devolution of power to the grass-roots level. The Panchayat Act of Assam, recently amended, has endowed a large amount of power and responsibilities to the local bodies such as the Gaon Panchayat and the Anchalik Panchayat. Planning, preparation and execution of various local schemes will be done under supervision of these bodies. It will also ensure more accountability from the people in the long run.

Weakness

- Small landholding;
- No scientific and technological aids used for agriculture;
- No diversification of the economic activities;
- Subsistence level farming and no commercialization;
- No entrepreneurship; and
- No irrigation facilities.

As far as cultivation is concerned, improved methods of cultivation and planting of crops is not being followed. Only one crop of paddy is grown in a year. Double or multiple cropping is virtually unknown here. HYV seeds, fertilizers are not in much use over here. All this results in low yields and lower margins of profit. Allied to this, animal husbandry is not done in a scientific manner, hence, income arising out of these activities remains low. Monitoring and reviewing of various poverty alleviation programmes is not carried out in a timely and proper manner. For example, there were a lot of complaints regarding the quality of construction of a school under EAS. There is a marked lack of existence of any rural industry. Villagers do not know how to utilize their leisure time in additional profit making cottage industries and other activities. The practice of drinking rice beer and alcohol is very common among the ex-tea garden labourers in this area. A lot of their earnings get drained away by such useless habits.

Ever increasing population but without any corresponding expansion of employment opportunities in the tea estate resulting in increasing of both seasonal and permanent unemployment. Constant discouragement to the cultivators for taking to the farming activities as they are being demotivated by the abiotic factors like light soils, and biotic factors like poor technical know-how, poor credit facilities, etc. Completely ineffective gaon panchayat and poor participation of people in the decision making process. Health care infrastructure is lacking in the village. Maternity health centres do not exist in the village. Holding are fragmented and this causes reduction in total cropping area and crop intensity.

Opportunities

- Productivity of the agricultural sector can be enhanced very easily;

- Two crops pattern can be developed with irrigation and by tapping underground water;
- Pisciculture and horticulture have a wide scope; and
- With forward-backward linkages agro-based industry can be developed.

On the agricultural front, modern methods of cultivation such as use of fertilizers, pesticides, multiple cropping etc. could be introduced which could go a long way in improving the agricultural yield and indirectly the poverty situation in the area. There is a lot of scope for development of horticulture, sericulture, fisheries, floriculture etc. These could be on individual or cooperative society basis.

Expanding of Blocks and town adjoining the villages opens up new opportunities for employment, development of infrastructure and expanded trade and business activities. The cultivated low land fields though they are light, still fertile and being surrounded by the River Bhogdoi and River Kakodonga, there is a tremendous potential for development of minor irrigation schemes. It would not only increase the cropping intensity but also overall productivity of the land.

There is a need for more efforts in the rural development sector. With the coming of Panchayati Raj, the programme implementation has been handed over to the Panchayat bodies. These bodies need to be empowered. They should be given some powers of resources generation and also the responsibility of some basic local functions. Along with that some lower level departmental workers can also be brought under the control of the Panchayats.

Threats

- Insurgency problems;
- Unemployment, particularly among the literates;
- Floods;
- Overall laziness of the villagers; and
- Lack of spirit of cooperation in the long run can be suicidal for the proper developmental perspective.

Appendix I

District-wise Demographic Profile of Assam, 2001 (Provisional)

Sl. No.	*District*	*Area (Sq. Km.)*	*Population*	*Rural Population*	*Urban Population*	*Sex ratio*	*% of literacy*	*Density per Sq. Km.*
(1)	*(2)*	*(3)*	*(4)*	*(5)*	*(6)*	*(7)*	*(8)*	*(9)*
1.	Dhubri	2838	1634589	1444043	190546	944	49.86	584
2.	Kokrajhar	3129	930404	866772	63632	945	52.55	294
3.	Bongaigaon	2510	906315	796028	110287	945	60.27	361
4.	Goalpara	1824	822306	755017	67289	955	58.56	451
5.	Barpeta	3245	1642420	1517280	125140	941	57.35	506
6.	Nalbari	2257	1138184	1110706	27478	937	68.08	504
7.	Kamrup	4345	2515030	1614512	900518	894	74.69	579
8.	Darrang	3481	1503943	1430099	73844	943	55.92	432
9.	Sonitpur	5324	1677874	1530043	147831	942	60.29	315
10.	Lakhimpur	2277	889325	824196	65129	952	69.59	391
11.	Dhemaji	3237	569468	530138	39330	936	65.96	176
12.	Morigaon	1704	775874	737813	38061	945	59.46	455
13.	Nagaon	3831	2315387	2037466	277921	939	62.28	604
14.	Golaghat	3502	945781	866625	79156	929	70.36	270
15.	Jorhat	2851	1009197	838549	170648	903	77.91	354
16.	Sibsagar	2668	1052802	955701	97101	926	75.33	395
17.	Dibrugarh	3381	1172056	952080	219976	923	71.21	347
18.	Tinsukia	3790	1150146	925972	224174	909	63.28	303
19.	Karbi Anglong	10434	812320	719569	92751	922	58.83	78
20.	N.C. Hills	4888	186189	128110	58079	883	68.59	38
21.	Karimganj	1809	1003678	930131	73547	944	67.21	555
22.	Hailakandi	1327	542978	497421	45557	933	59.84	409
23.	Cachar	3786	1442141	1240723	201418	945	68.42	381
	Assam	**78438**	**26638407**	**23248994**	**3389413**	**932**	**64.28**	**340**

Source: Census of India, 2001 (http://www.assamgov.org/ecosurvey/Appendix.htm)

Appendix II

District-Wise Numbers of Village, Gaon Panchayat and Community Development Block in Assam

Sl. No.	District	Number of Villages (As per 2001 Census)	Number of Gaon Panchayat as on 31-8-03	Number of Community Development Block as on 31-3-03
1.	Dhuri	1333	172	14
2.	Kokrajhar	973	88	6
3.	Bongaigaon	917	93	6
4.	Goalpara	837	81	8
5.	Barpeta	1073	150	12
6.	Nalbari	827	110	12
7.	Kamrup	1393	178	17
8.	Darrang	1341	155	11
9.	Sonitpur	1874	158	14
10.	Lakhimpur	1170	81	9
11.	Dhemaji	1315	65	5
12.	Morigaon	636	85	5
13.	Nagaon	1421	240	18
14.	Golaghat	1086	102	8
15.	Jorhat	866	111	8
16.	Sibsagar	881	118	9
17.	Dibrugarh	1348	93	7
18.	Tinsukia	1151	88	7
19.	Karbi Anglong	2843	—	11
20.	N.C. Hills	640	—	5
21.	Karimganj	940	96	7
22.	Hailakandi	331	62	5
23.	Cachar	1051	163	15
	Assam	**26247**	**2489**	**219**

Source: Directorate of Economics and Statistics, Assam. (Economic Survey Assam, 2003-04).

REFERENCES

Agriculture Statistices, Assam 1998-1999.

Ashokvardhan, C. *Socio-Economic Profile of Rural India,* Volume 2 (North East India), Concept Publishing Company, New Delhi, 2004.

Ashokvardhan, C. *Tribal Land Rights in India*, Centre for Rural Studies, LBSNAA, Mussoorie, 2006.

BPL Census, Assam 1998.

Census of Assam 1991.

Census of Assam 2001.

Census of India, 1991 (http://www.assamgov.org/ecosurvey/Appendix.htm)

Census of India, 2001 (http://www.assamgov.org/ecosurvey/Appendix.htm).

Das, Bhakta, *A Glimpse of the Scheduled Castes and their Socio Economic Development in Assam*, Omsons Publications, Guwahati, 1986.

Directorate of Economics and Statistics, Assam. (Economic Survey Assam 2003-2004)

http://assamgovt.nic.in/

http://planassam.org/stateProfile/economicProfile.htm

http://planningcommission.nic.in/plans/stateplan/sdr_assam/sdr_assexesum.pdf

http://pnrdassam.nic.in/setSchms.htm

http://rural.nic.in (official website of Ministry of Rural Development, Govt. India)

http://www.indiainbusiness.nic.in/indian-states/assam/general.htm

http://www.indiainbusiness.nic.in/indian-states/assam/socialinfra-assam.htm

Phukan Umananda, Agricultural Development in Assam, Mittal Publications, New Delhi, 1990, Bora A. K., Pattern of Land Utilisation in Assam, Manas Publications, Delhi, 1986.

Tamuli Ranjit, *Institutional Finance for Rural Development*, Himalayan Publishers, New Delhi, 2003

2

Nagaland

ASHISH VACHHANI, JAI SINGH SHEKHAWAT and VARUNENDRA VIKRAM SINGH

INTRODUCTION

Nagaland, part of Assam and North East Frontier Agency (NEFA) in 1947, became the 16th State of India in 1963. Statehood came as a result of a political agreement. In this respect Nagaland's case is unique and special constitutional protection was also provided under Article 371(A) of the Constitution of India to safeguard the culture, traditions and way of life of the Nagas. One of the smaller hill States of India, Nagaland is known for its myriad tribes with their rich culture and traditions. The State has a distinct character both in terms of its social composition as well as in its developmental history.

LOCATION

Nagaland is one of the 'seven sisters' of the North-East. The State is bounded by Assam in the west, Myanmar on the East, Manipur in the south and Arunachal Pradesh and part of Assam on the north. It lies between 25°6′ and 27°4′ northern latitudes and between 93°20′ and 95°15′ eastern longitudes. The State has an area of 16,579 sq. km (which constitutes 0.5 per cent of the country's geographical area) with a population of 19,88,636 (0.2% of the country's population) as per 2001 Census. The number of households in the State was 1.49 lakh in 1981, which increased to 2.17 lakh in 1991. The State is predominantly rural, with 82.26 percent of the population living in villages, generally situated on high hilltops or slopes overlooking verdant valleys.

Till January 2004, Nagaland consisted of eight administrative districts, with 52 Blocks, nine census towns and 1,286 inhabited villages. Each district generally has predominant concentration of one of the major/minor tribes of the State, making the districts distinct in their socio-political, traditional, cultural and linguistic characteristics. Of the eight districts, Tuensang is the largest, occupying 25.5 percent of the total area of the State, followed by Kohima with 18.79 percent. In January 2004, three new districts were inaugurated by the State Government, viz. Longleng, Kiphire and Peren. At the time of preparing this Report, Longleng and Kiphire were sub-divisions of Tuensang district and Peren was a sub-division of Kohima district. Therefore, the analysis for Tuensang includes information/statistics for Kiphire and Longleng and that of Kohima includes the data of Peren.

DEMOGRAPHY

The total population of Nagaland as per 2001 Census is 19.88 lakh, of which males form 10.42 lakh and females 9.47 lakh. Among the various districts, Tuensang has the largest population (4.14 lakh), followed by Kohima (3.14 lakh). The least populated district is Phek (1.48 lakh). Nagaland witnessed the highest growth rate in population over the last decade. This unprecedented growth rate of population is a cause of serious concern to the demographers and policy planners in the State. A total fertility rate (TFR) of 2.1 is considered to be the replacement level of fertility, which needs to be achieved in all States for population stabilisation. As per the National Family Health Survey, Nagaland had a TFR of 3.77 during 1998, amongst the highest in the country. There is thus a need for policy intervention to tackle this spiralling population growth, which can seriously hamper the planning process and development aspirations of the State. The density of population is another factor of concern in Nagaland because of the alarming increase in the population. The density, which was 47 per sq. km in 1981, increased to 73 in 1991 and 120 per sq. km in 2001. This will have serious implications on the ability of the State to meet the infrastructure requirements of its people, especially in the urban areas.

Table 2.1: Nagaland at a Glance

Total Area	*16,579 sq. km*
State Capital	Kohima (1,44,412 m. above sea level)
State Boundaries	East—Myanmar, West—Assam, North—Assam and Arunachal Pradesh, South—Manipur
Population	19,88,636 (2001 census)
Rural Population	16,35,815 (82.26%) (2001 census)
Urban Population	3,52,821 (17.74%) (2001 census)
Density of Population	120 per sq.km. (2001 census)
Sex Ratio	909: 1000 Female: Male (2001 census)
Literacy Rate	Persons: 67.11%
Male	71.77%
Female	61.92%
District with HQs	(1) Kohima, (2) Mokokchung, (3) Tuensang, (4) Mon, (5) Wokha, (6) Zunheboto (7) Phek, (8) Dimapur
Newly created districts	(1) Longleng, (2) Kiphire, (3) Peren
Number of Villages	1286 (2001 census)
Number of Census towns	9 (2001 census)
Biggest Village	Kohima village (3965 households: 13,705 persons)
Official Language	English
Average Rainfall	2500 mm
Highest Peak	Mount Saramati, 3840 metres (Tuensang district)
Other Important Peaks	Mount Japfu, 3015 metres (Kohima district), Mount Zanubou, 2750 metres (Phek district), Mount Kupamedzu, 2650 metres (Phek district)
Forest Cover	13,345 sq.km. (80.49% of State's Geographical Area)
Main Rivers	Dhansiri, Doyang, Dikhu, Tizu, Melak
Railway Head	Dimapur
Airport	Dimapur
Commercial Centre	Dimapur

DECADAL GROWTH

Nagaland has recorded progressively high decadal growth in population, increasing from 39.9 percent in 1979 to 64.4 percent in 2001. This decadal growth has been one of the highest in the country. The population grew by 5.0 percent per annum during 1971-81, which increased to 5.6 percent per annum during 1981-91, which again increased to 6.4 percent per annum during 1991-2001. During the decade 1991-2001 Wokha district registered a maximum growth rate of 95 percent, followed by Tuensang (78 percent). The district of Mokokchung registered the lowest growth rate of 43 percent during the period. The high growth rates over the decades have impacted the percentage of young people who form part of Naga society. Close to 40 percent of the population are below the age of 18. As a result, the dependency ratio has also increased.

URBAN-RURAL DISTRIBUTION

People living in rural areas constituted 82.3 percent of Nagaland's population in 2001, as against 90 percent in 1971. This is an indication of the migration that is taking place in the State from rural to urban areas. Though growth of urbanisation and economic growth are generally accepted as having a positive correlation, the high rate of migration into urban areas also implies a need for policy focus on the creation of employment opportunities as well as urban infrastructure to meet the requirements of the growing urban population. During the decade 1991-2001, there was a decrease in the percentage of urban population in the towns of Mon, Mokokchung and Tuensang. This is indicative of migration of urban population from these towns to other towns, possibly for access to better urban amenities and entrepreneurial opportunities. An urban management strategy, specific to local needs is required for Dimapur and Kohima, which play host to majority (36% and 21.6% respectively) of the urban population of the State. Besides, there is the usual presence of a floating urban population, which the two regions attract because one is the main commercial centre while the other is the State capital. It is, at the same time, necessary to explore ways to develop the smaller towns as growth centres for uniform development in the State.

Table 2.2 : Demographic Profile of Nagaland

Sl. No.	*Particulars*	*1961*	*1971*	*1981*	*1991*	*2001*
1.	Total Population ('000)	369	516	775	1210	1989
2.	Decennial Growth of Population (%)	—	39.88	50.05	56.08	64.41
3.	Density of Population (per sq. km)	22	31	47	73	120
4.	Percentage of Rural Population	94.80	90.00	84.48	82.79	82.26
5.	Level of Urbanization (%)	5.20	10.0	15.52	17.21	17.74
6.	Growth of Urbanization (%)	16.6	10.4	8.9	5.6	5.4
7.	Literacy Rate (%)	20.40	27.40	42.57	61.65	67.11
8.	Literacy Rate: Male (%)	27.2	35.02	50.1	67.52	71.8
9.	Literacy Rate: Female (%)	13.0	18.65	33.9	61.65	61.9
10.	Sex Ratio (females per 1000 males)	933	871	863	886	909
11.	Percentage of Workers	NA	NA	48.23	42.68	42.74

Source : Census of India; National Family Health Survey, 1998-99.

LITERACY

The literacy rate, which was 20.4 percent in 1961, increased to 42.57 percent in 1981, and further increased to 67.11 percent in 2001. A positive element here is the increase in the female literacy level, which was 13 percent in 1961 but steadily increased to 39.9 percent in 1981 and to 61.92 percent in 2001. Among the various districts, Mokokchung and Wokha had the highest literacy rates of 84.27 percent and 81.28 percent respectively. These districts also achieved female literacy levels of more than 75 percent during 2001. Mon and Tuensang ranked the least with literacy rates of 42.25 percent and 51.30 percent respectively.

THE GENDER DIMENSION : REVERSING THE SEX RATIO

The sex ratio in Nagaland, which had steadily declined from 933 in 1961 to 863 in 1981, showed a positive, reverse trend during the last two decades. From 863 in 1981, it rose to 886 in 1991 and finally, to 909 in 2001. This is a welcome feature as far as the demographic pattern is concerned. Among the various districts, Zunheboto and Kohima had the highest sex ratio of 945 and 944 respectively. The State's socio-cultural practices, which value the girl child, have contributed to the success of reversing the sex ratio, besides governmental and civil society interventions.

WORKFORCE

The workforce constitutes 42.74 percent of the population in Nagaland. Though in absolute numbers, the total number of workers has increased from 5.16 lakh in 1991 to 8.49 lakh in 2001, the percentage of workers to the population has remained at 42.7 percent. However, among the workers, the share of main workers has fallen from 42.29 percent to 35.62 percent, while the share of marginal workers has increased from 0.39 percent in 1991 to 7.12 percent in 2001. The near stagnant proportion of workers and increasing share of marginal workers is indicative of increased prevalence of unemployment and disguised unemployment in the State. In Mon, Tuensang, Zunheboto, Wokha and Dimapur, there was a fall in the percentage of workers in the districts over the period 1991-2001.

Among the workers, 68.03 percent were engaged in agricultural activities while only 2.12 percent were engaged in household industry and 29.18 percent constituted other workers during 2001.

CULTURAL AND LINGUISTIC TRADITIONS

Nagaland is inhabited by 16 major tribes along with a number of sub-tribes. Ao, Angami, Chang, Konyak, Lotha, Sumi, Chakhesang, Khiamniungam, Kachari, Phom, Rengma, Sangtam, Yimchungrü, Kuki, Zeliang and Pochury are the major tribes. Each tribe is distinct and unique in character from the others in terms of customs, language and attire. The colourful and intricately designed costumes and ornaments, that were traditionally worn, can easily distinguish each of the tribes and sub-tribes.

Table 2.3 : Tribes and Festivals of Nagaland

Tribe	*Subdivision/District*	*Main Festival*	*Celebrated during*
Angami	Kohima	Sekrenyi	February
Ao	Mokokchung	Moatsu, Tsungremong	May, August
Chakhesang	Phek	Tsukhenyie, Sukrenyi	April/May, January
Chang	Tuensang	Kundanglem, Nuknyu Lem	April, July
Kachari	Dimapur	Bushu Jiba, Baisagn	January, April
Khiamniungam	Noklak in Tuensang	Miu Festival, Tsokum	May, October
Konyak	Mon	Aoleang Monyu	April
Kuki	Dimapur; Peren	Mimkut	January
Lotha	Wokha	Tokhu Emong	November
Phom	Longleng	Monyu, Moha, Bongvum	April, May, October
Pochury	Meluri in Phek	Yemshe	October
Rengma	Tseminyu in Kohima	Ngadah	September
Sangtam	Kiphire; Tuensang	Amongmong	September
Sumi	Zunheboto	Ahuna, Tuluni	November, July
Yimchungru	Shamator in Tuensang and Kiphire	Metumniu, Tsungkamniu	August, January
Zeliang	Peren	Hega, Langsimyi/Changa Gadi, and Mileinyi	February, October, March

The multiplicity of tribes, within such a limited space, could be due to the fact that the Naga ancestors migrated to the present location in different groups and they remained confined to their ridges and mountainous terrain. This, subsequently, resulted in their unique characteristic of appearing to be both one people and many tribes, displaying both unity and diversity in their customs, traditions, attire and political systems.

The State is replete with festivities throughout the year, as all tribes celebrate their own festivals with a pageantry of colour, music and dance. A common feature is that the festivals revolve around agriculture, the mainstay of Naga economy. These festivals hark back to times prior to the advent of Christianity. The predominant theme of the festivals is offering prayers to the Supreme Being, known by different names in different Naga tribal languages.

Nagaland has a rich linguistic tradition with as many languages as there are tribes, each exclusive to itself. What is even more remarkable is that even within the language of a particular tribe, there are dialects mutually unintelligible. For instance, in some tribes like the Angami, every village has a slightly different variation even within the same dialect—this variance progressively increasing with the geographical distance. This makes inter-tribe and intra-tribe communication very difficult. In the circumstances, English has come to serve as the State language while Nagamese, a kind of pidgin Assamese, has become the common lingua. Each of the languages continues to be spoken and used. The music, ballads, knowledge systems, art and colour combinations of the beautiful Naga shawls, etc., represent times of leisure and the fact that at least some of the tribes may have belonged to an ancient civilisation.

HISTORY

The early history of the Nagas is sketchy. Ancient Sanskrit scriptures mention Kiratas, golden skinned people of the sub-Himalayan region, with distinct culture, who migrated from their original home to the Himalayan slopes and mountains of the East. Another view is that the Nagas belong to the Mongoloid race, and they migrated and settled in the north-eastern part of present India and established their respective sovereign village-states although when they came and how they came to their present habitations are still unsettled questions. The only things that are clear is that all the tribes say their ancestors came from the east and that they were settled in the area before the arrival of the Ahoms in 1228 A.D. Even the origin of the word 'Naga' is yet to be settled finally. Many scholars have made an attempt to define the word 'Naga'. A popularly accepted view is that it originated from the Burmese word 'Naka', meaning people with earrings. It is believed that as the British came to this part of the country through Burma and asked questions about the people living therein, the reply of 'Naka' from their Burmese guides was recorded as 'Naga', and thus used subsequently.

In the years before Indian independence, the Nagas of North-East India came to exemplify an exotic society. People of the hills, radically different in culture and beliefs, were renowned for their fierce resistance to British rule and their past practice of head taking. Their frequent raids into the plains of Assam prompted the British to penetrate into the dense forests of Naga Hills in the nineteenth century to establish their control over the region.

The first Europeans to enter the hills were Captains Jenkins and Pemberton, who marched across the land in 1832. The early British relations with the tribes were one of perpetual conflict. Between 1839 and 1850, 10 military expeditions were led to the hills, to explore the region, punish the Nagas for their raids and to establish British control. The policy of military expeditions and involvement in Naga affairs was changed after the bloody battle at Kikrüma in 1852 and the British adopted a policy of non-interference with the hill men. However, this policy did not bear fruit. During 1851 to 1865 there were persistent raids by the Nagas on British subjects in the plains.

Therefore, the British India Government, reviewing its earlier policy, in 1866, decided to form a new district, with its headquarters at Samaguting, present Chümukedima. Establishment of the British post at Samaguting was a landmark in the history of British-Naga relations. It signified the Government's determination to control the Nagas effectively. Captain Butler, who was appointed to this charge in 1869, did much to consolidate the British presence in the hills. These advances were resisted by the tribesmen. In 1878, the headquarters of the district was transferred to Kohima with the objective of effectively controlling and influencing the Naga Hills.

During 1879, Political Officer Damant was determined to control the powerful village of Khonoma. He marched on to Khonoma with his troops, where he was shot dead with 35 of his escorts. The whole countryside then rose and proceeded to besiege the stockade at

Kohima, and the garrison was under severe attack before it was relieved. The subsequent defeat of Khonoma marked the end of serious trouble and hostility in the Naga Hills. Between 1880 and 1922, the British consolidated their position over a large area of the Naga Hills. Those Nagas who still remained outside British administration were referred to as 'Free Nagas' in the 'Unadministered Areas'. These 'Free Nagas' included the tribes now living in Mon and Tuensang districts of present day Nagaland.

When India won independence, the Naga Hills was a district in the State of Assam. The Naga People's Convention in 1957 proposed the formation of a separate administrative unit by merging the Tuensang Frontier Division of the North East Frontier Agency (NEFA—present Arunachal Pradesh) with the Naga Hills district of Assam. The Government of India accepted this proposal and on December 1, 1957, the Union Government took over the administration of Naga Hills district of Assam and Tuensang division of NEFA to form a separate administrative unit called 'Naga Hills-Tuensang Area (NHTA)'.

In July 1960, the Sixteen Point Agreement between the then Prime Minister of India and representatives of Naga People's Convention resulted in the creation of Nagaland as a constituent State of the Indian Union. With the enactment of the Constitution (Thirteenth Amendment) Act, 1962, the State of Nagaland came into existence on 1st December, 1963 as the sixteenth State in the country. It comprised the Naga Hills-Tuensang Area, which was formed in 1957. A distinctive feature of the new State was the special protection guaranteed under Article 371(A) of the Constitution of India to safeguard the tribal law, traditional institutions and practices of the Nagas.

POLITICAL PROCESS

Nagaland has had a troubled political history for many decades, with insurgency pre-dating statehood. What had begun as a non-violent struggle for self-determination later took the form of a violent and armed conflict in the 1950s.

Concerned over the continued violence, the Nagaland Baptist Church Council initiated peace efforts. This took concrete and positive shape during its Convention in early 1964 and the historic Peace

Mission was launched the same year. The relentless endeavour of the Peace Mission actively supported by the Church resulted in an agreement for cessation of fire, on May 23, 1964, which came into effect on September 6. Several rounds of talks followed, including at the Prime Ministerial level, but the talks finally deadlocked, and the ceasefire was effectively over by 1972. The Church, however, continued with its peace efforts and formed the Nagaland Peace Council in 1972. Three years of efforts resulted in the Shillong Accord of November 11, 1975. Subsequently, the National Socialist Council of Nagaland (NSCN) was formed in 1980. Active fighting resumed in the eighties.

On 25th July, 1997, the Government of India announced a cease-fire with the National Socialist Council of Nagaland (Isaac-Muivah) with effect from 1st August, 1997—the NSCN had split into two groups in the latter part of the 1980s. Subsequently, in April 2001, the Government of India also extended the cease-fire agreement to the National Socialist Council of Nagaland (Khaplang). These cease-fire agreements have led to the generation of optimism, hope and creation of a supportive macro environment. Government and the civil society are engaged in a purposeful conversation aimed at societal development. People of the State are desirous of permanent peace. They are willing and eager to contribute to the process of change.

OVERALL ECONOMY AND SECTORAL CONTRIBUTIONS

Nagaland started the planned process of development much later than the rest of the country. It missed out on the benefits of the first three Five Year Plans. The State has also been inhibited in its growth because of insurgency and much of its scarce resources had to be spent on establishment costs. Given these constraints, the State's rapid strides in planned socio-economic development, especially in the fields of infrastructure and development indicators, are commendable. Table 2.3 gives an indication of the progress made. Despite the progress made in a span of 40 years, Nagaland's economy still confronts many developmental challenges. Foremost among them are relative isolation, the difficult terrain, inaccessibility to the rest of the world and continued insurgency. These handicap the State's endeavours towards industrial and entrepreneurial development, private sector partnership in spearheading development initiatives and all round regional planning. Remoteness and inaccessibility are also the predominant cause for regional disparities in the State. An Index for Social and Economic Infrastructure by the Eleventh Finance Commission, during 1999, ranked Nagaland, with an index of 76.14, as the seventh most remote State in the country. (Arunachal Pradesh, with an index of 69.71, was adjudged the most inaccessible while Goa, with an index of 200.57, was given the highest index).

Table 2.4 : Progress made during 40 years of Statehood

Sl. No.	*Item*	*Unit*	*1962-63*	*2002-03*
1.	Total Length of Roads	Km	837	9860
2.	Villages connected with Roads	Number	NA	1092 (79.4%)
3.	Water Supply Provided	No. of Villages/Habitations	Nil	1304 (94.77%)
4.	Generation of Electric Power	MW	0.20	29.00 (98.2%)
5.	Villages Electrified	Number	6	1216
6.	Literacy	Percent	17.91	67.11
7.	Life Expectancy	Years	NA	73.4
8.	Primary Schools	Number	592	1311
9.	Middle Schools/High Schools	Number	22	121
10.	Government Hospitals	Number	8	13
11.	Dispensaries/Sub-Centres	Number	3	422
12.	Hospital Beds	Number	613	2065
13.	Area under irrigation	'000 Ha	1.51	65.63
14.	Foodgrain Production	'000 tonnes	61.82	386.30

Source: Directorate of Economics & Statistics, Nagaland.

Nagaland's remoteness is one of the factors that has adversely impacted the spread of banking infrastructure, availability of credit, and consequently, industrial development in the State. During 2001, credit deposit ratio (CDR) for Nagaland was only 13.6, the lowest in the country. The low CDR has hampered the ability of the State to break the vicious cycle of remoteness and inability and attract capital flows due to overall resource-deficiency, which is made worse by the presence of continuous insurgency. Thus, Nagaland has been unable to affect key investments (government and private) to develop infrastructure and accelerate the growth of the economy.

Macro-economic Trend

This is a chart of trend of gross State domestic product of Nagaland at market prices estimated by Ministry of Statistics and Programme Implementation with figures in millions of Indian Rupees.

Year	*Gross State Domestic Product*
1980	1,027
1985	2,730
1990	6,550
1995	18,140
2000	36,790

Nagaland's gross State domestic product for 2004 is estimated at $1.4 billion in current prices. Agriculture is the most important economic activity in Nagaland, with more than 90 per cent of the population employed crops include rice, corn, millets, pulses, tobacco, oilseeds, sugarcane, potatoes and fibres. However, Nagaland still depends on the import of food supplies from other States. The widespread practice of *jhum*—clearing for cultivation—has led to soil erosion and loss of fertility. Only the Angami and Chakesang tribes in the Kohima district use terracing and irrigation techniques. Forestry is also an important source of income. Cottage industries such as weaving, woodwork and pottery are also an important source of revenue. Tourism is important, but largely limited owing to the State's geographic isolation and political instability in recent years.

REGIONAL DISPARITIES

On the whole, the level of socio-economic development in the western regions of Nagaland is higher than in the eastern side. This is because contiguity to Assam provides better connectivity while on the Myanmarese side accessibility still presents formidable problems.

It must, however, be mentioned that dynamics of poverty in Nagaland are quite different from other parts of the country. Due to strong community spirit and social capital, the poor are looked after, and cared for, by kith and kin and the community. As a result, there is no case of starvation deaths and no one is shelterless. The State has identified Mon and Tuensang districts as well as Meluri subdivision in Phek, Bhandari in Wokha, Peren in Kohima and Pughoboto in

Zunheboto as its backward areas. These areas were 'traditionally' remote and inaccessible. Present Mon and Tuensang districts were also part of the 'unadministered areas' during the British period.

In order to expedite the process of development in the less developed and remote areas, the State Government has created a new department for underdeveloped areas. It has also decided to create three new districts, viz. Longleng, Kiphire (erstwhile sub-divisions of Tuensang district) and Peren (under Kohima district). The Government hopes the new status for these regions would result in focused attention so as to bring them to the level of the more developed areas.

STATE DOMESTIC PRODUCT

The net State domestic product (NSDP) of Nagaland has shown an increase from Rs. 10,547 lakh in 1980-81 to Rs. 57,898 lakh in 1990-91 (at constant 1980-81 prices) and to Rs. 223,042 lakh during 2000-01 (at constant 1993-94 prices). The per capita income in the State increased from Rs. 1,361 during 1980-81 to Rs. 5,520 during 1990-91. During 2000-01, per capita income was Rs. 11,473 (at constant 1993-94 prices) as against Rs. 10,306 for the country as a whole.

An estimation of district incomes (district domestic product) has not been carried out by the State Government or other agencies of the Government of India. In order to quantify the achievements of the different districts in income generation, sample survey was conducted to determine the district domestic products. The results of the survey quantify that the per capita income of the State is Rs. 11,119, with Dimapur having the highest per capita income among the districts (Rs. 16,837) and Mon having the least (Rs. 4,500).

A look at the share of the various sectors in the NSDP during the last two decades shows that the share of the primary sector declined from 32.5 percent in 1980-81 to 31.01 percent in 2000-01. Among the primary sectors, agriculture formed the major component and its share declined from 28.65 percent to 27.48 percent during the above period. During the same period, the share of secondary sector rose from 14.13 percent to 15.18 percent. These figures show that Nagaland's economy has not witnessed many structural changes in the past two decades.

The share of the tertiary sector has shown some fluctuations—it increased from 53.4 percent in 1980-81 to 58.14 percent in 1995-1996, and declined to 53.81 percent in 2000-01. Within the tertiary sector, transport, storage and communication formed a major share. Their share in the NSDP, which was 1.68 percent in 1980-81, increased to 18.14 percent in 1999-2000. Public administration and finance and real estate are the other important components in the tertiary sector.

AGRICULTURE DEVELOPMENT

Agriculture has traditionally been and continues to be the mainstay of Naga life—the numerous festivals are centred around agriculture and have their roots in cultivation practices. Seventy-three percent of the people in Nagaland are engaged in agriculture. Rice is the staple food. It occupies about 70 percent of the total cultivated area and constitutes about 75 percent of the total foodgrain production in the State. Other crops include maize, linseed, potato, pulses, soya bean, sugarcane, jute, gram, cotton, castor, etc. However, like most of the world's tribal population, the production system in Nagaland has been close to proto-agriculture, which has enabled close links between nature and people from generation to generation. These linkages and traditional practices have been formalised through experiences and empirical observations, and interwoven with social, religious and traditional values. The impact of modern scientific practices has not been appreciable as most high external input technologies are not suitable for high altitudes and rain-fed conditions.

Major land-use pattern in Nagaland continues to be shifting cultivation, known as Jhum. Though often considered primitive and unproductive, Jhum is a complex agricultural system that is well adapted under certain conditions, which require exhaustive comprehension of the environment to succeed. The major challenge continuing to face Nagaland is how to adapt its land-use pattern and production systems to the increased population and changing lifestyles, making them biologically and economically sustainable. Shifting cultivation covers over 73 percent of the total arable area of the State. It is mostly concentrated in the districts of Mokokchung, Tuensang, Wokha, Zunheboto and Mon. In other areas, terraced rice cultivation (TRC) or combined Jhum and TRC are practised.

Table 2.5: Land Use Pattern

	Total Area	*16579*	*Sq. km*
1.	Forest Cover	13345 (80.49%)	Sq. km.
2.	Forest Area	8629 (52.04%)	Sq. km
3.	Area under Agriculture	389120	Ha
4.	(a) Gross Sown Area	260000	Ha
	(b) Net Sown Area	248354	Ha
	(c) Area Sown more than Once	9000	Ha
	Area under Irrigation		
5.	(a) Irrigated Area	66000	Ha
	(b) Net Irrigated Area	62000	Ha
	Area under Shifting Cultivation	190	Sq. km
6.	No. of Cultivators	5.444	lakh
7.	No. of Agricultural Labourers	0.338	lakh
8.	No. of Families Practicing Shifting Cultivation	116046	

Source : Basic Statistics of NER, 2002; Forest Survey of India 2001.

During the last four decades, the foodgrain production in Nagaland has shown an upward trend from 62,000 metric tonnes in 1964-65 to 386,390 tonnes in 2001-02. The productivity increased from 700 kg per hectare to 1300 kg per hectare over the period. However, the State is not self-sufficient in production of foodgrains. Non-traditional crops such as wheat, barley, spices, rubber and sugarcane are also gaining popularity in recent years, promising to convert agriculture from subsistence farming to commercially viable activity. The land is extremely fertile and can produce the best quality of agro-based, horticulture and floriculture products through organic farming. The potential of Nagaland becoming an 'organic State', and for exports and foreign exchange, is real. Strategic initiatives in the fields of animal husbandry, fishery and sericulture could result in generation of resources and overall development of the rural economy.

FOREST COVER

As shown in Table 2.5, forest cover is 80.49 percent of the total area of Nagaland. As such, forests represent the richest natural resource of the State. Nagaland is also very rich in biodiversity with abundance of animal, insect and plant species. The State has a wealth of herbal, medicinal and aromatic plants with tremendous economic potentials.

The rich forest cover holds tremendous potential for bio-technological manipulations and also indicates strength for a sustainable timber industry, especially through tree cultivation.

INDUSTRIAL DEVELOPMENT

The industrial base of Nagaland is narrow. The majority of the industrial units/village industries are based on local forest products, agroproducts and traditional handloom and cottage industries. The State has established six growth centres for industrial development. However, they have not been able to satisfactorily meet the objectives for which they were envisioned. Nagaland had only 73 industrial units including small scale industries, government emporiums, district industrial centres and specialised farms in 1980. This increased to 1,160 in 1999-2000. This includes 1064 small-scale units. The paper mill established at Tuli in Mokokchung district and sugar mill in Dimapur faced serious difficulties. The sugar mill has since been closed down. New initiatives are necessary after careful survey of the developmental potentials of different regions.

MINERAL WEALTH

Coal, limestone, nickel, cobalt, chromium, magnetite, copper, zinc, and recently discovered platinum, petroleum and natural gas are the major minerals available in Nagaland. The State has huge caches of unutilized and unexploited limestone, marble, granite, petroleum and natural gas. Coal is found in Nazira, Borjan and Teru valley of Mon district. Limestone of grey to whitish grey colour is found at Wazeho and Satuza in Phek district and at Nimi belt in Tuensang district. Ores of nickeliferrous chromite-magnetite occur in the Ultra Basic Belt at Pokhpur in Tuensang district. Nagaland is yet to fully explore its huge estimated reserves of natural oil.

The hydrocarbons are found in the western portion of Nagaland, where connectivity is available in the foothills. The metallic and non-metallic minerals are located in the remote and backward eastern parts bordering Myanmar, ideal for export to the South East Asian region. If the discovered minerals are economically exploited, these would turn out to be a rich resource base and the mineral-related trade can make a huge contribution to the State economy.

Unfortunately, though the potential exists, not much has been achieved so far due to funding and planning process constraints. In this connection, the proposed 'X Road' of the Government could provide good connectivity for exploiting the mineral wealth of the State and for trade and commerce both in the State and the country and with South East and East Asian countries.

INFRASTRUCTURE DEVELOPMENT

The strategy and approach of the State Government have been to provide the basic infrastructure requirements of the people such as roads, water supply, power supply, schools, hospitals, etc. The State has been largely successful in this and a large part of the infrastructure is now in place. The achievements of the State in providing infrastructure showed that 13.96 percent of the villages had pucca roads as on 31 March 1986, which increased to 29.24 percent as on 31 March 2000. Similarly, the percentage of villages having primary schools increased from 92.0 percent to 96.6 percent during the above period. There was an increase in the percentage of villages with primary health centre from 18.0 percent to 26.3 percent. The percentage of villages having facilities for potable drinking water increased from 67.6 percent to 75.2 percent during the same period. However, the State has been grappling with challenges to maintain the assets created in this hilly, geologically fragile, high-rainfall State.

Though significant progress has been made, Nagaland still remains underdeveloped and inaccessible. The High Level Commission on Transforming the North-East constituted under Shri R.P. Shukla, Member of Union Planning Commission, during 1996 estimated that the infrastructure (Nagaland State Human Development Report) gap for North-East India was Rs. 97,000 crore. For Nagaland, the estimate was Rs. 11,000 crore. These figures reflect the extent of further investments required in the state for it to come at par with other States of India. Such requirement of funds cannot be met from plan funding or assistance from Central Government alone. The State will also have to evolve a model of development, which will require people's participation and willingness to be partners with the Government in the process of development, change and prosperity.

TRANSPORTATION

The rail network in Nagaland is nominal (13 km). The only airport in the State is at Dimapur. Surface transport is the main method of communication in this land-locked hilly State. This has resulted in the development of an impressive network of public and private sector road transport system. The road length of national highways is 365.38 km and of State roads is 1094 km. During 1996-97, the road density was 1,107 per thousand sq. km as against the all India road density of 749 per thousand sq. km. However, road transport has been handicapped by inadequate development and poor maintenance of roads. All-weather roads linking the scattered villages are a prerequisite for development of potential areas. This holds true for agriculture, social, industrial, entrepreneurial and mineral development. As many villages are still not covered by all-weather roads, the villagers have been deprived of proper socio-economic development in education, primary health care, and ready access of farmers' products to the market.

POWER

Nagaland is not self-sufficient in power, generating only 29 MW (2001). The State purchases power from neighbouring States to meet its requirement. The annual energy consumption of 225 MU (2001) provides a very low per capita consumption of about 130 units per year only compared to an Indian average of 370 units. The current peak demand is estimated at about 75 MW but it is restricted to only 50 MW. The quality too is low, with frequent curtailment and interruption, transformer failures and low voltage.

The bulk of the power in Nagaland is purchased from the North-Eastern Grid, which is expected to be power surplus, with large hydel projects coming on-stream in other States. The total existing installed State generation capacity is 29 MW, all based on hydropower. Current mean availability from this is about 90 MU (2002 onwards). Under the central sector there is an operational 75 MW hydel plant, from which the State receives a share of 12 percent of the generated power. The 24 MW Likimro Hydro Electric Project has been commissioned and a few minihydro projects are under construction, which will add about 3 MW to the existing generation. A thermal power plant is planned to be set up at Dimapur within the next two years.

Power generation, transmission and distribution are managed by the Nagaland Department of Power (DoP). The DoP's current financial situation is dire with a revenue collection of Rs. 19 crore against a power purchase bill of Rs. 36 crore (2001). The State suffers from high transmission and distribution (T&D) losses, estimated at 58 percent. Due to old and overloaded T&D infrastructure, technical losses form a significant fraction. In this regard, it may be mentioned that the State Power Department does not have the facility to undertake an audit of power transmission or distribution. Consequently, no detailed projection or analysis of segment-wise demand is available in the State. However, an investment projection of Rs. 4,500 crore (US$ 900 million) has been made to raise the generating capacity of the State to 450 MW, based on a notional per capita consumption target of 1,000 units.

WATER SUPPLY

Most of the Naga villages are located on hilltops, which make supply of drinking water a challenging task. Therefore, water has to be normally supplied, through gravity, from a source located at a higher altitude than the village. The number of villages having protected water supply sources in 1963 was only 59. Now, 1,304 (fully covered 261, partially covered 1,043) of the 1,376 villages/habitations (approximately 95%) have been provided with drinking water supply. Under the ongoing water supply schemes, the remaining 72 villages/ habitations will also be covered during 2004. Efforts are also being made to augment the water supply/distribution in the State, both in the rural and urban areas, to keep pace with the increasing requirement of water as the population grows. The objective is to achieve the recommended norm of 40 lpcd (litres per capita per day). Attempts are being made to involve the community in implementation and maintenance of the water supply schemes.

HEALTH

In spite of the high decadal growth rate in population, the health profile of Nagaland has shown tremendous success, particularly in the expansion of primary health care system, the progressive increase in the number of trained health providers and the low infant mortality rate. Nagaland's crude birth rate is higher than the all-India figures but the State's infant mortality rate is much lower. The vital statistics of every married woman producing four children during her productive phase has resulted in a total fertility rate of 3.77. The couple protection rate, i.e. use of contraceptives, is 30.3 percent. This shows there is need for improvement in the health profile indicators in the State.

The programmes carried out during the last 40 years have resulted in fairly good infrastructure facilities for health for the people of Nagaland. During 1980, the State had 204 health centres, including urban hospitals, rural hospitals, primary health centres and sub-centres with a total of 1,367 beds and 156 doctors. By 1999-2000, the number of health centres increased to 425, with 1,633 beds and 394 doctors. The coverage was roughly 20 doctors and 30 hospitals/health centres per lakh population. The health professional to total population ratio was 1: 4000, against the recommended ratio of 1: 3500. This showed inadequacy of health facilities to meet the requirements of the State. Specialized services were even more limited. The State has, so far, not taken full advantage of its vast potential of indigenous medicines, readily available, to take health to all its citizens. Ethno-medicinal practitioners too enjoy the confidence of the people, who often go to them first before approaching modern health providers.

During 1999-2000, 37.1 percent of rural households approached government hospitals for health care whereas 34 percent went to private clinics. The corresponding figures for urban areas were 34.8 percent and 57 percent. This showed that people, especially in urban areas, were willing to pay for good health facilities.

Communitisation of health services has been initiated since July 2002 to delegate powers for management of the health centres to the community. The initiative has resulted in a marked improvement in the quality of health care facilities available in the villages.

EDUCATION

There has been a phenomenal increase in the levels of literacy, which was 67.11 percent in 2001 as compared to 21 percent in 1963. However, against a national increase of 21.39 percent in the literacy rate during the period 1991 to 2001, the State witnessed an increase of only 8.86 percent in the same period. Consequently, there was lead of a mere 3.73 percent above the national average in the State's literacy during 1991-2001 as compared to a lead of 9.24 percent during 1971-81.

In spite of the laudable achievements made by Nagaland in terms of the educational infrastructure and the improvements in literacy percentage, the quality of education being made available is a matter of concern. Improvement of existing educational infrastructure, extensive human resource development and support for teachers' training will be vital. The pass percentage in the matriculation examination is only 48.6 percent, whereas in higher secondary it is 76.5 percent. The dropout rates at class 10 and 12 levels are considerable. Unfortunately, vocational training and entrepreneurial skills building still remain weak.

There is need for at least one college each for medicine and engineering. At the moment, the Government of Nagaland nominates and sends students on stipend, annually, to various institutions in the country as per allotment of seats made by the Union Government. Other sectors like IT, biotechnology and environmental studies need to be built up, considering the inherent strengths of the State in these areas. The existing two government polytechnics (a third polytechnic is in the offing) need to be revitalised by inculcating the spirit and attitude towards work, introducing relevant trades, and by providing adequate support for physical facilities and equipment.

With a view to revitalising education, the Government passed an Act in 2002, communitising elementary school education in the State. Under this initiative, the management and development of elementary schools have been transferred to the community. It is anticipated that community involvement and participation would not only ensure universalisation of education but also yield quality results.

THE WAY AHEAD

Development in Nagaland started under very challenging circumstances. Besides near absolute lack of any infrastructure, its remoteness and inaccessibility, the State was also engulfed in protracted and violent insurgency, which disrupted development efforts at every stage.

Nevertheless, in 40 years of statehood, Nagaland has made significant progress. The administrative reach has extended to the far corners of the State, which is one way of addressing the problem of 'remoteness'. Important infrastructure has been laid and connectivity within the State has improved. Nagaland has also made tremendous progress in all major sectors of human development. Its literacy rate has reached 67.11 percent from a mere 20.40 percent in 1961. Its sex ratio, CBR, CDR, IMR and MMR rates are better than the national average. Life expectancy is 73.4 years. The per capita income has also climbed above the national average as per 2001 figures. However, the major challenges which confronted the State in the beginning still remain. Because of this, in most cases, the figures and statistics, even though impressive, do not reveal the complete picture. For instance, while the literacy rate is encouraging, the quality of education has suffered and the unemployment rates, especially of educated youth, are a real cause for concern. Problems related to infrastructure remain. There is also the question of mobilisation of internal resources, especially through exploitation of the State's natural resources. Strategic planning and intelligent investments will be as important as finding sources of funding.

The State is at a crucial stage in its trajectory of growth. The rich social capital of Naga communities, the general resilience of the society, the varied and rich environmental capital and the mineral wealth are the inherent strengths to build upon for a faster and sustainable progress. Through various innovative policy interventions, the State Government is making efforts to tap into this rich social capital and to bring the people back into the centre of decision-making. One of them is the Nagaland Communitisation of Public Institutions and Services Act, 2002, where management of Government assets is being turned over to the village communities. The people have responded favourably although the initiative is still in its infancy.

As Nagaland looks forward, the following areas have to be addressed :

- Conditions to overcome the immediate impacts of violence.
- Development initiatives to improve infrastructure, living and working conditions.
- Special attention for the youth of Nagaland in the fields of technical education, recreation and gainful employment.
- New strategies for a 'Developed Nagaland'.

- A purposeful model of interaction between the people, administrators and political leadership has to achieve this vision of a 'Developed Nagaland'.

The last few years of ceasefire have given the people renewed hope. Naga society is now poised at a critical juncture. The time to build is now.

ADMINISTRATION

The Governor of Nagaland is the constitutional head of State, representative of the President of India. He possesses largely ceremonial responsibilities. A 60 member Vidhan Sabha is the State of ministers, led by a Chief Minister—all elected members of legislature—forms the government executive. Unlike most Indian States, Nagaland has been granted a great degree of state autonomy, as well as special powers and autonomy for Naga tribes to conduct their own affairs. Each tribe has a hierarchy of councils—at the village, range and tribal levels dealing with local disputes. There is a special regional council for the Tuensang district, elected by the tribes of the area.

The State is divided into eleven districts. Mokokchung District is Nagaland's most advanced District.

Districts	*District Headquarters*
Dimapur District	Chumukedima (Dimapur)
Kiphire District	Kiphire
Kohima District	Kohima
Longleng District	Longleng
Mokokchung District	Mokokchung
Mon District	Mon
Peren District	Peren
Phek District	Phek
Tuensang District	Tuensang
Wokha District	Wokha
Zunheboto District	Zunheboto

E-GOVERNANCE PLAN OF NAGALAND

The Government of Nagaland (GoN) envisions to implement e-governance in the State of Nagaland with a view to enhance transparency, efficiency and provide quality and prompt services to its citizens. National Informatics Centre (NIC) was entrusted to chalk out an Action Plan detailing the existing status, proposed activities, roles and responsibilities, and implementation methodology. Accordingly, First Draft of the Action Plan has been prepared and submitted to GoN for consideration.

METHODOLOGY ADOPTED FOR THE PREPARATION OF ACTION PLAN

The activities involved in the formulation of the e-governance plan are as follows :

- Interaction with various Departments of GoN
- Needs Assessment Survey at 40 Departments
- Research on various international and national ICT initiatives on e-governance
- Compilation and Analysis of Survey Feedback
- Preparation of Draft Action Plan Document
- Draft Document for approval of GoN

STRATEGY BEHIND ACTION PLAN

The key points taken into account while formulating the Action Plan are as follows :

- The Plan has been developed within the overall framework, objectives and guidelines as discussed with Chief Minister, IT Minister and Senior Officers of State of Nagaland.
- Before proposing a future course of action, an assessment of requirements and existing status of computerization has been done to know the current ICT scenario and establish a base line.
- Priority departments have been identified to initiate and implement e-governance in a phased manner. Further, an exercise has been done to identify priority functions within the selected departments. Functions that have direct interface with public have also been identified to effectively address G2C and citizen-oriented services.

- Current availability of computing and communication environment and future requirement has also been assessed in these departments.
- The Plan also takes into account the recommendations of National and International studies on e-governance carried out for developing countries.
- Taking input from the needs assessment study, the e-governance Plan proposes reuse of the existing IT services and infrastructure wherever possible. Accordingly, a list of the software packages for the identified functions that are already available in the inventory of NIC has been indicated in the plan.

ACTION PLAN HIGHLIGHTS

The e-governance Action Plan document has been prepared keeping in view the following :

- Communitised structure of grass root administration;
- Plan, policies and schemes/projects highlighted in tenth Five Year Plan Document of Government of Nagaland;
- Information requirement gathered from Need Assessment Study and Departmental websites;
- Emphasis on web portals for all the Departments/ Directorates/Districts/State and District Level Autonomous agencies with citizen charter;
- Efficient and effective delivery of government services to the citizens;
- Better dissemination of information on government functions, through setting up of Integrated Citizen Service Centre (ICSC) and using various channel of delivery of services and information namely CICs, IVRS, Web and Kiosk;
- Improved efficiency, transparency and productivity;
- Improving IT literacy and culture; and
- Better financial management.

The State shall establish a backbone network—Nagaland State Wide Area Network (NAGALAND-ONLINE) that will connect State

Secretariat, Directorate, districts, ADC/SDO office and Blocks which will be further extended to cover villages and schools. The network shall be utilized for the inter-departmental connectivity, multi-user and multi-service facilities, Video Conferencing, e-mail, on line application processing and query. NAGALAND-ONLINE shall enable better communication and information sharing to allow the officers to work more effectively resulting in cohesive administration. Phased implementation of Nagaland-online will cover strengthening of existing and future internet connectivity in the State. The Nagaland online shall be a secured network for the State of Nagaland and would be based on VSAT/Leased Circuit/Radio frequency links. Since Nagaland is hilly terrain coverage of RF connectivity will reach up to village without much investment which will be a boon for IT literacy spread in the State.

40 departments (and their Directorates) have been identified to initiate the e-governance exercise. An assessment survey within these departments has resulted in identification of priority functions and assessment of existing status of computerization. The plan document also proposes the information systems for district and Block level offices and Village Development Board (VDB). E-Governance Project Activities: Based on the above approach, the participating Departments identified their Governance requirements. The E-Governance requirements of the State government can be classified into:

- Citizen facing requirements;
- Employee facing requirements; and
- Improve internal control.

The proposed design of IT infrastructure and E-Governance services envisages setting up of NAGALAND-ONLINE (http://nagalandonline.nic.in) connecting the State Secretariat with District, ADC/SDO and CIC at Block level offices of the various departments along with VDBs for secured transmission of voice, data and video. The various services falling into category of G2C, G2B (if any approved by government) and G2G will be offered in integrated manner through the portal acting as a single gateway.

Intra Naga Portal (G2E and E2G) : This web portal (http://intranaga.nic.in) would capture all the requirements catering to employee of government departments. Each of the departments should continuously provide the content and ensure that the portal information is current.

e-Delivery: Delivery of services has to be one stop agenda for achieving digital democracy. Every information and service should be delivered over one's preferred medium like CICs, Web, Kiosk, IVRS and ICSC at Kohima and Dimapur. Delivery of Professional Services will also be provided through the proposed Call Centres or any of the above channels. The requests will be routed to the specialists/experts in the respective domain. The inputs/requirements will be plain text or graphical images.

The inventory of software packages already available with NIC has been assessed and it has been found out that software packages for many of the identified functions could be made available readily or after customization. The areas where software applications are not available with NIC, action plan recommends fresh development for such functions with resources being made available by GoN. The projected time frame for fresh software development has been indicated in the Plan.

The Governance Plan proposes to set up E-governance Steering Committee, Technical Evaluation Committee and Department Action Committee for implementation and monitoring of the Plan.

Major IT projects to be taken up in phases:

Citizen Relation Management Centre (CzRMC) : Back End State Level Operations—Citizen Relation Management (CzRM) Centre will manage and control the Nagaland-Online Portal. This will be 24 × 7 infrastructure for Nagaland-Online consisting of Web Server. Mail Server, database server, storage devices, IVRS system with adequate network security.

Naga-Smart Village Net : In order to interconnect each of 1200 Village Development Boards/Council, wireless based network needs to be established in Nagaland. Each VDB/VDC centre will be equipped with one PC with wireless card and necessary peripheral. Necessary feasibility and pilot testing for network will be carried out before establishing this network and details (architecture, equipments details, time duration, cost, etc.) would be part of network plan. This could be harmonized with PURA Scheme to optimize the benefit for the people of rural areas. **Deliverables**—The structure, functions and assets will be online available through Nagaland-Online Portal.

School-Net: The Nagaland State Wide Network will link all Government Educational Institutes (702) up to middle level schools to enable e-learning and good education content. These entire educational institutes will be provided two network PCs with related accessories. **Deliverables**—Student enrollment, dropouts, teacher ratio and interrelation with VDC and sharing of course content and teaching material through e-learning process.

Integrated Citizen Service Centres (ICSC) : This envisages establishment of two Integrated Citizen Service Centres (ICSC), one at Kohima and another at Dimapur. The main objectives behind this effort would be to provide a single counter to the citizens to remit utility bill payments, obtain statutory certificates, submit applications, seek information on government programmes and schemes, access other special services etc. Thus it would act as a public interface for the government. **Deliverables**—Easy facilities for common man to make financial transactions with government (such as payment of bills and taxes).

Treasuries : Majority of Treasuries functioning are being carried out at Kohima, Dimapur and Mokokchung treasuries. It is planned to computerize and connect these 4 treasuries to its Directorate to streamline its functioning. **Deliverables**—Improving fiscal management of the State.

Commercial Taxes : 4 Major check posts located at Dimapur, Mokokchung, Kohima and Mon, which require day-to-day operations to be computerized and its linkage to Directorate at Dimapur. **Deliverables**—Enhancement in revenue realization and transparency in the tax management.

RD-Net : Under Naga-Smart Village-Net, the appropriate software packages in the area of Land Resource Management including Land Records and Resurvey, Poverty Alleviation Management and Drinking Water and Sanitation will be provided by NIC and accordingly customized as per local needs. This includes the fund management by Rural Local Bodies (PriaSoft) and strengthening marketing needs of the products produced by rural people through Rural Bazar application package available with NIC. **Deliverables**—The structure, functions and assets of Rural

Development Agencies along with Scheme monitoring will be available through Nagaland-Online Portal.

Modernization of Information and Public Relation Functions: 11 offices and State directorate need to be strengthened with modern computing equipment, content management software and appropriate manpower skills to manage the dissemination of Government information through various medias including the Nagaland Online, IntraNaga Portal, District Portal, DRDA Portal and Block Community Portal. This will bring high order of transparency of Government functions and availability of information to the people at large within/outside State. **Deliverables**—This will establish IPR laboratories through the State for providing better publicity about Government Activities and Projects.

Capacity Building : It is proposed that all the employees at the level of Section Officers, Steno, UDC, and LDC should be trained on fundamentals of computers, internet, and MS Office tools on continuous basis every year by NIC/CIC, SIRD and ATI. This will be include setting up of State of art training laboratory and e-learning packages and material. **Deliverables**—This will lead to better awareness, change in work culture and human resources development.

E-Literacy among masses and Elected Representatives : One person per family as nominated by VDC/Village (limiting to maximum of 20 persons per village) may be trained on basic ICT Concepts, e-mail, browsing, MS Office at respective CIC, for five days per year, with token contribution of Rs. 100 per person making it participatory learning. Government may have to bear the remaining cost, if any. This will enhance e-literacy among masses, exposure and utilization of already established ICT infrastructure. **Deliverable**—This will create pool of IT trained manpower for better employment opportunities. It is also proposed to train elected representatives of various bodies including legislative assembly on internet, office automations and appropriate e-governance applications.

Monitoring Mechanism—Close and qualitative monitoring of the project will be done by E-Governance Steering Committee under Chief Secretary, Nagaland. This committee will frame policy guidelines and review the project milestones while guiding Departmental Implementation Committees. Departmental Committee will work out project action plan and fix interim milestones for the implementation.

SOCIO-ECONOMIC PROFILE OF VILLAGES

This State paper is based on the socio-economic village study assignments of IAS Officer Trainees. Reference from some books, Internet material and secondary data sources are used in between to make the State paper significant and relevant. The study attempts to bring out the trends and current status in the socio-economic scenario in the rural Assam, covering the last 8 years of study (1994-2002) solely depending on the micro-level socio-economic surveys conducted by the officer trainees. The broad areas covered are :

- Rural Infrastructure,
- Health and Family Welfare,
- Education,
- Agrarian Relations,
- Social Structure,
- Economic Activites,
- Anti-poverty and other Rural Development Programmes, and
- Panchayati Raj System.

List of IAS officer trainees (1994-2002) whose assignments were available and used for socio-economic State paper of Nagaland is given in Table 2.6.

Table 2.6 : IAS Officer Trainees and the Assignments

Sl. No.	*Name of OTs*	*Year*	*Name of Village*	*Name of District*
1.	Anu Agarwal	2001	Medziphema	Dimapur
2.	Abhishek Singh	1995	Longkhum	Mokokchung
3.	V. Shashank Shekhar	1996	Tsiese Basa	Kohima
4.	Abhijit Sinha	2000	Longjemdang	Mokokchung
5.	Amardeep Singh Bhatia	1995	Nerhema	Kohima

VILLAGE STUDY—INTRODUCTION

This socio-economic survey, to be taken up as a part of the district training, aims to make the officer trainee to understand more of the people, of the development schemes as they are undertaken at the grassroots level and the government-people interaction at the lowest level as also to understand the social dynamics operating in the area.

The selection of the village was done partly because of convenience and partly by the sampling process given in the guidelines for the socio-economic survey. Some villages had to be eliminated from the entire list of census villages because of factors like geographical accessibility and law and order situation. An attempt was made to conduct an exhaustive village and household survey as required by the guidelines for the socio-economic survey. However, there were certain limitations with regard to the special situation prevailing in the State as per the landholding patterns and agricultural practices of the people of this place.

It should be noted that there is no individual ownership of land in the Ao Naga tribal society. Land is owned by various clans and so it was impossible to collect data in the format provided. Nagaland State has a special status in the Indian Union as per the ownership of land is concerned. Article 371A of the Constitution provides that the customs and traditions of Naga people should be protected and that land ownership should continue to remain in the hands of the villagers. As such the Government of Nagaland is not the owner of land and villagers are the actual owners of the land. Of course, the government does own the land which was handed over by the British when they left and the land that has been acquired either by paying compensation or through donations from villagers for specific purposes of community benefit. Thus, since the government does not own any land, it can also not levy any tax as land revenue. Moreover, there has not been any survey of the village lands as the villagers have this fear that once land is surveyed, the government might pass a legislation imposing land revenue. Due to these very reasons, the villages of Nagaland are yet to be surveyed and hence no land records exist for the village lands. The villagers also do not follow the standard systems of measuring land. Land belongs to the individuals and to the clans to which the individuals belong. Most of the village lands in Mokokchung district are hilly. For the requirements of this survey, the absence of land records was a major problem as the survey basically relies on the land ownership details for the socio-economic classification of the people. To get over this problem, I have recorded the agricultural produce of each household during the *field survey*.

Another rough estimate will be that under *jhum* cultivation, around 40-50 tins of rice is obtained from one hectare of land.

Similarly, the agricultural practices are different in the sense that it primarily consists of *jhum* (shifting cultivation) in which the villagers clear and cultivate a piece of land for 2 years and then move on to new lands, only to return back to the same piece of land after about 9-10 years. Thus the agricultural practice consists of clearing of the jungle, burning it and then sowing. It does not involve the use of any chemical fertilizers. The entire cultivation is rain fed. In some parts of the State, terrace cultivation is practiced, but in the village under survey, it is entirely *jhum* cultivation. In *jhum*, there is only one crop of rice that is grown, along with minor crops of maize, vegetables like chillies, sweet potato, pumpkin, cucumber, ginger, beans, cabbage, etc. and some local varieties of pulses. Thus it can be said that the entire village has only mono cropping. More details about *jhum* cultivation will be given in the section that deals specifically with agriculture.

Thus, this survey is a bit different from the standard format that has been prescribed by the booklet on socio-economic survey. Since, there is no proper system of land records in the State of Nagaland, there is no question of land reforms in the conventional sense. Moreover, land reforms are not relevant in the society here as there is no landless family. Since land is owned by the clans, every household is a landowner. Hence, nothing with regard to land reforms can be written.

This report will deal with various aspects of the life of the people in the selected village. The data was collected in the month of February by actually going to the village and staying with the villagers for 4 days. During this period, one learnt a lot about the rural life in this part of the country and also the customs, traditions of the people along with the way the villagers practice *jhum* cultivation and the problems and hardships faced by them.

As required, an attempt has been made to study the way the rural development programmes operate in the village and what are the shortcomings in their working. Once again, the State of Nagaland seems to be quite different from other mainstream States as the rural development schemes are implemented (or more appropriately, not implemented) in an entirely different way. The various schemes that have been studied are JRY, IRDP, EAS, IAY and the VDB schemes of the State.

The power structure and the internal administration of the villages in the region is also quite different. The 73rd Amendment of the Constitution is not applicable to Nagaland and so there are no elected panchayats. Instead, there is a system of village councils, which are constituted as per the traditions of the people. Its working is quite interesting and has been studied in detail.

Nagaland is occupied by 17 major tribes. Angami tribe is one of the bigger tribes with wide influence over the other tribes and the administration of the State. The culture and tradition, however, vary a lot and there is a lot of diversity in culture, language and other ethnological considerations. The study of one village cannot thus be used to characterize the other villages in the other regions of Nagaland. There is a wide variance in practices—both social and administrative—all over the State.

Nagaland State with an area of 16,579 sq km is a small (the third smallest in the country), remote, mountainous region in the extreme North-East of India. The State was carved out in 1957 from the Naga hill district of Assam and the unadministered areas of Tuensang part of the then North Eastern Frontier Agency (NEFA). Subsequently, on 1st December, 1963, it was given the status of the sixteenth State of the Indian Union with the capital at Kohima. The State lies between 25°6′N and 27°4′N latitudes and between 93°20′E and 95°15′ E longitudes.

The history of how the Naga tribes came precisely to occupy their present position is clothed in the dim obscurity of various traditions. But enough of them remain to give some indication of the course which the migrations took. The Angamis, according to legends, spring from ancestors who emerged from the bowels of the earth, but that not in Angami country, but in some other land to the south. And all the weight of the tradition points to migration from the south, i.e. via Mao via Manipur from Burma (though difficult to pinpoint).

As mentioned in the village assignment of **Nerhema village** many stories about the origin and settlement of the tribes of Nagaland abound. But the most prominent and the most oft-repeated story traces the origin of the Naga tribes in the Kezami village of Kezakenoma. The story is worth mentioning. There was, the story goes, once upon a time an old couple with three sons living in that village. Everyday they used to spread paddy to dry upon a great flat stone, and at dusk a single load spread to dry had become two loads, for the stone was inhabited by a spirit. The three sons used to take it in turns to spread their paddy on this stone, but one day they quarrelled bitterly as to whose turn it was, and their parents, fearing bloodshed, broke eggs on the stone, covered it with brushwood, laid faggots about it, and set the whole on fire. The stone burst with a crack like thunder, the spirit went up to heaven in a cloud of smoke, and the virtue of the stone departed. The three sons then separated and became the ancestors for the Angami, Lotha, and Sema tribes, while from the parents who remained are the descendants of the seven Kezami villages.

Although the village may be regarded as the unit of the political and the religious side of the Angami life, the real unit of the social side is the clan. In the old days, the clans used to be close knit villages within villages. In fact, sometimes the rivalry used to be so great that the clans used to be at frequent war with each other. However, this clan (almost equivalent to a *khel*) system was useful in settling new people in the village in the old times. In Gariphema, with a mixture of Angami and Sema population, when the original Angami and Sema inhabitants, they settled along the two sides of the hill dividing themselves along tribal lines into different *khels* (in spite of the fact that amongst the Semas no *khel* system exists), thus making co-existence possible while retaining the original customs of their own tribes and, of course, creating new amalgams.

The Angami race is believed to be descended from two men, sometimes described as brothers (or cousins) who came up out of the earth (the exact place of this occurrence is not known and is shrouded in myths). From the elder of the two (called Thevo) sprung the division of the Angamis known as the Kepezoma and from the younger (called Thekrono) the other, the Kepepfuma. The Kepezoma call their father *apuo* and mother *azuo* while the Kepepfuma call their fathers *apfu* and mothers *apfu*. The descendants from these have started their own *khels* but the appellations for the mother and father remains similar. These *khels* were exogamous, marrying mutually into one another. Till quite recent times, the Kepezoma clan split into Thevoma and SatsUma, for exogamous purposes, however, for practical purposes, only the Thevoma *khel* exists now. *SatsUma* being limited to only 3-

4 villages, and the Kepepfuma *khel* Thekronoma (also called as Solhima *khel* in some parts—Northern Angami areas in particular).

DISTRICT PROFILE

Dimapur is the youngest of the 8 districts of Nagaland. It was inaugurated in December 1997. There are 4 subdivisions with 4 coterminous Rural Development Blocks in the district. The Blocks are Dhansiripar, Medziphema, Niuland and Kuhuboto. There are 188 recognized villages in Dimapur. Most of the villages are new settlements. Very few of the villages are traditional villages. The total population of the district is 2.9 lakh. It has a mixture of almost all the tribes in the State with a predominance of Semas, Angamis and Aos. It is the only district in the State with a sizable population of Marwaris, Bengalis, Keralites and Muslims. The latter mostly reside in the district HQ, i.e. Dimapur town. It is the main commercial town of the State with its only railhead and airship. It is well connected to the biggest commercial town of North-East, i.e. Guwahati by rail, road and air. And Dimapur is rated as the second most important commercial town in the North-East.

Historically, it was the capital of Dimasa Kachari kingdom. This is evident from the existence of the Kachari Rajbari Fort ruins, housing the ancient stone monoliths and the many evacuated tanks dug by the royalty. History and legends trace the civilization to the epic age of *Mahabharata* where Bheema, the second Pandava, while in exile married the Kachari Princess, Hidimba. In Kachari dialect, Dimapur means—Di = river, ma = big/great, pur = city, i.e. the city near the great river.

Geographically, Dimapur is the only plain area in the whole State and thus, is hot and humid during summer with temperature reaching a maximum of 36 degree Celsius with humidity upto 93 per cent while the winter months are cool and pleasant. Average annual rainfall is 1504.7 mm. Major rivers are Dhansiri and Diphu.

The present site of **Mokokchung** town used to be a heavily forested area before the arrival of the British. Only after their coming, the area slowly and slowly started to develop into a town. In 1889 Mokokchung was created as Sub-Division. In 1957 it was created as a District having Mokokchung. Wokha and Zunheboto as its Sub-

Divisions. Later, in December 1973, Wokha and Zunheboto were made separate districts.

The district is bounded by the State of Assam to the north, Tuensang district to the east, Zunheboto to the south and Wokha district and State of Assam to the west. The populace of the district mainly comprises the Ao tribe, one of the major tribes of Nagaland. However, a sizable number of people belonging to other tribes also live in the district though mostly in the towns.

The area of the district is 1,615 square kilometres. The number of Blocks are 6 and the number of villages come to 93. The average rainfall is around 2200 mm. Since rainfall is heavy the growth of vegetation is quick and dense. The region looks very green, more so during the rains. The important rivers flowing in the district are Melak, Dikhu and Tsurang. The population of the district according to the latest census is 2,27,230 and the density is 140 per square kilometre. Literacy is quite high around 84 per cent.

Almost the whole of the district is hilly. Whichever direction one looks, one finds a range of hills cutting across. The whole district is divided into six ranges of varying altitudes. The highest range has a height of around 1,600 metres while the range near Assam is just 300 metres. Mokokchung town is at an altitude of 1,325 metres. There are areas bordering Assam, which are in the plains.

Kohima district lies in the southern part of the State. Bounded by the State of Assam and the district of Wokha on the north, the districts of Phek and Zunheboto on the east, by Manipur on the south and the State of Assam on the west, it forms an irregular plateau with elevated ridges and peaks, except for the north-western portion which is a plains territory merging into the Sibsagar and Mikir plains of Assam. Kohima, the State headquarters of Nagaland is situated in the heart of the district, known as the Switzerland of the East, it commands a charming scenery and a magnificent landscape.

VILLAGE PROFILE

The selected village was **Mediziphema** village in the Block of the same name. Though the village fulfils the criteria of number of households as required by the guidelines of rural study, but random sampling method was not followed in selecting this village. This village was not a representative of the entire district. As already mentioned, most of the villages in the district have been recently established. But, this village was a traditional Angami Naga village, established in 1100 A.D. This was selected to study the traditional village culture of the State, especially that of Angami area. The total area of the village is appoximately 6,000 acres. It is located at 18 miles or about 30 km from Dimapur district headquarters and 4 km from the Block headquarters. Nearest bus stop is in the Block headquarters whereas the nearest railway station is in Dimapur town. Nearest town is the Block headquarters.

The village is located on a hilltop as all the traditional Naga villages used to be. This was a mechanism to defend themselves from the approaching enemies in the days of warfare and head hunting. The traditions of warfare and head hunting have long ceased to exist but those costumes are still worn during folk dance performances. Themes of folk dances revolve around hunting and cultivation. *Jhuming* is being practiced as a mode of cultivation. To reach this hilltop village, the villagers have made steps under the Rural Development Programme. This is especially helpful for the villagers for commutation in rainy season.

The life of the villagers revolves around the Church. They have a weekly service in the Church on Sundays when the pastor teaches them sermons from the Bible. After church service, women gather together and discuss about their problems. There is a Sunday school for the children before the villagers have the regular Sunday service.

Educated youth in the village have taken an initiative to help and guide the younger school students in their education. They take classes free of charge in the evenings. These are a kind of tuitions for the younger students. Some sports freaks play football in the local ground.

Most of the villagers get up early in the morning, fill up water, finish their daily chores and send children to school. Thereafter, with their bamboo baskets called *khans* at their backs, they go to their fields located in the foothills and do cultivation there. In the evening, they carry head loads of agricultural produce in their baskets and bring it back home. They have their second meal after that and sit together or visit each other's place to discuss the events of the day and their problems.

There is a unique system of Age-sets in this village. All the villagers belong to a particular age-set. These are like 1 age-set for persons in age group of 30-39 years. These age-sets cut across clans and *khels*. Members of these groups do social work and collect money. Out of that money, some of the groups arrange for Christmas feast, some make footsteps in the village, organize sports, etc. This is a system of social organization.

Another organization is based on heredity. All the descendants of a grandfather form a lineage. Many lineages form a clan and the latter merge to form a *khel*. There are 5 *khels* in this village and all of them occupy a separate locality. Thus, there are 5 localities in the village based on hereditary grounds.

Name of the hamlet	*No. of households*	*Percentage of households*	*No. of households proportion sampled*
A	40	15	0.15 x 80 = 12
B	82	30	0.30 x 80 = 24
C	64	24	0.24 x 80 = 19
D	61	23	0.23 x 80 = 18
E	23	08	0.08 x 80 = 7
Total	**270**	**100**	**80**

The village has a strong administrative structure. It has an elected village council, which is the administrative body of the village. The Central and State governments sponsored rural development schemes are implemented through the village development boards.

Longkhum village has a distinct place in the history and the origin of the Aos. As per Ao tradition, the ancestors of the tribe came out of the earth at Lungterok (six stones), sometimes called the Ungterok, lying on the top of a spur on the right bank of Dikhu river, just opposite Mokongtsu (Mokokchung). The Aos basically have two main linguistic groups—the Mongsen and the Chungli. The Mongsen came out of the earth first and settled at Kubok, a vacant site on a spur running down from Mokongtsu towards the Dikhu. The Chungli emerged and settled at Chungliyimti. For quite some time, the Mongsen people used to kill the Chungli people, who unknowingly used to get into the Mongsen territory. The Chungli had no idea of the existence of the Mongsen. Sometime later, Shiluti, an enterprising Chungli youth saw the huge village of Kubok, across the Dikhu valley. He along with twenty-nine other youth organized a raid on Kubok and defeated them. They then forced the Mongsen to come to Chungliyimti and form a *khel* (sector) side by side with the Chungli. Thereafter, the Aos from Chungliyimti began their invasion of their present country. All except a few crossed the Dikhu, and one big group founded the Longkhum village. The majority settled around Koridang, which is part of the Ungma village. Later on the villages of Kubza and Setsu were founded. Those who did not cross the Dikhu river stayed back in the Longsa village, which is on the other side of the Dikhu. In fact the name Ao is also derived from this crossing over of Dikhu. The name Ao is from Aor, meaning those who came (i.e. across Dikhu), as distinct from Mirir, meaning those who did not come, the term used for Sangtams, Chang, Phoms and Konyaks. Thus the Longkhum village has got a distinct and prominent place in the history of the Aos and still the village has retained the customs and traditions of the old time Aos.

Tsiese Basa village is situated in Chiephobozou Block of Kohima district in Nagaland. It is located about 14 km from the district headquarters. There is neither a PHC nor a bank in the village. The nearest PHC is about 3 km and the nearest bank is in the district headquarters, about 14 km. The village is electrified with many houses having electricity connection. It is a comparatively new and small village with a population of 280, 160 males and 120 females. The language spoken is the Angami. The locals all come under scheduled tribes. The religion followed is Christianity. The village is clustered together and there are no separate hamlet. As the village is not too large, the people might have found it more convenient to settle together.

Nerhema village situated towards the south of Chiephobozou is one of the oldest village in the region. After extensive touring of the Northern Angami area (which is said to be the most backward amongst the Angami areas), I chose to conduct my socio-economic study in this village because of various practical reasons—I had first chosen the village of Gariphema Bawe because of its peculiar composition of Sema and Angami population, but decided to discard the idea after going there on foot (around 18 km), collecting some of the basic data there and staying the night there (the main reason was the inconvenience which my coming and staying there had caused to the simple village people). Since Nerhema was closer to Chiephobozou, and the fact that most of the population of Chiephobozou town (village) comprised Nerhema villagers, it was much more easier to observe and interact with the people of Nerhema village without inconveniencing them. Also the village of Nerhema has an interesting history regarding its participation in the underground movement in the 1960s.

Longjemdang, is around sixty-nine kilometres from the district headquarters. It is near Mangkolemba town, some three kilometres from it. The town Mangkolemba, one of the three important towns in the district (the district headquarters and Tuli being the other two) is sixty-six kilometres from Mokokchung towards north-west.

Longjemdang is in the Mongkolemba Block at a distance of three kilometres from the Block headquarters, which is in Mangkolemba itself. Being so near a town as big as Mangkolemba, the village is quite dependent on it. The path to the village is not black topped. The last two kilometres is just a path. However it is jeepable and it is open throughout the year even during the rains. The village is on top of a hill whose height is some 651 metres from sea level. At the top, the hill flattens out a bit and the whole of the village is spread on it. This hill is apart of the Japukong range, one of the six ranges of Mokokchung district. Being at such a height the climate of the village is moderate. The winters are pleasant and summers though not so cool as other places in the district are nevertheless comfortable.

DEMOGRAPHY AND INFRASTRUCTURE IN THE VILLAGE

According to the village assignment of **Medziphema** village, the total population of the village, as per 2001 census is 1,332 and sex ratio is one. The rate of growth of population in the previous decade in the village has been 30 per cent. Still the pressure on land for building houses is not substantial as the population density is very low. However, the *jhum* cycle has shortened alarmingly from as long as 30 years to just 6-7 years.

More than 70 per cent of the people live in mud plastered bamboo houses with CGI sheet roof. The floor is made of mud. The rest have pucca houses made of cement and bricks but they also have CGI sheet roof.

All the villagers fetch water from a common tank from a distant stream. From there water is brought to the tank through a rubber pipe. From this common reservoir the entire village takes water for household use. Bathing and washing of clothes is done there whereas for cooking, washing utensils and for cleaning the house, water is taken by women early in the morning and stored in the houses. These days people store water in big plastic drums. However, traditionally, people used bamboo pipes to collect and store water. They used to collect water from the streams directly.

There are no hand pumps or ring wells in the village for drawing underground water. Though Dimapur district has got central aid under District Water and Sanitation Mission, to provide facilities for sanitation in the villages but it has not yet reached **Medziphema** village. All the houses have made enclosures with plastic sheets for purpose of defecation in the house compound.

All the households use firewood for cooking food. The fireplace has a chimney whereby smoke can escape outside. The kitchen is kept very clean and maize can be seen hanging from the roof for drying. Some houses likewise hang meat while it is awaiting consumption. The foodgrains for consumption through the year are kept in granary made of bamboo. This is raised on stilts. Only lower half portion is mud plastered and the upper half allows free air flow thus helping keep the grains dry. They keep a pet cat to eat the rats attacking the stored foodgrains.

All the houses are electrified though the power supply is quite erratic. The community hall in the village has a solar panel for capturing solar energy and for lighting a tube in the hall. Still, the solar energy potential has not been widely explored. In fact, because of the location of the village on a hilltop, there is a great potential for tapping solar energy. Moreover, erratic power supply in the area requires using non-conventional energy sources in the village.

Table 2.7 : Basic Amenities of Houses

Basic Amenities	*No. of Households*
Straw thatched hut	58
Katcha pucca	22
Pucca house	0
Public reservoir	80
Own water source	0
Defecation in house compound	80
Sanitary latrine	0
Wood as fuel	80
Gobar gas or LPG	0
Electricity in homes	80
Use of NCES	0

It is a custom amongst the villagers to give separate piece of land for establishing a homestead to their son after his marriage. Thus, most of the families in the village are nuclear families.

Caste	*Joint Family*	*%*	*Nuclear Family*	*%*	*Total*
S .T.	13	16.3	67	83.8	80

Marriage is a norm in the society. Remarriage of widowed and divorced people is also common.

Marital status of head of household	
Unmarried	3
Married	69
Widowed	8
Divorced	0

The widows and orphans are well taken care of. On any occasion, where money is to be collected from the entire village, nobody can dare to ask a widow to pay. If anyone does, they are liable to be fined by the village. On remarriage of a widow/divorce, his/her children form a part of the household of the spouse. If there's any scheme given from the government side, first of all the benefit shall go to the widows or sick and poor people.

As is true of the rest of the State, this village also lacks proper infrastructure facilities. The approach road to the village is very narrow and is full of potholes. Therefore, villagers have made stone steps to reach up to the village but no vehicles can ply on these steps. Especially during rainy days, the approach road becomes non-usable. There is no source of drinking water within the village. The water is brought by pipe from a distant stream to be stored in a tank in the village. They do not filter, sediment chlorinate this water. Only the water meant for drinking is boiled and consumed. There are no sanitary latrine in the individual households. However, under the district water and sanitation mission, they have made 2 community latrines but these are not functional as of now.

Longkhum is a village situated 20 km from Mokokchung district. The village is located at about 8 km from the Mokokchung-Kohima State highway. It is a relatively big village, with 325 households and a population of 1946. The altitude of the village is the highest in the district and the height would be around 1700 metres above the sea level. It is one of the most important villages of the Ao Nagas as some of the traditional customs of the Aos is still practiced in the village. In spite of about 125 years of Christianity in the State, there are still about 20 households in the village who are animists—the Naga Hindus. Thus, the village has a rich cultural heritage and tradition, which is not seen in other villages of the district.

As one takes the road leading to Longkhum from the Mokokchung-Kohima highway, from Alichen, one cannot fail to notice the picturesque and beautiful trees on both sides of the road. Longkhum is a beautiful village, with lots of pine and other trees. There are some rhododendrons also in the village, which make the surroundings more beautiful when they flower. Apart from this, the village is quite clean and that adds to the overall beauty.

The area of the village is quite large and its boundaries touches the districts of Wokha and Zunheboto. The neighbouring villages in Mokokchung are Setsu, Alichen and Ungma. The village as such is divided into 3 *khels* (sectors) which are referred to as A, B and C *khels*. The A *khel* is the biggest and the *khels* are basically inhabited by people of one or more clans. Longkhum has got clans of both Chungli and Mongsen linguistic branches of the Aos. The Chungli clans are Jamir, Pongener and Longkumer and they reside in A *khel*. The Mongsen clans are Imchen and Longchar and they reside in B *khel*. Each *khel* elects some representatives which are called *gram buras* (GBs). The village has 13 GBs with 5 each from A and B *khels* and 3 from C *khel*.

Like all villages of the region, Longkhum is also located on the highest point of a long, straight range, which is a conspicuous feature of the region. The prime reason for locating a village on the top of a hill seems to be security of the village. Most villages in the region have gates, which in the olden days, used to have wooden doors. Longkhum, however, has no such gate. The village is quite developed in the sense that it has got metalled, black topped road, right till the main village. The houses are located close to each other and the three *khels* in the village are as per their geographic location. The A *khel* is higher than the B and C *khels* and is referred to as the upper *khel*.

The village is electrified. But for a few houses, almost all have electricity, which however is not all that regular. There is an all-weather approach road which reaches right upto the village centre, where the church is located. The village has a bus stop and there is a regular bus going to the district headquarters and the bus makes several trips in the day. There is a branch post office located at Alichen, about 6 km from the village, but for the services of the bank, people have to go to the district headquarters. There is a primary school and a middle school. Apart from the government schools, there is a private school also. But the well off in the village, send their children to Mokokchung for studies. There is no high school. Primary health centre and primary health sub-centre is there, but the villagers had no knowledge about ORS packets. There is no veterinary dispensary. There is a PDS shop, which sells only kerosene and sugar. The village does not have a *haat*. There is no adult literacy centre as the adult literacy is quite high. There are 4 community latrines in each *khel*, 2 for men and 2 for women. But the interesting aspect is that they are very poorly maintained and most villagers go in the open to defecate. The village has community tap and water is pumped from the stream and thus supply of pure drinking water is ensured. The village had some phones installed through the MARR scheme, but the phones work only within the village. The ICDS centre is there but it is hardly doing anything for the last 1-2 years. A Panchayat Bhavan has been built in each *khel*, by JRY funds. There are functioning streetlights and as expected they are placed near the church in the village. The village does not have any primary agricultural cooperative society, but there is a cooperative society in the village, which presently is not doing any work but operating a bus to the district headquarters.

The **Tsiese Basa** village is electrified and most of the houses have taken electricity connection. There is no bank, post office or PHC. The nearest bank is in the district headquarters, about 14 km away. The nearest post office and PHC are in the Block headquarters about 3 km away. There is an all-weather approach road. There is no PDS shop in the village. There is only a primary school and no middle or high school. Veterinary dispensary and public telephone are not functioning.

The male to female ratio is 4 : 3 in the village. The religion followed is Christianity by all the members of the village. The caste is ST for all the members. All the local people of Nagaland have been categorised as STs. The population less than 14 years of age constitutes almost 40 per cent of the total population. The working population (lying in the range 20-50 yrs) is about 40 per cent of the population.

There is no migration from the village as such. During the lean season some people do go out of the village to work in nearby areas. But they go out in the morning and come back in the evening.

Many of the houses have CGI sheet roofing. The CGI sheets are provided by the government but the rest of the building material is arranged by the beneficiaries. The government plans to have CGI sheet roofing for all the people of the State by the year 2000. Many of the houses are electrified. But the electricity supply is very erratic, especially during the day. For drinking water most of the people are dependent on tanks in the village. The source of fuel is wood for all the households.

As mentioned in the village study assignment of **Nerhema** village, it is typical Angami (for that matter Naga) village is invariably built either on the summit of a hill, on a high saddle, or perhaps more frequently on the ridge of some spur running down from a high range. This used to be done mainly to give the village an impregnable security against all types of attacks from the other villages. With changing time, this has become unnecessary and now the Nagas are settling all along. But the old tradition still continues. **Nerhema** village is no exception to this and is also situated on a hilltop, though with no threats from any raiding parties from neighbouring villages, the people are expanding out a little.

The villagers believe that the original settlers of the village were from the Thevoma *khel*, the first persons being apuo and azuo. A monument has also been erected tracing out the genealogy of this *khel*, over the generations this *khel* has further split into five parts, the five Thevoma khels being:

1. Chadi ZiephrU A,
2. Chadi ZiephrU B,
3. CUzerUlho A,
4. CUzerUlho B, and
5. Khrama.

The present Thevoma *khels* are running into their twelfth generation. The split into the five *khels* occurred between the ninth and the tenth generations. The exact reasons for the split or the rules along which the new *khels* are set up (involves when and why) nobody seems to know (at least I failed to get them out). However, it seems to be based on the genealogy trees.

The other major settlers in the village are from the Solhima *khel* whose first persons in the village were called apfu and apfU. These *khel* people came to the village around six generations back and around two generations back split into three (some village elders said that they were split right from the beginning) :

1. Solhi I,
2. Solhi II, and
3. Solhi III.

From this account it seems that some sort of consolidation of nearby hamlets took place around six generations back when 2-3 small clans from outside joined the already established big hamlet for some reasons (may be protection from other raiders).

Although the village is divided into clans for social functions, the tribal society is characterized by a sense of equality where there is no discrimination towards any individual on any basis. People from the richest to the poorest have all an equal say in matters relating to village affairs. The tribal society is a casteless society, not suffering from the ills of a caste based society like the Hindus. In fact, the social structure amongst the tribals where there is no restriction to a person from doing anything, moving around, etc. is a much superior society than the mainland Indian society.

The concept of rich and poor was generally associated with the amount of rice a person was able to accumulate. The larger the rice accumulated/harvested, the richer he was. This depended on the hard work the person and his family could put in and the maximum amount of his land, for land is a plenty for almost everybody, which he can put into use productively. Now-a-days, though this yardstick is still used in some villages of the area, the concept of richness is getting closely associated to the money, the buildings he has and the lifestyle led by the person. In Nerhema, this modern concept of richness has crept in (in another village, Seiyhama, which I visited the old concept of the amount of rice which the person has is still prevalent).

In the annual calendar of **Nerhema** village there are seven major traditional festivals. Most of them are mainly associated with agriculture. The festivals are :

1. Sekrenyi,
2. TerhUnye,
3. Ngonyi,
4. Kerunyi,
5. Terhuonye,
6. Chadanye, and
7. Khupfuṇye.

The houses in the village are mostly made of mud plastered/un-plastered bamboo walls having CGI sheets as roofs (these have been mostly bought under some government scheme or the other). The flooring is also made of earth. Some of the houses (around 20) are made of RCC. Churches and community buildings are all made of RCC. Very few houses (around 10) have thatched roofs (no CGI sheets). Every family has a house, however, small and none is roofless.

The village constructed two kutcha road connecting it to the nearby Chiephobozou and the Kohima—Wokha district road which is blacktopped. The village is 30 km from Kohima. The nearest post office is at Chiechama which is almost non-functional. There are no telephone lines to the village. Nearby Chiephobozou was provided with a rural phone by the Dot which is not functioning. For post and telecommunications, the village people have to rely only on Kohima. The village through the VDB funds has acquired a community bus which makes two daily trips to Kohima to take the villagers to make their purchases, etc. there. This bus service is doing quite well. The bus service has also been taken up by almost all the other villages in this area. The government run bus service (Nagaland State Transport) is off the road. In the old days, the villagers used to walk their way to Kohima.

195 houses out of a total of 357 have been electrified. This does not, however, mean that the villagers can enjoy the benefit of electricity throughout the day. The power situation in Nagaland is that of acute shortage, because of which even towns like Kohima have to undergo heavy load shedding. The power is supplied to the village and adjoining areas, but the reliability of this—when and for how much time—is not there (the power supply varies from 10 minutes to 4-5 hours, but not continuous).

The main fuel in the village is still fuel wood collected from the village forests. Kerosene is also used, but mainly limited to hurricane lamps, etc. The main reasons are tradition, easy availability of fuel wood, unreliability of supply of kerosene, etc.

The village is the residence of the Angami group of tribes falling in the northern Angami region. The Angamis are the only tribes residing in the village. They are further divided into *khels* on genealogical lines for social functions only. There is no discrimination among the *khels*. In the olden days there used to be inter-*khel* clashes, but these have been forgotten in the modern days. All the *khels* have an equal say in the matters relating to the village and have equal representation in the village council. There are no division on caste basis.

The women in the Angami society in this village have a low status as far as inheritance of land is concerned. They are totally debarred from inheriting any land. However, this does not debar them from purchasing any land. The women have, however, an equal say in household matters. She is supposed to look after all the household chores, attend to cultivation along with the male members of the family, do weaving work, etc. The male counterpart is supposed to collect firewood from the forests, hunt and look after the money matters. The husband expects absolute fidelity from the wife, but as far as an ordinary villager is concerned will have to render the same himself also. May be because she shoulders the major responsibility of work in the household, she can dictate the terms in certain cases also.

In the case of marriage the women are allowed a degree of freedom which can be compared to anywhere else in the world. The parents can, at the most, resort to persuasion, but can never force the girl to marry against her wishes. The final decision is always hers. Divorce is also easy to obtain; and unless she is herself divorced for adultery she obtains a third of the joint property exclusive of land. A widow can remarry where and when she pleases, provided that she may not remarry from her deceased husband's house. Before marriage the Angami girl is given a great deal of liberty. The intermixing and movement of women and men, married or unmarried, is not restricted at all. It is not uncommon for a girl to have a lover before marriage. The participation in the festivals by members of both the sexes equally also is another indication that there are no social restrictions. In fact, sometimes the leg pulling and the jokes cracked at the gatherings are more ribald and embarrassing coming from the women's side. Thus, it can be said that though the women in the Angami village are not discriminated against except in the case of land, a certain amount of superiority is still kept with the men folk for decisions regarding the village, etc.

Christianity has been a great influence over the Naga villagers, and as elsewhere, in this village also the fact is there to be seen. The families practicing the traditional Naga religions (peculiarly called Hindus by the villagers) can be counted on the fingers. The church—be it the Baptist, the Catholic, the Revivalist, the three of which are present in this village—look down upon the traditional customs and do not encourage even the practice of the traditional festivals and functions involving dance, etc. However, the villagers have been able to retain this colourful part of their tradition and still celebrate many of the festivals outlined elsewhere in the report. The customs of head hunting and related activities, have however been left behind long time back in the quest of modernity under guidance of Christianity and modern administration.

An interesting custom: The boys (unmarried) of the village roam around in the village in the evening visiting the houses of the unmarried young girls in the village. The girl is supposed to entertain them with rice beer and other eatables (which are sometimes brought along by the boys themselves). They drink, sometimes even the girl (s) joining in, and make jokes during such visits. The girl who does not receive any visitor is looked down upon, as not beautiful and are not considered fit for marriage. The girl who receives the maximum number of such visitors is the most sought after for marriage. It is during such visits only that hearts joined, lovers chosen and matches made.

This village was actively involved in the underground movements during the 1950s and 1960s. It also faced a lot of hardship during the army operations to curb the insurgency during those times. The whole of the village was burnt during those times and the whole of the village was forced to take shelter in the jungles for many weeks. A number of ex-UGs, who were rehabilitated during this period are residing in the village and it is an experience talking with them. Even now, quite a few recruits from this village are there. In fact, it is difficult to distinguish between a UG and non-UG here, so openly are they found to be moving around.

While there is hardly any crime committed inside the village, except for petty thefts, which are also rare, the youth of the village have been involved in the past in many highway robberies and killings on the adjoining Kohima-Wokha district road. The crime situation depends to a large extent on the leadership of the village—the VC Chairman, members and the GBs. If the VC Chairman is strong and able to control the youths, there is less likelihood of anybody committing any crime.

The total population of the **Longjemdang** village is 438 according to 2001 census. Out of this, the population of males is 217 and females' 221. The population of children below six years is 118. The whole of the village is inhabited by the people of the Ao tribe. In fact, almost all the villages in Mokokchung are Ao villages. The Aos are one of the major tribes of Nagaland. The Aos are more educated than the other tribes in Nagaland and all of them have now embraced Christianity. The Ao people do not practice any such thing as caste system as we understand. They are rather divided into clans. There are six clans in all. In Longjemdang, people of four clans are living. The four clans are:

1. Longcher,
2. Kubzar,
3. Sungmir, and
4. Lusang.

All the clans have equal status and nobody is superior to the other. One important thing about the clans is that intra-clan marriage is prohibited. The wife or husband may be from the same village but he or she must be from some other clan. The son after getting married gets separated from his father and he sets up his own household. The father gives him a plot of land to build his house and a land for doing cultivation. Every household in the village has a number of plots, which can be used for constructing houses. As and when sons get married they are given the plots. If there are not any plots then they have to buy from others. Thus the family structure is nuclear in all the households.

The houses in Ao villages consist mostly of thatched house but the church buildings made of concrete are outstanding features in every village. The churches are of good modern design and located at the most central and dominating places in each village. In this village too, the grandest building is the church. It is of concrete and is very well maintained when compared to the other buildings. The church building being big is visible from quite a distance.

The houses in this village are not entirely thatched. A lot of houses have walls of bamboo and timber and the roof consisting of CGI sheets. Of course, there are a few which can be labelled as entirely thatched. Out of the 30 households I surveyed, the number of houses which are entirely of thatched variety are 6 which is 20 per cent. For the whole village too, the percentage of thatched houses would be around this. Fully pucca houses are very few. In my survey I came across only one house which was totally pucca.

The latrine in all the households is within the house itself. The survey showed that most of the people's latrine is of pit type. At one corner of the house, the toilet is made which is connected to a pit dug some distance below. The cost of building such a latrine is not much. It is quite affordable for the villagers and everybody has it. Of course, there are a few who have the modern type and there are even some whose latrines are open. In some households, a small area at a corner of the house to be used as a latrine is surrounded by a bamboo wall and the waste is allowed to run down the slope. It is to be noted that the houses in the village are at the top with land sloping all-around it. So the waste just goes down. In the household survey I did, the breakup of different type of latrines is as follows: Pit—80 per cent, Modern—7 per cent and Open 13 per cent.

The villagers mostly use firewood for cooking purposes. About 87 per cent of the households that I interviewed use firewood. Wood is available in plenty in and around the village. The total land of the village is big and it is pretty forested too. So the households without any difficulty get firewood. The people who are using liquid petroleum gas are very few and it is only in the last few years that they have started using them. One thing to note is that a large number of households are using pressure cookers for cooking. About half of the households I surveyed had pressure cookers.

Water is a bit of problem in the village. There are a few sources where water brought by streams get collected. People go to these sources to collect water. These sources are at some distance from the place where people have their houses. Daily the women folk trudge to these points and come back with the water on their backs. The water is taken after it is boiled. The villagers do not suffer from any water diseases, which shows that the water is safe. One interesting thing is that the village has not always faced the water problem. Till thirty years back, the villagers use to get water through pipes. The water used to come from a stream source at a higher altitude from the village and at some distance lying in the area of another village, Khar. It so happened that there arose a dispute between the two villages regarding something, which resulted in the Khar villagers cutting the supply. The dispute is still unresolved. It is to be noted that in Nagaland water sources are owned by the villages in which it lies. If some one wants to use that, he has to take the permission of the Village Council, which is normally given if there is enough water.

The approach road of the village is not black topped. The last two kilometres is just a path. It is jeepable, however, and is open during the monsoon too. The nearest town to the village is Mangkolemba, some three kilometres away. The people if they are going on foot to the town, rather than using this path, use a shortcut to the town, which is along the slope and would be about two kilometres. Whatever the villagers require, they get from Mangkolemba. However the grocery items they manage from the shops in the village. Two such shops are there which take care of the day-to-day needs of the people.

The whole village is electrified. Almost all the households have electricity connection. The supply of power is satisfactory. A phone connection has been given to the Village Council Chairman's house. In case of emergency it can be used by the villagers.

HEALTH FACILITY

There is no primary health centre in the **Medziphema** village. All villagers go to the community health centre located in Medziphema town whenever they want to see the doctor. This CHC is 4 km from the village and they have to go on foot, as there is no mode of transport plying on that road. Therefore, the villagers go to the community health centre only in case they fall sick. The pregnant women and mothers are the other category of people visiting the health centre. The pregnant women visit the CHC for antenatal check up and for getting tetanus injections whereas, the mothers visit to get their children vaccinated. There is one gynecologist in CHC, Medziphema. She does antenatal check-up of the pregnant women. Children are getting regular vaccination because of proper maintenance of cold chain for keeping the vaccines in the CHC. The general nutritional status of the children in the village is excellent. There is no case of malnutrition among children in the village. 12 children were born in the village in the past year of which, 6 were females and 6 were males. There is no preference for any sex and both are taken care of well. In fact, most of the villagers feel that they shall be giving their lands to their sons but nothing to their daughters. Abortions are heathen to the Catholics of this village. Almost 11 of the 12 births in the past year were home deliveries, conducted by a trained *dai*. There were 5 cases of deaths in the village in past 1 year's time and those were all due to old age. On the family planning front, the church does not allow adoption of family planning methods except for abstinence and safe period. Despite this, almost one-third of the females in the reproductive age group have undergone tubectomy. Another two-third are adopting temporary method like Copper T or oral contraceptives.

No. of eligible couples studied	*F.P. Method (permanent)*		*F.P. Method (temporary)*		*Couples with 2 living children*
	Female	*Male*	*Female*	*Male*	
80	23	0	57	0	

More needs to be done to widen the health services network, to provide emergency services as also laboratory testing service. There is a high incidence of AIDS/HIV and drug addiction in Nagaland but this village seems to be quite unaffected by these afflictions.

In the **Tsiese Basa** village, the family planning methods used are only temporary and are not very prevalent. The childbirth is mostly at home and done by the village ladies themselves. Though the child has been immunized in most of the cases it is only partial immunization.

There is no dispensary or any other medical facility in the **Nerhema** village. The nearest dispensary is at Chiephobozou, manned by a doctor and para-medical staff. The doctor remains half of the time in Kohima. The availability of medicines also is not adequate. However, because of the nearness of Kohima, the facilities are availed quite frequently—whenever needed. Under the VDB schemes the village has undertaken the construction of community latrines for each *khel*. These are quite infrequently used. The water supply is through the various ring wells constructed in the village by the VDB. There are some storage places for water from the streams which are quite far off. The supply of water from nearby is still a problem in the village and no perennial source is there causing much hardship in the lean season from December to May.

The people in **Longjemdang** village in general are enjoying good health. All the households I interviewed. I did not come across a very sick or a very seriously diseased person. The health of the people looked good. The children also appeared to be well fed and not suffering from anything in particular.

The houses are clean and the surroundings are also taken care of. Though a large number of households rear one to two pigs and also keep some poultry, it is ensured that they are outside and do not in any way dirty the house. The toilets are outside the house at some corner. The village lanes are all well maintained. Besides the households, the Village Council also takes interest in this.

The fact that the village is enjoying good health does not mean that the villagers have access to good medical facilities right there in the village itself. As a matter of fact there is no Primary Health Centre or Sub-PHC in the village. For their medical needs the villagers almost always depend on the medical facilities in Mangkolemba, a town, which is quite near, just three kilometres, and if one goes by a footpath along the slope, not even two kilometres. Whenever somebody is in dire need of medical help, someone from the village rushes down, gets a vehicle, comes back and then takes the patient to the doctor. The villagers have always done this and it appears that they are quite satisfied with this scheme. Because, during my whole stay I did not come across a single villager mentioning that the absence of a PHC is unfortunate. Of course, they could not come up with a reasonable answer as to what they would do if there is an emergency, and the patient is in need of medical attention right there at the spot itself, because all this going and coming back from Mangkilemba requires half an hour or so. Since such emergencies are quite rare they did not bother much about this thing but I feel that a PHC is a must. Emergencies may not have occurred till now but it is not that they are never going to occur.

There are two Anganwadi workers in the village. Their names are T. Amenla and T. Alila. However, they do not seem to be very active because very few people are clear as to what their work is.

Last year the number of births were 3; 2 boys and 1 girl. However, one boy died just ten days after birth. He died in the hospital itself and the cause was jaundice. The people, however, say that deaths like this are rare and in the years before last, there has not been any cases of infants or mothers dying during childbirth. The medical facilities are quite good in Mangkolemba and people know the importance of taking proper care during childbirth. Unless the situation demands so, all the births are at home itself. There is one woman in the village who is a bit trained in all this and whenever a case arises, her help is taken.

Almost all the households surveyed, the people knew about immunization and have taken care to get their children immunized, partially though. The infants have been administered BCG, OPV and measles doses, but not DPT. The villagers go to Mangkolemba for getting their infants immunized and the hospitals there have not been keeping DPT vaccines. However, two cases I found the infants to be fully immunized and I learnt that the initial years the kids passed in Dimapur and there they got all the doses.

The Pulse polio programmes have been conducted in the village and they have quite successful. The first team that came for this programme went from door to door to administer the dose and all the children of the village were given the dose.

A lot of people go for family planning methods as is evident from the survey. About 70 per cent of the eligible couples said that they are using family planning methods and out of this, 80 per cent have opted for a permanent method, namely tubectomy in all the cases. The couples are opting for permanent family planning after having 3 to 4 kids. I found that nobody is willing to stop after just two kids. Those who have not yet opted for any family planning method are exactly those having fewer than 3 kids. One more thing to be noticed is that there is no connection between income level and the adoption of family planning. The important thing is the size of the family.

The number of deaths last year was 4 and the year before that 6. Almost all these deaths were due to old age. Deaths due to diseases are rare though cases of malaria are seen during the time when people are in fields for wet rice cultivation. Last year some 3 people were down with malaria. Alcoholism is not a major problem and for this the church of the village can take the credit.

The household schedule was filled in for the 40 households, selected proportionately and randomly from the three *khels* of the village. Many sections of the survey could not be filled because of the special conditions prevailing in the State of Nagaland as has been enumerated elsewhere also. First we shall analyse the distribution of the population of the sample of 40 households by age and sex. The Table 2.8 gives this distribution:

Table 2.8 : Age and Sex-wise Distribution of Population

Sl. No.	*Age group*	*Male*	*%*	*Female*	*%*	*Total*	*%*
1.	< 1	1	1.14	2	2.35	3	1.73
2.	1 to 4	3	3.41	3	3.53	6	3.47
3.	5 to 9	8	9.09	5	5.88	13	7.51
4.	10 to 14	7	7.95	9	10.59	16	9.25
5.	15 to 19	11	12.50	12	14.12	23	13.29
6.	20 to 24	8	9.09	14	16.47	22	12.72
7.	25 to 29	8	9.09	4	4.71	12	6.94
8.	30 to 34	7	7.95	2	2.35	9	5.20
9.	35 to 39	4	4.55	7	8.24	11	6.36
10.	40 to 44	4	4.55	5	5.88	9	5.20
11.	45 to 49	2	2.27	3	3.53	5	2.89
12.	50 to 54	7	7.95	9	10.59	16	9.25
13.	55 to 59	5	5.68	2	2.35	7	4.05
14.	60 plus	13	14.77	8	9.41	21	12.14
	Total	**88**	**100.00**	**85**	**100.00**	**173**	**100.00**
	Sex Ratio				966		

From this distribution of the population, it can be concluded that people in the village do live long, as 12 per cent of the population is in the age group of 60 plus. Moreover, there were a number of people in their 80s and 90s. The sex ratio of 966 is pretty high, especially compared to the all-India average. However, this figure is smaller than the one mentioned in the 1991 Census data. This is indeed strange. Also around 38 per cent of the population is in the age group of 15 to 35 and in my view, this should be the target population group which should be the focus of all developmental and future plans.

EDUCATION

The Naga villagers are becoming increasingly education conscious and everybody wants their children to be educated and do government service. The villagers in general are quite aware of the importance and the opportunities that a good education provides. Hence, they are demanding not only education but also quality education, something, which the government schools are not able to provide. Hence, the apathy towards the primary school in the village can be seen.

According to the village study assignment of **Medziphema** village, there is a marked difference in literacy rates amongst those less than 14 years and those greater than 14 years. Amongst those grater than 14 years of age, the literacy rates are as low as 50 per cent. However, 95 per cent of those less than 14 years of age are attending schools.

More than 14 years

Illiterate	*Upto primary*	*Upto secondary*	*Above secondary*
46%	10%	14%	30%

Less than 14 years

Never enrolled	*Dropped out*	*Enrolled but doesn't go*	*Those attending government schools*	*Those attending private schools*
0	2%	3%	15%	80%

Education has been brought to Nagaland along with the Christian missionaries. They have introduced the Nagas to education and that too with English as the medium. Now-a-days, parents strive hard for education of their children. They do not have a tradition of selling their agricultural produce but they do so to educate their children. The present government primary school was established first as mission school by Khonoma Baptist Church in 1952. It was recognized and taken over by the government in 1959. However, the school infrastructure is not upto the mark. The building has many rooms whose walls are made of cement and bricks in half its length and the rest are bamboo. The roof is made of CGI sheet. The floor is cemented. The school has adequate furniture. The blackboards are not permanent ones. There is an excess of teaching staff in the village school. There are 135 students in the primary school with 6 government appointed teachers. Thus, the teacher pupil ratio is 1 : 22, which is much above the prescribed limit. However, 5 of these teachers are under matric and not trained as teachers. Teaching aids as charts, maps etc. are not available. There is no playground on any sports goods to promote habit of playing amongst the school children. There are no extracurricular activities or even morning assembly in the school. There are no vocational activities either in the village school or in the private school being attended. There is lack of drinking water and sanitation facilities in the school premises. An interesting trend is that there are more students in the school in A and B classes and number gradually dwindles by the time they reach class III and IV. This is because the parents find it more convenient to keep their children in the village school at a younger age but send them to a better private school later. Almost all those enrolled attend the school till matric but only a few pursue further studies. The government has not taken up any literacy campaign, as the awareness levels are already very high. However, to check teacher absenteeism in the school, the power has been delegated to the village council. The latter has also been entrusted with the task of maintenance of school assets.

Nerhema being a big village has a primary school. Nearby Chiephobozou has facilities upto class 10 (being extended upto class 12 from this year). Both government schools and private schools are there, however, there is a large percentage of dropouts, mostly due to lack of interest, pressure of work at home, expenses involved, etc. Very few are able to make it to college (as can be seen from the data in the Appendix II). There is not much of a discrimination based on sex in providing education, though in some cases the girls are discriminated against because of the pressure at work at home—these cases are few.

The total number of literates in the **Longjemdang** village is 278. This gives a literacy rate of 86.9 per cent. This is after removing the population of those below six years of age. The male literacy rate is 89.4 per cent and the rate for female is 84.3 per cent. Thus literacy rate is pretty high. The survey also showed so. There are very few who have not been ever to school. The importance of education even in the villages of Nagaland was realized quite early on and the Church must take a lot of credit for this. They brought education in a big way and now as a result illiterates are hard to come across in Naga villages.

Table 2.9 the educational status of the people of the village whom I interviewed. Since the sample has been drawn at random, the percent can be taken as representing the whole village. This data is for people who are not studying any more or not going to any educational institution and if studying have completed matriculate.

Table 2.9 : Sex-wise Educational Status

Status	*Male*	*Female*	*Total*
Illiterate	5 %	8 %	7 %
Primary	13 %	25 %	19 %
Middle	30 %	39 %	34 %
High School	34 %	14 %	24 %
Matriculation	8 %	8 %	8 %
Pre University	8 %	3 %	5 %
Graduate	3 %	3 %	3 %

From the above figures it is clear that the educational level of most of the people is middle school. Almost one-third of the people have been to middle school. The number of people going for further studies drops down a bit after that. Matriculates are not many and only 3 per cent of the people are graduates.

Another noticeable thing is that the percentage of men continuing with their studies even after the middle school level is more than the women. 34 per cent of the males have been to high school whereas most of the females have gone up to middle school. This shows quite clearly that females do not prefer going further. Many have dropped out after finishing middle school.

A survey of the people below 20 years helps in understanding some more things. Out of the 56 people, I found that 10 are dropouts, not going to any educational institution. Thus the dropout percentage is around 18 per cent. And among the dropouts 80 per cent are females showing yet again that the females do not have much urge for continuing with their studies.

Another thing to note is that a lot of parents send their children outside for studies. Many have relatives at places like Kohima or Dimapur. The children stay there for studies. If not with relatives then they stay in the hostels. Out of the 49 children who are studying and whose households I interviewed, 18 are living outside giving a percentage of 37 per cent which is definitely a high one. This is a bit surprising because there are quite a number of schools in Mangkolemba and some of them are High Schools too. Besides the town is also quite near. But those who are keeping their children outside feel that the schools are not that good and knowing fully well the importance of good education are willing to send their children outside. About 17 per cent of the households have an annual income of more than Rs. 40,000 and these people can easily keep some of their kids outside. The others of lesser income also manage if they have some relatives in the bigger cities.

There is one primary school in the village. 18 students are enrolled in it. However, the day I visited I found only 5 students in the school. It seems that when the kids turn three to four they are enrolled in the village school. But then they are not regular. Before long many get admitted in some private school in Mangkolemba and rather than coming to the Government school start going over there. So of the 18 enrolled one cannot find many in the school. The school has 5 teachers, 2 of them women. The teachers are regular and the villagers told me that this is because some are from the village itself while others are staying in Mangkolemba quite near. The school has a building of itself, build some years ago with some money provided under some scheme. I also saw some books in the office to be provided to those students unable to buy the books.

One being asked about mid day meals the teachers said that they in the past have got something in this regard but mostly it has been irregular. Hence, it was not possible to comment on its effectiveness. Some teachers are of the view that in spite of having everything, it is difficult to increase the number of students in the school because people have a bad impression about government schools and Mangkolemba being so near they have to difficulty in sending their kids to some private school. However, the village people are of the opinion and though things are there, the standard of teaching in low and if their kids study there then they would not be able to cope up with the academic pressure later on.

LAND AND AGRICULTURE ACTIVITIES

In Nagaland, unlike in other States and as taught in the Academy, all land is not owned by the government. As provided for in Article 371A of our Constitution, the land ownership has been left with the tribal people only. As a result, except for in the Dimapur mouza and in the urban areas where land has been acquired from the surrounding villages by the State government at some point of time, all the land is owned privately by the villages. It is because of this reason mainly (and partly for the impotency of the government departments like the land revenue and settlement) that survey and settlement has not been done for areas other than the government owned (even this is not complete and not done in all the areas, in fact may be only in Kohima town and Dimapur mouza, and the records are never found to be complete). The land revenue system is not at all evolved in any place except for the Dimapur mouza, which is a plains area and was under Assam during the British times.

The **Medziphema** village owns 6,000 acres of land. No revenue is collected by the administration for this land and it is totally owned by the villagers. There has been no survey of the land and thus, no land records have been made and maintained. 80 per cent of the total lands are community lands, 15-16 per cent are private lands and 45 per cent are clan lands. Out of the private lands 2-3 per cent are used for building houses. The rest are used for household gardens etc. Of the community lands, 1/4th each are under *jhuming, panikheti*, forests and plantation. The village has a general body meeting at the beginning of each agricultural season where they decide who is going to cultivate which *jhum* field in the following year. Since, the land is freely available but there is a constraint of manpower, the migrant Muslims work as sharecroppers and are given 50 per cent of the total produce by the land owners who keep the rest unto themselves. In return, they are allowed to stay on the land of the villagers. Their numbers are almost two times the total population of the village. The *jhum* cycle is only 4 years now and thus, the productivity of land is drastically coming down. This is the result of increasing population pressure on the land. They practice both *jhum* and *panikheti*. They cultivate rice, maize, pineapple and vegetables. *Jhum* fields are sown in May and harvested in October whereas; *panikhetis* are sown in July and harvested in November. The fields are left for the rest of the months as there is no water for *jhum* and there is a custom of leaving animals open in the *jhum* fields to graze there. The seeds for sowing are taken from the previous year's harvest. No HYV seeds are used. They practice organic farming and do not add manure to their fields. The *panikhetis* are ploughed using bullock ploughs and not tractors.

Particular	*No. of Households*
Only family labour	0
Mainly family labour	0
Only hired labour	0
Mainly hired labour	80
Exchange labour	0
Using HYV seeds	0
Using bullock plough	71

The villagers have a traditional system of making canals for irrigation in their fields. This has been highly commended by the British in their records also. The villagers have, on their own, diverted waters of a river to their village and into fields and have made canals in such a way that the water reaches each and every field. All this has been done based on traditional knowledge of the farmers and not with any kind of engineering help. Each household gets about 200 kg of rice/year. Normally, they do not sell rice in the market. Only in case of dire need for money they sell it to the local traders. The rate of sale is Rs. 3.50 per kg of paddy. Pineapples are grown for sale in the market. Each family, which cultivates pineapples, gets Rs. 10 thousand to 15 thousand per year from sale of pineapples alone. Most of the pineapples are sold in small marketing sheds along the National Highway No. 39 at Rs. 10 per pineapple. This is the main source of income for the villagers. Some wage labour is also used during sowing and harvest season. However, the local male labour is paid at the rate of Rs. 70 per day and women at the rate of Rs. 50 per day and Rs. 50 per day is paid to outside labour. The village maintains Gamari and Arecanut plantations. From the forest, they collect firewood and other minor forest produce.

As mentioned earlier, the only form of cultivation in the **Longkhum** village is *jhum* or shifting cultivation. Of course, in other parts of the district and the State terrace cultivation is also practiced. The villagers of **Longkhum** practice *jhum*, in the traditional pattern, just like the other Aos of the district. The practice involves shifting of land on the part of cultivators who undertake an arduous work to cut the heavy jungle and convert it into a field where mixed cropping is practiced. The cultivation in the same field is done only for two years, and these two years of cultivation is referred to as *nootan kheti* and *poorana kheti*. In the second year, the output and yield is significantly lower than the first year. Hence, each year some new areas are brought under *jhum* and cultivation is done simultaneously in both the fields.

Under the system of *jhum*, an area selected for cultivation is cleared of its shrubs and undergrowth. Then the smaller trees are also felled, but the big trees are not. Branches of the big trees are slashed so that the tree does not die and can bear fruits for its propagation. This work is generally carried out in the month of October-November. The logs are fixed with pegs to keep its position. It is a kind of making flat plots, but the plots are never very flat nor do the logs form actual steps. It helps a lot in preventing soil erosion. But still the top soil is washed to some extent and is mostly deposited on the upper side of the log step and as a result of this the crop grows better on the immediate upper side of the log than its far upper side or down.

As a result of burning, the land becomes more fertile because of the ash which contains lime and phosphate. Before burning the field, care is taken to clear about 3 to 6 metres round the field of the dry substances as file path so that the fire may not extend to other areas.

The soil is quite soft as it is formed by falling of leaves and decayed annual undergrowth and shrubs. But it still requires some tilling with spade and hoe. Thereafter, paddy is broadcast in the month of March or April, depending on the pre-monsoon showers. In the fields, in which cultivation is being carried out for the second year, this is generally done in April. Thereafter, there is sufficient rain and the crop ripens by August-September. In between, weeding is required at least two to three times. But it should be noted that the yield in *jhum* is quite low, it is about 477.51 kg per hectare in *jhum* as compared to 982.73 kg per hectare in terrace cultivation.

The major crops grown by the villagers and the seasonality of their cropping can be listed as :

Crops	*Months of sowing*	*Months of harvesting*
Rice	March-April	September-October
Maize	March-April	July-August
Chilli	May	July
Sweet potato	March-April	November-December
Naga Dal	April	November
Pumpkin, cucumber	April	October-November
Ginger	March-April	February
Karela, beans, cabbage	April	June

According to the estimates provided by the villages (as mentioned above, no survey of the land has been done) about 60 per cent of the land is used for cultivation. About 10 per cent is under forest cover. But these figures may not be very reliable, as they are only very rough estimates.

In **Tsiese Basa** village the land is estimated to be equally divided between these two forms, viz., individual and community ownership. Majority of the land in the village is used for cultivation. It is single crop cultivation, the crop being paddy. In addition fruits and vegetables like tomato are grown. It is interesting to note that almost 10 different varieties of paddy are used. The crop produced is used for internal consumption.

There are about 30 cows, 5 buffaloes and 5 pigs in the village. The soil is extremely fertile and neither HYV seeds nor fertilizers are used (this is true of almost the entire State). There are no government irrigation projects. The people are dependent on canals and rainfall for their irrigation.

The moneylender as an institution does not exist in the **Tsiese Basa** village. The people would borrow from friends and relatives or from their clans. At times the respondents mentioned moneylender but they meant individuals from whom they had taken loan. In the output 3 moneylenders have been mentioned where it only indicates various individuals. There are very few landless families in the village and they are also provided land to cultivate by the clan. Almost everyone has land, individual as well as community. Almost all of the cultivable land is used for sowing and the cultivation is single crop.

There is no tenancy/land ownership system in the village. In Nagaland almost everyone has land, if not individual then community land. The village community takes care of its inhabitants. There has been very little transaction of land in the last 5 years.

The study of land ownership, its classification and measurement are very difficult in Nagaland as no cadastral survey has been conducted before there is no detailed official record in respect of land in Nagaland. Owing to the absence of required authentic data on land ownership system, operational holdings, land-use pattern etc., it is difficult to make a study of land ownership. The figure given for land in the survey is also approximate ones only.

When Nagaland was part of Assam, a small portion of land, about 259 sq. km was surveyed and it now falls under Dimapur Mauza. The Government of Nagaland, Department of Land Records, has also surveyed some of the important administrative headquarters (township areas). But except this portion of land, no area in Nagaland has so far been surveyed and no standard or uniform laws have been framed. The Department of Agriculture conducts agricultural census from time to time, but they also do not have proper records on land-use pattern etc. The only legal framework for the right to cultivate land is the Nagaland Jhumland Act, which has certain limitations.

Invariably the ownership of land, exercise of ownership rights, controlling system, land-use pattern, land boundary and land-man relations are based on traditions, which are simply guided by customary laws. The customary laws are not yet codified, but they are used very effectively as guiding principles in the socio-economic life of the community. Every Naga tribe follows its own customs and there is no uniform custom or tradition for the tribes. Because of the diverse nature of the socio-cultural background no land reform measures like ceiling on landholdings, consolidation of holdings, ownership rights, distribution of land to the landless etc. have been attempted. Article 371(A) of the Constitution of India provides certain special privileges to the State of Nagaland relating to religion, social practices and land ownership system of the Nagas. No Act of Parliament on the above subjects can constitutionally be enforced in the State of Nagaland unless the Legislative Assembly of Nagaland by a resolution so decides.

The crop grown is paddy, though there are some 10 different varieties of paddy in use. The produce is used for self consumption in the village and there is nothing left for selling outside the village. There is no use of HYV seeds or fertilizers. The farmers rely on traditional methods of farming. For irrigation all the households depend on canals and rainfall. The reasons for not using fertilizers etc. are that for one the land is very fertile and the people are also wary of using fertilizers as it may create imbalance in the soil composition. In addition, in hilly areas it is difficult, if not impossible, to use many of the newer technologies like the tractor.

Nerhema village, like most of the other villages, is located on a hilltop. It is one of the richest villages in this area with an ownership of over 11,250 ha of land. According to official records, however, as no land survey or settlement has even been done, and all the data available is based only on the traditional records passed from generation to generation orally. Despite there being no land records system, there is hardly any dispute over the land ownership and if at all there are disputes these are resolved at the village level itself by the traditional laws (which again is an oral tradition) and is decided by the village council. In a very few cases, being an exception rather than the rule, the village council is not able to resolve the matter and then the case is referred to the DB's court or even the higher judicial authority. There are very few cases of land disputes overall, however.

All the lands in the village can be classified as:

1. Agricultural Land: This can be further classified as (a) terraced cultivated lands (*paani kheti*) and (b) land under shifting cultivation (*jhum* land, *sukha kheti*);
2. Forest Land; and
3. Land under use for housing.

The land ownership is of two kinds—individual and communal. The communal land is divided amongst each *khel* and the *khel* is the real owner of this land. The land ownership passes along the male line of the family. The girls are not entitled to ancestral property. One of the reason given for this is that since their is an exogamous society with intra-clan marriages not allowed, this is to ensure that the property of a clan and hence the *khel* (which can be of more than one clan) is not transferred out of the *khel*. Even if the girl is the sole heir, then also on marriage the land ownership passes to the *kehl* or other close relatives. All these traditional rules are not written down anywhere but are passed from generation to generation by practice and narration.

The agricultural land constitutes the major portion of land under the ownership of the village. With the increasing pressure of the population, more and more forest land is also being brought under agriculture. The Angami people have an old tradition of using terracing along with the shifting cultivation areas. The areas under each depends on the availability of water, the soil type and the population of the village. The terraced fields are found closer to the inhabited areas of the villages while the *jhum* lands are farther away.

In the old days, the Angamis, and the other tribes also, realized the importance of the forests and allowed a certain portion of the village to be forest land. From this forest the village requirements of animal meat, vegetables, fruit, etc. was met. But now, even though that realization for the forests is there, the logging operations for commercial purposes having taken over, almost all the original forests have vanished and what remains is only regrowth. But, even this regrowth constitutes more than half of the total village owned land.

The land ownership varies from 1 ha to 10-12 ha. However, the average size of the holding will be around 3 ha (these are all educated guesses, as the data given by the villagers is not very reliable, and there being no survey and settlement, the data from the land records is not available). However, there is no case of any landless family (there is a tradition in this village according to which if anybody wants to settle in this village, after getting himself adopted by somebody from the village, he is provided with a piece of land for his personal cultivation absolutely free). However, to supplement the land needs of the families having inadequate land, some land is rented by these families. The rental lands are either from the *khel* community lands or the personal lands of those having larger quantity of land. As a rental, some percentage of the produce, which can extend upto half of the produce is taken. This, however, is highly relaxable if the family is found to be in dire need. In some cases, some sort of labour is also expected from the family renting in the land. However, in all these no indication of any sort of exploitation is to be observed. Although, some of the families having good amounts of land are living outside, most of these lands are lying unattended and not being cultivated by anybody, except for those lands which are being used for logging operations. 4-5 plantations have also been started as well as some fishery ponds.

The villagers in **Nerhema** (and most of the other villages in the Kohima district) practice the terraced type of cultivation supplemented by the shifting cultivation (*jhuming*). These two are also known as *paani kheti* and *sukha kheti* respectively in this region. Terraced cultivation is in practice amongst the Angamis since old days and is not a modern introduction. The expertise in this type of cultivation varies from village to village. The experts are to be found in the southern Angami villages—Viswema, Kigwema, etc. and some of the western Angami villages—especially Khonoma, Mezoma. The villages of the Northern Angami region are considered backward in this area. Nerhema village terraces are impressive but cannot match those of the advanced villages.

Jhum cultivation is an inherent part of the cultivation which is a tradition of the Angamis (and the Nagas). While in the other districts it occupies as much as 90 per cent of the total cultivated area in the district of Kohima, this is restricted to around 20 per cent and hence is used only to supplement the yields from the terrace type of cultivation. This practice arises out of the necessities of the area. Though seemingly wasteful, *jhum* cultivation is done very methodically and is the only mode of cultivation which is possible in some areas. The soil in this area is a very loose variety of soil which forms a thin layer over a very rocky undersurface. Because of this it is very difficult to cut terraces in this area. The *jhum* cultivation involves felling of the vegetation of a chosen patch and then setting it on fire. However, this felling in done very systematically with the useful trees being allowed to remain standing (e.g. in the Khonoma area, the Alder tree because of its nitrogen fixing properties is allowed to remain standing). This patch is then cultivated for 3-4 years, with the yield falling down every year, in the first two years it being even more than that of the terraced fields. After the yield gets considerably reduced, the patch is abandoned and the vegetation is allowed to regrow in the area over a period varying from 7 to 14 years. With the pressure of population, this period is getting reduced and thus the land is now-a-days not being allowed to retain its full fertility.

The weather, the soil and the level of availability of water for irrigation purposes does not allow the villagers to go for multiple cropping pattern or intensive cropping. The conditions allow for cropping only once a year. The principal crop in the village is rice (paddy). This being the staple food of all the villagers. Rice is also used for making rice beer which is the most popular drink in the villages. Both amongst the menfolk and the ladies. Thus the only economic reason behind the cultivation of paddy only is its need as one of the basic needs of existence—food and hence a strive towards self-sufficiency in at least this area. Some other crops like maize, certain pulses, jowar, etc. are also cultivated in small quantities.

The productivity depends upon the type of cultivation being practiced. From *paani kheti* (terraced type) the average yield varies from 18 bags/ha (1 bag = 80 kg). In the case of *sukha kheti* (*jhum* type) the average yield varies from 18 bags/ha (for 2-3 years old) to 22 bags/ha (for new fields). When the yield from the jhumed fields go down below that of the *paani kheti* (which happens in 3-4 years), that patch of land is abandoned and allowed to regrow.

The irrigation system in the village should not be understood to be equivalent to the irrigation systems as found in the plains areas of India. There are no canal systems as are to be found in the plains of Punjab, Haryana, Andhra Pradesh, etc. The only system of irrigation available to the villagers in this hill village is the one which has been developed over the years through the traditional intellect of the villagers. The irrigation of the fields is through harnessing of the streams, natural springs and rivers flowing at a higher level in some adjoining area. This is done by digging small channels (small in width, because sometimes they can be of great length), sometimes using bamboo poles cut in half as supplemental irrigation means to channelize the water down the slopes where the terraces are located. The water is made to flow by the use of gradient only. This irrigation system is an inherent part of the terrace system. No modern systems are used. It is only a simple system. No electric pumps (hardly any electricity) or wells are used. Irrigation in the hill areas is an area which needs to be researched into and new systems developed.

As only a single cropping pattern is followed uniformly, there is no question of any differentiation on this basis. It should be noted that by the traditional definition followed throughout the plains area of the country, most of the area will be marked as unirrigated.

The farmer-villagers are almost self sufficient for their needs as regards seeds, etc. no fertilizer is used. The HYV seeds are not suitable for this area and though once or twice they were tried to be introduced they failed. Some seeds, of course, are sourced from the government (but minimal). The villagers store the paddy in big cane containers in their houses. This paddy is used throughout the year for their own consumption. Out of this also comes the seed. The credit needs are also minimal and whatever is needed is either earned through personal labour (on daily wages, working in others' fields) or borrowed from relatives and clan people on easy terms, or in some cases also borrowed from the VDB. In fact it is not feasible for a bank to operate in other areas of lending also owing to the almost 100 per cent default rate—one suggestion is to use the VDBs as a source of lending also because the authority of the Village Council will ensure that there are no defaulters. Since cultivation is done only to meet internal needs and not for commercial purposes, that way also the credit needs are minimal.

The produce from the land is just sufficient, and that also not always, enough for the internal consumption of the family. Thus, there is no question of the produce being used for any commercial purposes, except, of course, for the small exchanges/redistributions (e.g. contribution to the church, providing for the destitute, old and those who are unable to look after themselves, small lending, etc.) which go on inside the village. So, no marketing arrangements have ever been made or should even be thought of at this stage.

The climate is congenial to the domestication of the animals as is the favourable availability of grass and vast pasture grounds. However, the main purpose for which the livestock is kept is for the meat. Consumption of milk and milk products is not practiced because of which large scale dairying operations cannot be thought of in spite of other favourable factors. The animals which are popularly reared up in **Nerhema** village are:

1. Pigs,
2. Poultry, and
3. Cattle.

Some well off households also keep dogs which are treated as a delicacy. Goats are also provided under the IRDP scheme but are not popular (I could not find even a single goat in the village).

Keeping pigs is very popular as pork is the favourite dish amongst the Nagas and almost every household tries to keep at least one pig. This can also be seen from the number of schemes allocated for piggery in the district plan and under the IRDP. Although the hybrid breeds have also been introduced through the veterinary department, due to lack of availability of these piglets these varieties are not widely kept. The villagers recognize the better quality of these pigs but are still keeping the old varieties because of non-availability of the new varieties. There exists a captive market for pork, especially around the festive season of Christmas and other traditional festivals.

Poultry products in the form of chicken are also taken. Though eggs are eaten, it is preferred to get them hatched to have more poultry.

Nowhere is poultry kept mainly for production of eggs. Cattle is usually imported from the neighbouring State of Assam and is usually brought on foot in herds. Some years back, the cattle was also used to be kept inside the village, but now-a-days a cattle shed, known as a *khuti* is maintained outside the inhabited area, where all the cattle of the village is kept.

Most of the meat is used for internal consumption in the village during regular use, festivals, marriages, etc. though some is taken out to Kohima for selling purposes. This activity can be increased by providing adequate linkages which involves a larger involvement of the department of veterinary and animal husbandry. The inputs which need to be there are adequate supply of good quality piglets, calves at an affordable price, adequate supply of animal feed, and good medical facilities (death due to some disease is a regular feature. A veterinary medical officer is supposed to be there in the village, but none is to be found in the neighbouring Chiephobozou)—stress should be given to training a person from the village itself so that he can cater to the local needs or a mobile dispensary should be regularly organized. In some villages, the village council has passed orders banning sale of pork below certain price. This can also be passed by the village council of this village so that people do not sell below the economical price (there are cases where villagers in need of money sell the meat even below the price which they had borne for rearing it up).

The **Longjemdang** village has never been surveyed. So, there is no data as to how much land it has, how much, is under cultivation or how much forest it has. Cultivators in Nagaland do not pay any land revenue to the government and hence there is no department as land revenue, which would have been expected to keep such data. However, I tried to get a rough idea of the land of the village by trying to ascertain the boundaries, then making a rough sketch and doing a calculation.

The oval at the centre shows the place where people have houses. The lands of the village are all around it. To the north the land extends for 10 kilometres. The land of Lakhuni village forms the boundary on that side. In the south it is 2 kilometres, bounded by the land of Japu village. Towards the east, 2 kilometres, on that side lies the Mangkolemba town and a range of hills known as Changki range. Towards the west it extends upto 8 kilometres, a stream passes on that side known as Tzurang river. The land of the village lies beyond the river too and borders the Tzurangkong villages. The whole area of the village can be approximated as equivalent to a rectangle of sides, 12 and 10 kilometres having an area of 120 square kilometres. However the area all around the village is not flat. The village itself is on the top of a hill, having a height of 672 metres. Towards the west the hill slopes gradually flattens out before reaching Tzurang river, so that some land on that side is even. On all the other sides, however, it descends and then rises. It is difficult to correctly know the slope or gauge the distance. Anyway, looking at the topography, one can assume that the total area of the village would be 1.1 to 1.2 times the rectangular area we calculated above. This gives us an area between 132 to 144 square kilometres. In acres it is 33,000 to 36,000. Not many villages in Mokokchung district have this much land and number of households also being low and the per capita land would be one of the highest in the whole area.

The villagers are doing both *jhum* and wet rice cultivation, though now more of the later. A larger portion of the land, especially towards the north and south are on the hill slopes. Here the people of the village have done *jhum* cultivation since ages. Land is cleared somewhere in January and February. The trees are cut and the logs are taken away to be used as firewood. In March, the cleared land is set to fire. Next month, the crops are sown. The sowing is quite easy. Seeds of rice, maize are just thrown on the land. No fertilizer or manure is used. The land is fertile because of being kept fallow for long. Harvest comes in September to November depending on the crop sown. In winters vegetable crops are sown. Sometimes the field is cultivated for the next year too. Otherwise it is abandoned and the household moves to another land. After this the field is left fallow for the next nine to ten years depending on the availability of land. The longer the fallow period; the richer the soil for the next cultivation.

In **Longjemdang** village, however, the stress on *jhum* has decreased, and now every year only ten to twelve households do some *jhum* cultivation. The reason is that unlike most other Naga villages in Mokokchung, this village has around 500 acres of land, which is even and fit for wet rice cultivation. All this land is towards the west where the hill slopes give rise to a flat land. There are three streams also in this part, which enables irrigation. One stream, called Ailong was dammed by the villagers with some help from the government some thirty years back, allowing the farmers to use its water for rice cultivation. Ever since then, more and more households have moved towards wet rice cultivation.

In **Longjemdang** village there is not a single household, which does not have land to speak of. Land here can be divided into two categories: *jhum* land lying on the slopes; and even land on which wet rice cultivation can be carried out.

In survey it was found that 50 per cent of the people have land above 500 acres. Rest below that, and only one household with no *jhum* land at all. This household too had *jhum* land earlier but it was taken away from them by the Village Council due to some reason. Otherwise, every household in the village has a lot of *jhum* land. However, this land is not being used much now. With the start of wet rice cultivation people have stopped *jhumming* and now only those who do not have any land for wet rice cultivation do some *jhum* cultivation. The *jhum* land of a particular household is scattered at many places, in some cases as many as ten places.

Rather than cultivation people are using land for raising betel leaf and betel nut farms. Betel leaves grow well on the sloping *jhum* land especially those which are in shade About 80 per cent of the households, I surveyed have a betel leaf farm. Similarly a large number of households have betel nut farms but their number would be less than the betel leaf farms. There are other plantations too but their number is quite less.

The more valuable land to possess is the land fit for wet rice cultivation. For the people, this land is what matters. However, compared to *jhum* land, people have less of this. In my survey the biggest plot was of just 6 acres with some having just 1 acre and 3 had none. This is understandable because anyway the total land fit for wet rice cultivation is less, only 500 acres.

The following figure shows the percentage of people in the village having different land holdings fit for wet rice cultivation. It is evident that bulk of people has around 2 to 3 acres of land. Out of the 500 acres of land fit for wet rice cultivation about 300 acres is being used. The rest is still undeveloped. The reason for this is that the villagers are not in a position to provide irrigation to all the land. The undeveloped portions are those areas, which are far from Ailong river, the river which has been dammed. The villagers are of the view that it Tsurang and Aloshi streams, the other two flowing in the area are also dammed, then they would be in a position to utilize all of the lands.

The village depends heavily on hired labour for cultivation. No household on its own can hope to cultivate the fields. For one, the fields for wet rice cultivation are quite far from the village. It takes almost an hour to reach from the village. Further, there, are not enough hands to do all the work. Hence, the dependence on hired labour. The people who are doing labour in the fields are from places like Assam, Bengal and Bihar. Some come just before the sowing season and work thereafter but majority are those who stay throughout the year there itself and look after the fields. Those who work on daily basis are given Rs. 45 with two meals or Rs. 50 with one meal. These rates are if the workers are from outside. If the persons doing labour are from the village itself then the rate is Rs. 100 for man and Rs. 75 for woman. There is a reason behind the difference in wages for non-locals and locals. All the households in the village have land and if they have to labour, they would do in their own fields. If they are working in some other field, it means that they have very less land or due to some reason unable to cultivate on it, which implies that their condition is not good. Hence they get more than the others. All the above mentioned rates have been fixed by the Village Council.

Many of the labourers who remain throughout the year in the fields are not daily wage earners. These people: till the land, sow it, and do all the other things and after harvest take half of the produce. The owner also helps his labourer when some direction is required. However, there are some households, which give the land to the labourers and come back only to collect their share. People who are very old or those in jobs do this.

The labourers who come to work live in the fields in a small hut made by themselves or sometimes provided by the owner of the land. In some cases the same person has been looking after the land for many years. There are some who have been living for quite some time and have brought their families too. There would be thirty such families living in the lands.

The number of the labourers taken together is quite substantial. Some decades back there were not so many because the village at that time as only doing *jhum* cultivation. But as more and more land began to be opened for wet rice cultivation, need for labourers increased. The labourers have always enjoyed good relationship with the villagers. A meeting with them in the rice fields made this clear. If ever a difference between a labourer and villager arise and if it cannot be sorted out then it may be taken to the Village Council for settlement. However, till now no such dispute has occurred. Rather disputes between the labourer families have been occurring every now and then. To sort it out, the Village Council has appointed one person among the labourers as Gaon Bura. This person has to intervene in case of any dispute and liaise with the Village Council if something occurs and is important enough to be told to them. Some years back, the Village Council, opened a school in the fields to take care of the education of the children of the labourers. It, however, was not successful because the teachers chosen for this purpose were not fluent in the languages, which the kids of the labourers understood and the school had to be eventually closed down.

The villagers have bullocks for ploughing the fields. Most of the households have more than a pair of bullocks. These animals are kept in the rice fields and the labourers take care of them. Sometimes there are cows too. The milk of these cows is not used by the Nagas. They are not very fond of milk. They keep these cows for raising bullocks and at times for meat; not for milk purpose.

The villagers do not use kilograms or quintals for estimating their farm produce. Rather they use tins. One tin of rice is equal to the amount of rice that a 15 kilograms edible oil container made of tin may hold. Since every household buys edible oil, each has such a tin container, which is used for weighing. Three tins of rice roughly equals 40 kilograms.

Rice is the most important produce of the village. Maize is also grown but not much. Quite a number of vegetables are grown, potato being the most important. Other vegetables like cabbage, cauliflower, tomato, chilies are mostly grown in kitchen garden. Most of the households maintain a kitchen garden.

The total produce of rice would be around 350 tonnes. Some village people came up with this figure which seems correct because the survey results, if they are scaled up, they also come to something of this sort. Regarding the productivity it is difficult to come to any figure because it varies so much. In the survey I came across these figures :

Produce per acre in quintals	Percent of household doing wet rice cultivation
20–40	42
40 60	38
60–80	17
More than 60	3

Thus more than 80 per cent of the lands have productivity less than 60 quintals. A mean calculation shows that it is around 40 quintals. The villagers are not using any fertilizer. They are not even using manures. However, they know about all these things. It is just that economic constraints prevent them from using them. The villagers have an idea about high yielding variety of seeds. The Agriculture Department sometimes gives them seeds to try it out in the fields on an experimental basis. The seeds that they are currently using in the fields are a variety known as Pankaj supplied many years ago by the Agricultural Department.

About 1000 acres of land in the village belongs to the Village Council. Almost all of this land is in the *jhum* area except some, which is in the wet rice area. This land is covered with trees and belongs to all the inhabitants of the village. However, to get anything from it the Village Council's permission is required. Some households do not have any land for doing wet rice cultivation. Their *jhum* land is also quite less. These households with the permission of the Council may do *jhum* cultivation in these lands. The Council does not charge anything from these households. Further, the amount of land that can be used by the household is upto them. If it can manage more, it can have more. Since very few households would be going for such a thing, the land available is plenty. The trees in the common land can be cut if some community structure has to be built. Individuals also get wood from it if they want to. It is another matter that they do not because each has sufficient *jhum* land of his own which is now quite forested because *jhuming* is not carried out anymore by most of the people.

Of late, some villagers have wanted to develop plantations. They can do in their lands too but since it is scattered they have approached the Council to allow them to do this in the community land because here a large tract of land is available at one place itself. Many people have developed plantations of betel nut and in some case oranges.

Land is plenty so whoever approaches gets, though preference is given to the one who is older.

The streams flowing through the village lands are accessible to all. Anybody can fish and use its water. Sometimes the whole village goes for community fishing. The catch, which at times is substantial, is then distributed among the people taking part in the fishing.

The village church is an important place for the whole village. The whole population is Christian and members of the church. Every Sunday all the grown ups gather in the church for the service. There is a Pastor who looks after the church. He is from some other village but stays in the village itself. His needs are taken care of by the Village Council. The building of the church is the best in the village and for its construction the whole village had contributed their labour. The wood was obtained from the trees growing in the common land of the village.

There is a rice mill in the village. It was set up some time ago by the Village Development Board. One man has been assigned the work of running the mill. He charges some amount from the people coming to the mill with their rice. Whenever a community project is taken up in the village, the whole village has to get involved. They have to work in that project and at times also advance money. This is true not only for projects taken up by the villagers all by themselves, but also for projects under some government scheme.

OCCUPATIONAL PATTERN AND INCOME

Nagaland is characterized by the almost total lack of organized industries, not to talk of the rural industries. This does not mean, however, that there is a total lack of artisanship at the rural level or a total absence of hard workmanship amongst the Nagas. As agriculture forms the basic occupation of almost everybody in the village. Most of the hard work of the family is put into agriculture related activities. However, despite this, the women folk in almost every house undertake hand weaving. Cane work, wood work, blacksmithy and pottery are some of the other rural activities to be found in the village. Weaving is entirely confined to the women folk who besides shouldering the domestic and cultivation works, weave their apparels, the tradition of weaving being handed from mother to daughter. In the old days, the ginning and dyeing was also done at the village level using traditional methods. Now-a-days, however, with the easy availability of cotton and woollen thread of the required colours in the nearby town of Kohima or Dimapur, this is used instead. The loom is a simple loin loom. The products of weaving are mainly wrappers (maikhlas) and shawls, waist clothes and bodices, bags, etc. all woven in the basic traditional patterns with slight modern modifications. Cane work is also popular because of the easy availability of cane. While waterproof hats, bowls, mugs, etc. are made they are not very popular now-a-days. The main product is the cane basket. Baskets are made in wide range and number with different shapes and sizes, used for different purposes—as containers for crops and other household goods, as carrying baskets for cultivation equipment, water, paddy, etc. In fact, a girl is not supposed to go to a field without carrying her basket along with. Wood carving, having more of an artistic than commercial value is also carried out. Dolls, statues, saucers, platters, cups and other utensils, spear shafts, etc. are made from wood.

Smithery was practiced to forge the agricultural instruments and war fighting equipments in the olden days. However, with the easy availability of cheaper agricultural instruments in the neighbourhood towns, and the extinction of old enmities and hence the wars and the tradition of head hunting, this has dwindled. Now-a-days, only occasionally, some *daos* or spears are forged in the villages to keep the tradition going on. Some villages are also known for crafts specific to that village only, e.g. Khonoma village is very well known for its expertise in stone carving. The main observation that can be made is that the skills of an artisan, except for the weavers and basket makers are considered as useless in the new age, and because of the easy availability of cheaper alternatives and the non-introduction of new technology, hardly anybody from the younger generation is taking up these professions. Also, the existing artisans practice there skills to supplement their income from agriculture and for in-house purposes.

Around 80 per cent of the villagers practice cultivation. While the rest are employed and doing service. During the farming season, the villagers are busy but during the non-farming season, they rear animals or do woodwork especially making furnitures. Both rearing of animals and carpentry is for use at home or within the village and not on a commercial scale.

Caste	*Self owned land*	*Tenant*	*Casual labour*	*Self employment*	*Traditional occupation*	*Govt. job*	*Unemployed*
S.T.	60	0	0	10	20	10	5

Though, income of the villagers in monetary terms is not very high, still there is no dearth of the three basic necessities of life-viz. house, food and clothing. Money is required mainly to pay for school fees or for clothing. Many women weave cloth at home for wearing also. They weave lovely traditional shawls and mekhlas. Money for starting self-employment ventures comes only through the rural development schemes but none through other agencies like the National, Rural and Cooperative Banks, KVIC, Industry Department, Horticulture, Agriculture or Sericulture Department. No training either in school or thereafter is being given to educated, unemployed youth in the village. The banks are not favourably inclined to give them loans on the pretext of non-repayment of advances. Each household has its even share of cattle (1-2 per household) for farming, poultry (9-10 per household) for consumption at home, ducks (4-5 per household) for consumption, cat (1 per household) for consuming rats attacking the granary. All these animals are fed by locally produced grains from the fields and boiled yams. Even the cows are consumed after they grow old and are unfit for carrying on work in *khetis*.

Women have five self help groups. 10 women are members of each of these groups. They started it in 1999 by collecting Rs. 50 per month from all its members. After two years, they made a building for renting out. From here, they get a rent of Rs. 9,600 per year. This has become a source of income for them. Another self help group tried ginger plantation but due to lack of proper marketing facilities they incurred a loss of Rs. 25,000 in one year. This was because all of them produced ginger in that year but no corresponding markets for that huge quantity were explored. Another self help group is growing vegetables and selling them in the local market. One of the SHGs gives loans at 10 per cent per annum and the members keep the return on it as a profit. Under integrated wasteland development scheme, villagers have planted teak, arecanut, gamari, black pepper, ginger and turmeric. Teak reduces the fertility of the soil and yields Rs. 5,000 per tree only after 30 years. Thus, most of the villagers are now shifting to arecanut. The latter starts yielding fruit within 5-6 years of its sowing. Each tree gives a profit of around Rs. 500-600 per year and it lasts for longer. Black pepper and turmeric are recent introduction and hence their results are yet to be seen. Main advantage of having plantation in hills is that there shall be reduction in soil erosion and conservation of natural environment. *Jhuming* can also be done away with and foodgrains can be grown in *panikhetis*. The villagers undertake a number of non farm activities also. The chief ones can be mentioned as :

1. Carpentry : 10 units, small scale;
2. Weaving : 1 unit;
3. Loom : Almost all households have handloom;
4. Handicraft : 1;
5. Rice Mill : 5 small scale units;
6. Dairy : 6 units;
7. Shops : 4.

Other than this almost all houses rear pigs, as pork forms an essential part of the diet for the people of Nagaland.

The nearest market from where people purchase seeds, saplings for plantations is in Mokokchung, which is also the only market for the produce of the **Longkhum** village. There is a multi-purpose cooperative society in the village but unfortunately it is not involved in agriculture related activities. At present, its only activity is in operating a bus service to the district headquarters. By a rough estimate, the agricultural surplus of the village that is sold by the villagers consists of :

1. Around 1000-1200 tins of rice @ Rs. 50 per tin; and
2. 500-600 trucks of firewood @ Rs. 2500 per truck.

The approximate number of milch and other cattle in the village is:

1. Cows/buffaloes; 25
2. Pigs: 1000

Other than this each family has few chickens. In the forests around the village, there are around 50-60 deer, and around 20-30 wolves and antelopes. These numbers are rough estimates, obtained by what the elders of the village told me.

Migration is not a major issue for this village. On an average about 30 people migrate to places like Kohima, Dimapur, Mokokchung, Wokha, Mon etc. for working in saw mills, running shops, selling meat, for government jobs, as labour or for carpentry.

There is a person called Ayin in the **Longkhum** village who produces beautiful wood carvings. He has a lathe, which he has himself modified for his needs. He produces numerous articles. The wood for the carvings is obtained from the Gamhari trees of the nearby forest. He has not had any formal education or training, but anybody who sees his unit will agree that he is a genius. Unfortunately, he is not interested in marketing his products. He just gifts these articles to people who visit him in his village. He earns his living by making iron agricultural implements, which are not only sold within the village, but outside too. He also has a rice mill in the same premises. His wood products definitely have an export potential, if marketed properly.

There is no migration from the **Tsiese Basa** village as such. During the lean season some people do go out of the village to work in nearby areas. But they go out in he morning and come back in the evening. Most of the workforce is engaged in cultivation with a few government employees. No one works as agricultural labour in the village. In case of shortage of labour, help is provided by the community.

With the encouragement by the Rural Development Department to take up schemes and also the large scope of leaking out funds through this scheme, fisheries have become very popular, especially with those who can manage funds from the government either through district plan fund or any other method. However, in **Nerhema** village the VDB has also allocated money for a fishery pond for each of the *khels*. These ponds have been made, though without any expert guidance from the department concerned. Proper guidance is needed to make good and viable fishery ponds which can last for an economical period of time.

Horticulture in the form of banana plantations have also been recently undertaken by using the women's share of the VDB funds, though they are not commensurate with the funds allocated for them. Nobody seems to have any idea as to what they will do with the produce, as of now. It does not seem that this has been taken up for commercial purpose.

The credit needs of the individual in the village are very limited. Whatever money or food an individual needs to borrow, he/she borrows from his/her *khel* mates. This lending is on easy terms and usually is returned on the loanee getting his/her harvest. In some cases, the VDB also lends, however, this tradition is not so much in vogue in this area, although it is popular in other areas. There is no presence of any banking institution in the village. No bank is also present in the sub-divisional headquarters of Chiephobozou. The banking needs of the village are very limited, confined to the VDB accounts and the accounts of some of the rich contractors and the churches. This is catered to by the branches of the various banks situated in Kohima. The lending experience of the banks in Kohima is not encouraging enough for the banks to think of any expansion on these lines in the villages and the subdivision. The default rate is as high as 99 per cent. No cooperatives are operative in the village.

The tribal society has many features which should be envied upon by the plains people of India. Amongst these, one of the features is a casteless society where everybody is treated with equal respect and has an equal share in the common resources of the village community. There are, because of this, very rare cases of any exploitation amongst the villagers. There are no permanent employers or employees. Whatever work is done, is done to supplement the basic income got from cultivation. The employers are the relatively bigger farmers with small families, government servants (for cultivation of their fields), the village council (for VDB works, etc.). The compensation is either in kind or cash. The wages given are much above the ones specified in the Minimum Wages Act and hence it is not applicable here. There is no instance of practice of any kind of bonded labour in this area.

The population of the village is engaged mainly in agriculture or agriculture related activities. Most of the population have only just enough to last them through the year. The question of savings in the form of money does not arise. The only savings which are done are in the form of rice/paddy. In the old days, even the criteria for determining the richness was the amount of paddy that the person has in store. Even now, in some of the remote villages this is followed, though with the creeping in of the modern civilization this is changing as has been the case in this village. Now-a-days, the concept of richness is more property oriented. In spite of this there are some rich persons and educated government servants, mostly having a foothold in the towns also who will be having certain savings in their accounts in the towns. The total absence of the banking facilities (even the post office is not there) certainly hampers whatever can be done towards this side.

As has been described elsewhere in the report also, there has been a limited penetration of the markets in the villages. The only real penetration which has really taken place is in the area of timber logging, where the effect has been the almost complete wiping out of the original forests (what is now-a-days to be seen is only the regrowth), and firewood export from the villages. Firewood is still exported to the plain areas and in the months from January to April, the roadsides are lined with stacks of firewood waiting to be carried away by trucks. The income from these firewood stacks is usually used to supplement for other expenditure like food for consumption. However, there are 8-9 cases where the families have become rich by selling their timbers (which may be more than the rest) and have built houses at Kohima or Dimapur. One case was there of a person running a bus service also.

Beyond this, there has not been any permanent creation of employment with the bulk of the trade from the towns being still routed through the Marwaris. The nearest town of Kohima caters to most of the commercial needs of the village. There are only a few shops in the village, which also stock only *pan* and a few groceries bought from Kohima and available at a much higher rate than in Kohima. The only source of employment other than self-employment is the government, with nobody in the village working in any private company/industry (there is no industry in the hills).

The main occupation of the majority of the people in the **Longjemdang** village is cultivation. All the households have land, either *jhum* land on the slopes, or flat land where they can do permanent cultivation. The villagers are carrying out wet rice cultivation on these lands. With the spread of wet rice cultivation *jhum* cultivation has come down and now only six to seven households out of 102 households are doing *jhum* cultivation, and these people are the ones, who do not have land for wet rice cultivation.

The cultivation is carried out mainly through hired labour. The labour is involved in all the things and he takes half of the produce in the end. The household also works along with him, provides him with directions, and if needs be, also advances him money and other things. Of course, there are a few households, which does not go for share cropping. They do hire labour, but the bulk of the work is done by themselves. Big households and especially those, whose lands are near and not scattered, go for this. In the survey of 30 households I came across only 4 households not going for share cropping.

Almost every household has a betel leaf farm of some acres. Many have betel nut farms too, but these are less than the betel leaf farms. The betel leaf farms are mostly of 1 to 3 acres. Both these farms have been developed by the villagers in the forests of the *jhum* fields. Since the betel leaf creepers love shade, these are towards the side of the hills where sunlight is not all that strong. The households, which have these farms, spend quite some time in looking after these and during the season collect the leaves for selling outside. Thus the most important subsidiary occupation of the households can be said to be plantation work.

The villagers are busy throughout the year. From August to December they are busy in the rice field. Since the fields are quite far, many go there and stay with the labourers, and do things along with them. From November to February many keep themselves busy in growing vegetables. Besides the plain fields, many households also grow them in the *jhum* fields. January onwards the households gets busy with the betel leaf farms. All the members of the household go to the farms, collect the leaves, make bundles and bring it back to the village to be sold later in the market. This thing lasts till April and by May end the household are again back into the field to make it suitable for rice cultivation. So we can see that the villagers are always at work on something or the other.

For arriving at the total income of the households in the village, one thing has to be looked into. The first thing is that very few households are selling their agricultural produce into the market. Out of the 30 interviewed only 4 had some surplus to sell in the market, which is 13 per cent of the total. For the village taken together too, the percentage would be 10 per cent. So when people are asked about their income, all those who used all the rice for themselves and had nothing to sell in the market did not count this as their income. But for the income purpose this has been counted as income because if they had not got this rice, then they would have had to buy from the market spending money on this. Hence, whatever rice a household has got, after leaving out the share given to the labourers has been put into the income, at the rate at which rice has been sold in the market. Similar is the case with potatoes too, which every household grows and very few manage to sell.

The income of the villagers is from many sources. Rice is the number one, followed by betel leaves. In some cases, however, betel leaf is the number one. Those who have jobs, for them their salaries is the most important source. A lot of households rear pigs and whenever they have sold pig meat, it has contributed a lot to the income. Every household has drought animals, but except one, I did not come across anybody else earning money out of it by hiring it out. The following brings out the importance of a particular income source. It shows the percentage of households for which a particular income source is number 1, number 2 or number 3.

Source	*Number 1*	*Number 2*	*Number 3*
Rice	57%	27%	—
Betel Leaf	20%	47%	7%
Job/Pension	10%	—	10%

It is seen that in more than half the cases the rice obtained from fields is the most important income source. Betel leaf is the number two source for many while for 20 per cent people it is the most important especially those who have large farms for these. 20 per cent of the people have jobs and some get pension, which make these sources important for them.

The total annual income of the households when taken from all the sources varies from Rs. 2,000 to Rs. 1,20,000. The minimum income of Rs. 2,000 is of an old widow who has just some land for wet rice cultivation whereas the highest income is of a household who is a Class III government servant.

In the village nobody having a problem of two square meals a day, not even those who are in the lowest income bracket. Everybody has land and further the community structure is so strong that if ever, somebody faces problems the others are there to help him. Besides, the people for their many minor needs are dependent on the forests that are there in the village land and which everybody has access to. Fish, many type of edible things, timber which otherwise would have cost money are available in the forests. Thus even those who are not having much visible income are able to live well enough.

In the end, it would not be out of place to mention that in many cases the villagers are not utilizing all their resources properly. They have a lot of land especially the *jhum* land, which they can use for increasing the area of the betel farm and thus earn more revenue. These betel leaves have a ready market not only in the nearby areas but also in Assam, which is some 40 kilometres from the village. The villagers can also increase the yield of their produce of rice by using things like fertilizer and good seeds. If these things along with some others are done the income would be much more than this.

POVERTY ALLEVIATION PROGRAMMES

The villages are getting funds through rural development department from the centrally sponsored schemes and the State government's grant in aid scheme. At the district level, DRDA is the implementing and monitoring agency. However, at the village level VDB gets the funds directly from the DRDA. The VDB is an elected body of the village with 10 members in this village. Each *khel* has elected 2 members for the VDB. These members in turn elect their secretary. The secretary should have a minimum educational qualification of matriculation and above. The VDB is elected for 3 years. The DC is ex-officio chairman of the VDB of the villages under his jurisdiction. He has appointed the Secretary of the VDB are being operated jointly by the chairman and secretary of the management committee of the VDB. Every year, VDB shall have a general body meeting, wherein all the villagers shall attend and decide upon which works are to be undertaken and which beneficiaries are to be selected. They shall make a resolution and submit it to the BDO who shall make a technical estimate of the selected schemes. This shall be submitted to the DRDA. After approval, these schemes shall be taken up by the VDB. The share of funds of the VDB shall be deposited in its account. After completion of the work, the BDO shall go and verify the work on the spot and give completion certificate, which they shall submit, to the DRDA. Only after submission of the completion certificate, the funds shall be released by the Bank through draft, which is signed by the chairman DRDA and VDB Secretary jointly. The VDB maintains accounts is great detail as these are subject to annual audit. Under the centrally sponsored schemes, money is equally divided among the house tax paying households in all the VDBs in the entire State. The State government's rural development department provides grants-in-aid to every VDB every year, according to the number of households therein.

Out of the grant in aid money, the VDBs are required to put 10 per cent into their fixed deposits with the Nagaland State Cooperative Bank. Also, whatever income they get out of the VDB schemes is supposed to be deposited into the post office savings account. Once their savings reach Rs. 2.5 lakh, the government gives on time matching cash grant to the VDB. The VDB is not allowed to withdraw any money from the fixed deposit until the VDB passes a resolution to that effect and the chairman VDB approves it.

This VDB was established in the year 1980 and has been getting regular funding from the government since then. Out of all the funds meant for the VDB, 25 per cent are exclusively for women and 20 per cent for youth welfare schemes.

Most of the works taken up are for making rural infrastructure as roads, ring wells, rural housing, marketing shed, etc. The works are thus chosen as shall benefit the entire village. Moreover, the income from them is also used as income of the village as a whole and not of a particular household. For construction of rural infrastructure, the labour employed is mainly Bangladeshi Muslim immigrants and the local villagers gain only through the infrastructure developed in the village as a result. Only under IAY, rural housing is given to the needy people.

In **Medziphema** village, people take up handloom, handicraft and animal rearing during the lean agricultural season. Thus, EAS does not have much significance in the State. However, the village does need funds for development of rural infrastructure, which is provided for under the EAS. Last year, the villagers took up metalling and soling of the village approach road for 1.82 km. For wages, Rs. 32,750 was given along with 2 bags of rice. Thus, generating 3,275 mandays of employment. In addition, Rs. 21,850 was given for buying materials required for construction of approach road. Again labour employed for this work was mainly hired one from outside the village though the infrastructure thus made shall be used by all the villagers.

Beneficiary	*Days for which employed*	*Wages received*	*Mode of wage payment*
Entire village	3275	Rs. 32750	Rs. 10 cash/day + rice

SGSY: No work has been taken up in the village under SGSY.

In the last one year—Out of women share (25%) of the total—one marketing shed costing Rs. 50,000 was constructed at **Medziphema** and it is being used on the weekly market day. Out of the youth share (20%) a youth welfare centre has been made at the cost of Rs. 27,300. Here, they have also saved some amount to celebrate annual sports meet.

Rest of the general share for the VDB has been used for tree plantation on 12 hectares of land.

Wasteland Department—Under the integrated wasteland development programme, the department has taken up construction of one public latrine as an entry point activity, according to the felt need of the villagers. They have also given Rs. 12,000 as seed money to one self help group in the village to take up piggery. Now, they have given teak, gamari, arecanut, black pepper, ginger and turmeric saplings, for planting on the fallow village land. They are planning to take up contour bunding to prevent soil erosion on the hilly terrain. Later, they shall make water tank and promote fishery in the village. This has been only a recent intervention and thus, is still under progress. Thus, it is difficult to evaluate it as yet.

As per the baseline survey conducted in the **Longkhum** village by the DRDA, there are around 200 households which are below the poverty line.

IRDP: The last baseline survey to identify the beneficiaries was done in 1990. The beneficiaries are selected by the Village Development Board through consultations with village council. The VDB has got representation of all the classes in the **Longkhum** village. The VDB lists down all the families below poverty line. There are 15 classes in all. Each year around 5 to 6 beneficiaries are selected by rotation among the various classes. The most poor person of a particular class is selected by the representative of the class in the VDB. The names are approved in a joint meeting of the VDB and the village council and their names are then sent to the government. The Block and bank officers, then verify the selected beneficiary. Forms, etc. are filled through the VDB by the beneficiaries. The favourite schemes under IRDP are piggery, dairy and fishery. The amount of money that is given under each is as below :

Sl. No.	*Schemes*	*Total*	*Loan*	*Subsidy*
1.	Piggery	14000	7000	7000
2.	Dairy	18000	9000	9000
3.	Fishery	12000	6000	6000

Most beneficiaries get the money, but do not start the work. The recovery also is not on schedule. Most beneficiaries do not understand the concept of loans and as a result, there is misuse of funds.

The selection of beneficiaries seems to be more or less fair. But there has been instances when names of people above the poverty line are recommended. In some cases wives of the government servant are selected as beneficiary.

TRYSEM : No IRDP beneficiary has been given training under TRYSEM. Some women members were given training in weaving.

IAY: Selection of beneficiaries is done by the **Longkhum** village council and the VDB. Mostly, the poorest, who are in need of houses are selected. Generally 3 beneficiaries are selected every year. This year, a woman with no male dependants was selected and the whole village is helping her to construct the house. The problem is that the full amount of Rs. 20,000 is not given to the beneficiary. They are provided with just 3 bundles of CGI sheets. Rest of the material required is arranged locally. Thus year the VDB has got 10 bundles of CGI sheets under IAY. There are four DWACRA groups in the village. Their groups have been formed through the Village Development Board's Women Welfare group. I met several groups and am giving the details of the functioning of one of the groups. There are 15 members and they belong to all the *khels* in the village. It was started in 1996 and they got Rs. 8,000 from the government. They started weaving on the powerloom in the village and made 40 shawls and sold them, they made a profit of Rs. 1,800 on a loan amount of Rs. 5,000. They also planted vegetables like ginger. The balance loan amount of Rs. 3,000 was given to the people in the village as loans at 5 per cent interest. They have a bank deposit of Rs. 1,000 and the group plans to put the money that is earned or saved in the bank. But they had no knowledge of the interest that they get in the bank. For using the powerloom in the village, they paid Rs. 25 per mekhla/shawl as hiring charges. The group feels that they can have greater profits in agriculture. The group was aware of schemes like MCY though there are very few accounts. They are not involved in adult literacy schemes. They have not been given any training

JRY: The **Longkhum** village is covered under JRY since 1989. The fund allocated to the village for the year 1995-96 is Rs. 1,30,000. This has been approved for the following schemes :

1. Link roads (2 km)—Rs. 1,00,000 (Lachenba)
2. Public wells: (a) Rs. 15,000 (Longpangtsuba); and (b) Rs. 15,000 (Sungumerok)

Of the two public wells, only one has been constructed. The interesting feature of JRY, here, is that no wages are paid for the works that are undertaken. The works are done through community participation by everyone. The funds earmarked for wages under JRY are then distributed proportionately among the three *khels* and there are then used to create more assets. The panchayat bhawan in the 3 *khels* have been constructed in this manner. Other schemes that have been completed include public well, stairs, playground, etc. People generally feel that the works are of good enough quality. Some of them are indeed in need of wages, but they cannot do anything as the village council takes decisions for the whole village.

The schemes that are undertaken under EAS are very confusing. There is lot of duplication under the sense that the same works are pointed out under the EAS, JRY and RD schemes of the VDB. However, some stairs have been made and there is a big plantation with a broad saying that it was done under EAS, 1995-96. The VDB secretary's records the expenditure under EAS for 1995-96 as follows :

1. Labour charge—Rs. 80,000
2. Purchase of materials—Rs. 28,940
3. Library Hall (Students)—Rs. 90,000

Village Development Board Schemes: The State government provides funds to the village development boards to undertake rural development schemes. The allocation of funds is at the rate of Rs. 750 per household. Thereafter, 25 per cent of the funds is given to the women BDB group and 20 per cent to the youth development programme to undertake schemes specific to women and to the youths. The breaking of the schemes planned for 1996-97 are :

RD Schemes

1. Community fishing pond Rs. 30,000
2. Marketing shed—Rs. 15,000
3. Culvert, 2 No.—Rs. 30,000
4. Block topping—Rs. 68,750 (Total Rs. 1,43,750)

Women VDB

1. Granary—Rs. 36,000
2. Weaving (2 units)—Rs. 20,000
3. Bee Keeping Box—Rs. 4,000 (Total Rs. 60,000)

Youth Development Programme

1. Waiting shed—Rs. 10,000
2. Experimental scheme—Rs. 10,000
3. Cultural Goods—Rs. 20,000 (Total Rs. 40,000)

The women VDB group has 4 handlooms. They have an instructor from Manipur, who is being paid Rs. 1,500 per month. They have 6 trainees per year. The looms have been brought from Imphal at a cost of Rs. 20,000. The money for these have been paid from the women's share of the VDB. The VDB gets hiring charges for the looms at the rate of Rs. 25 per mekhla or shawls. They plan to get into more activities and buy more :

1. Ginger : They sold it at the rate of Rs. 7 per kg and used the money for office expenditure.
2. Bee keeping : They have 5 boxes but do not have sufficient bees and so in a failure.
3. They want to undertake some experimental schemes but are not very clear, how to do and what to do.

They do not have any coordination with the DWACRA groups. They are also not aware of the schemes like MSY. The youth development programme is supposed to undertake schemes specific to youths. They do have a library which is fairly well equipped. But there is tremendous scope for they being able to undertake more schemes rather than just duplicating the work being done under the general RD schemes. They have 500 members and all are youths above the age of 13 and so should be playing a much greater role.

As the **Tsiese Basa** village is entirely composed of STs, there is no separate caste-wise distribution; the total BPL population would be 130. But the records of BPL are not properly updated. There was only one IRDP beneficiary during last year. The scheme taken up was piggery. Under JRY work was done on the school building. About 150 mandays were generated under JRY. There is one DWACRA group in the village, which has 15 members. The activity being undertaken is kitchen gardening. No training has been given under TRYSEM.

There was only one IRDP beneficiary in the Tsiese Basa village. He had been provided the loan for piggery. The beneficiary was selected by the village council. The loan component was Rs. 6,000 and the subsidy was Rs. 7,500. Subsidy component is given only after the repayment of the loan component.

The beneficiary was selected by the village council after going through the BPL list. The scheme is not functioning any longer. In JRY, work was done to improve the school building. The wage rates for men and women are different. While men get Rs. 70 per day, the women get only Rs. 40 per day. The payments were made in cash and no contractor was employed. Though there was a slight improvement in the living conditions, it was not very significant considering that the employment was for 5-7 days only.

The Jawahar Rozgar Yojana (JRY): handled in the State by RD Directorate through the 28 RD Blocks into which the State is divided. On the basis of suggestions made by the State government, the Government of India approved of the allotment of JRY funds directly to the VDBs on the basis of tax paying households in the government recognized village, subject to a minimum and maximum. This is done on the same principles and procedures as laid down for the administration of funds by the VDBs under the grant-in-aid programme of the State government. Various schemes, the selection of which is left with the VDB under a set of guidelines to ensure that the projects are best suited to the local conditions and needs, which include social forestry, rural housing and sanitation, school buildings, drinking water wells, rural roads and fishery ponds, etc. have been taken up. These schemes are also implemented by the VDBs under the supervision of the administrative staff. The BDOs prepare the estimates, the technical assistance is extended by the department concerned and the verification is done by both the administrative officer and the BDO (at least theoretically, this all needs to be done). The VDB was originally formed by the village councils in the form of a committee to manage the village funds generated from the common property resources. It was a delegated authority until 1980, when it was formalized in form of a set of Model Rules to regulate its functioning. Thus today in Nagaland, the VDBs are the development bodies in the villages, meant to function in coordination (as an arm of the village council) with the village council having a legal status. They have been constituted *vide* order (known as the Village Development Boards Model Rules, 1980 as revised lastly in 1989, by the State government in exercise of the powers conferred by Section 50 (1) of the Nagaland Village and Area Council Act, 1978.

The following points about the functioning of the VDB were noticed on interaction with the VDB and VC members, VDB Secretary, the villagers and going through the VDB accounts :

1. The accounts are maintained by the VDB Secretary appointed by the village council, according to rules laid down in the VDB Act and orders passed from time to time by the State government. These accounts, in this village (the practice varies from VDB to VDB) are audited and approved from time to time by a committee appointed by the village council (the persons auditing are not professionals).
2. The VDB Secretary in this village is given an allowance of 3 per cent of the JRY funds received in that year. This is only this VDBs innovation and is not necessarily found in the other VDBs. This allowance is to compensate the VDB Secretary for the work he puts in, since he does not receive any other amount for this work done by him. A commission at the rate of 1 per cent of the JRY funds for the year is given to the village council as its fees.

3. While in this village the VDB Secretary was/is quite honest because of the check of the village council and other members of the VDB, even to the extent of maintaining bills for photostating, tea, etc. in some cases the VDB members are not as honest and are prone to misappropriating the VDB money. However, the honesty of the VDB Secretary alone does not ensure the implementation of the schemes, because if the VDB/village council decides to just distribute the money without doing any work, there is no check on this as the administrative officers who are supposed to verify the schemes, due to various reasons, usually do not perform their duties.
4. The auditing and accounting, as can be seen from the accounts itself, is not an elaborate affair according to the traditional definition, in the absence of any guidelines for such auditing, but is just there to check any misappropriations (matching of the columns), and as the committee is appointed by the village council from amongst the educated villagers, that independence and objectivity is not there. The verification of the schemes is not there at all. In some villages, even this auditing and accounting is not done. In fact, even no accounts books are maintained.
5. Even from the above account keeping, it is not possible to trace out (all inquiries are also in vain) as to where the (a) Interest amount from FDs and Savings Account, (b) House rent from the buildings built in Dimapur, etc., (c) Interest on some loans extended by the VDB, and (d) Cash received from Ministers, etc., is utilized. Some instances are there of the interest being distributed amongst the different *khels* of the village.
6. There is a tendency, not only in this village but in other villages also to lay stress on approach roads and construction of buildings. An amount of Rs. 2,01,200 has already been spent on the laying down of roads from 1980-81 till 1992 and still an amount of Rs. 3,61,000+ has been laid down in the years 1993-94 and 1994-95 for this purpose. Even at the current approved rates of the PWD, this should have resulted in a length of road of at least 3 km (if we take inflation into account, then at least 1.10 kms stretch should have been

there). However, though some road is there, the quality is very poor, being a kutcha road and the length also will not be as much. This indicates distribution of money amongst the villagers. Though, this is a diversion of money but still the money is at least reaching the lowest levels.

Similarly, in the case of buildings, buying of CGI sheets for rooftops is an area which gives rise to some leakage of funds at the departmental level, as these are supplied by contractors, etc. Thus, even the RD department ensures some leakage by insisting on the model schemes like buildings, approach roads, etc. Steps which can be taken to improve the functioning of the VDBs :

1. The auditing and accounting can be tightened up. A specified format can be recommended for keeping the records. This will make it easier for the DC and other administrative officer to go through the accounts. This step should not be difficult as the format will be according to the rules only and as the VDB Secretary is an educated man, it will not be difficult for him to fill it up.
2. Although the step above can bring about a better accountability in terms of the account keeping, the implementation portion depends very highly on the verification to be carried out by the administrative officer. Usually, the administrative officer who is of the level of an EAC or SDO (C) and being a local succumbs to tribal pressures and signs without actual verification. This has to be rectified. One approach is through tightening of the administration by proper training underlining the importance of the schemes and its implementation, so that the officers are provided with the necessary moral authority and strength to resist these pressures. The other approach is to try out new systems, e.g. having photographs of the schemes along with, though this can be easily manipulated. The best approach is for the DC to sufficiently motivate his team of officers by providing various incentives, etc.
3. More schemes need to be introduced, otherwise the same schemes, e.g. playgrounds, etc. are being repeated. Stress needs to be shifted to some income generating schemes. Though some schemes, e.g. VDB buses are coming out by

the initiative of the VDBs themselves, the role of the innovator and the philosophical guide needs to be played more effectively and thoroughly by the administrative officers as well as the RD department officers.

4. The BDO does not come under the control of the administrative officer right now. This should be modified to have the BDO under the control of the DC/ADC.
5. A mechanism needs to be evolved to have a coordinated effort between the VDBs of an area to develop the total infrastructure of that area and not limit themselves only to the village concerned. For this, the area councils (modified from the original version) can be restarted.

The following points need to be noted in respect of the IRDP scheme implementation in this village (applicable in other villages of northern Angami area also) :

1. The choosing of beneficiaries is in the hand of the village council which decides as to which *khel* will be given the opportunity to choose the beneficiary. This is usually done by rotation. The *khel* elders then meet and decide as to which person to choose from amongst the *khel* people.
2. Usually the poorest/most needy person is chosen but at the discretion of the elders (depending on the clout they have) exceptions can be and are made. The most needy person chosen can be a person who for some reason has not been able to get any produce from his/her land that year. This can, thus be looked on as an extension of the already existing tradition in the villages/*khels* of looking after the basic needs (just the basic) of the old and the aged.
3. Except for 2-3 cases no training was ever imparted to any of the chosen beneficiaries.
4. The money is usually released by the government (SRDA is the nodal agency for implementing the IRDP scheme) in the last months of the financial year only. This indicates some sort of misuse of the funds throughout the year, e.g. by depositing them in short term fixed deposits and siphoning off the interest amount thereof.

5. No extension facilities, e.g. veterinary medical aid, education/training, help in choosing the right scheme, animals, etc. are ever provided. In fact, the extension officers who are supposed to be stationed at nearby Chiephobozou operate from Kohima only and never pay a visit to the village. A suggestion is to get the extension officers accountable to the village councils of the areas (or at least the SDOs) by having their ACRs go through them.
6. The money provided in some cases is used for consumption expenditure only and no assets are purchased. In some cases money is partly used for the scheme while the rest is used for consumption expenditure.
7. The animals kept under the scheme are used for consumption as meat (pigs, cattle especially) during some family function, e.g. marriage, etc. In cases where the animal is sold off, the money received is again used for some festivities. Also, the sale price is not commensurate with the inputs (in some villages, however, the village councils have fixed the minimum sale price of meat, so that no loss occurs). Also the mortality rate of animals is high.
8. As milk is not preferred as a food item, dairy schemes are only cattle schemes for production of meat.
9. There is no change in the poverty status of the family because of this scheme only. If no other inputs from other quarters are there, the family relapses to the same status after some time. So, the overall impact is just to raise the level of life (festivities) for some time. In fact, nobody seems to be bothered too much about these schemes. It is just a small aberration in the otherwise normal life of the villager (only a stop gap arrangement—sharing of the loot attitude).

In the **Longjemdang** village, out of 102 households, 42 are in the BPL list. Thus 41 per cent of the people are in the list. Looks a big figure, but actually it is quite possible because some 56 per cent of the households have income below Rs. 20,000 per annum, and to be in the list one should have an income below the level mentioned above. However, it is not that everybody who is in the list should have been necessarily there. In my survey I came across 15 BPL families and out of that 2 have income well beyond Rs. 20,000.

Similarly there are many people who have been left out. I came across 11 households whose income is less than Rs. 20,000 but they are not in the BPL list. Nobody has an answer as to why these people are not in the list. It seems that the survey for short listing people in the BPL list have not been done properly. The villagers say that those people who have been left out would be included the next time the list is made.

For the last many years, the schemes taken up in the village have been under four types of programmes. One is the Jawahar Rojgar Yojana now known as Jawahar Gram Samriddhi Yojana, the second one is Employment Assurance Programme, the third one is Swarn Gram Swarojgar Yojana and the last one programme under Grants-in-Aid.

Under the JGSY/JRY some 30 to 35 per cent people have been benefited. Almost always, the households have got money under this scheme for converting their houses from a totally thatched one to a semi-thatched one where the walls would be of bamboo and timber, and the roof made up of CGI sheets. The reason for this is that, sometimes in the last decade the government took a decision to make the roofs of all the houses in the village of CGI sheet. Initially, people used to be given only money but now, they are given 5 sheets of CGI alongwith some money. The money given is to be used in paying wages to the labourers who would be employed in building the house. However, in the village, people rather than hiring labour, do the work themselves. At times, the neighbours and other villagers also come and work. This they do, not for money, but because of a tradition where if a new house is being built, the villagers are to work there and help in building the house. This applies to everybody and hence there is no need to resort to wage labour. The money portion is used by the household in buying some more things needed for house construction. In the last three years, money has been given for construction of 3 houses. In 1999, an amount was also given for construction of approach road to the village.

The JGSY/JRY scheme has been for quite some time and people are well aware of it because many have been benefited from it. The scheme is supposed to generate wage labour, but here in the village it is not, because there is no need to hire labour. However, the benefit is visible because a lot of house have CGI roofs and since in Nagaland it rains a lot, it is good to have a sturdy roof.

Another programme, which though has not lead to a lot of visible changes but nevertheless known by all the people, is the EAP or Employment Assurance Programme. In the last three years money has been given under this programme for construction of approach road. The money provided is quite insufficient to build a concrete road. Hence, what is done is that, every year a stretch of road is taken up. The earth is dug, boulders and rocks are broken and the path is filled up with it, and finally it is made even by bulldozers. The path thus becomes good enough to be made use by the vehicles. For doing all this, the Village Council first calls a meeting of the people. Some days are decided on which everybody would have to come and work on the approach road. Wages are not given in cash, nor are foodgrains given. What is done is, food is cooked for all the people who come to work for those days. One of the items is necessarily pork, which the people here like very much. In the survey I found that people are quite happy with this arrangement. However, the thing is that while calling people for work no differentiation is made. All able-bodied males willing to work are welcome. It does not matter whether the household is really in the need of the work. Thus those households really in need of some extra money do not get the whole advantage, which they would have got if they were doing the whole thing unlike now where everybody comes and the work does not even three days. Anyway, this is a traditional way of doing things, and in fact all the community things are taken up in this way.

The SGSY is only 2 years old and under this, only two schemes have been taken up. One is the Self-Help Group or SHG of 18 members formed for betel nut plantation. A total of Rs. 49,500 have been allotted to this SHG, out of which, 50 per cent is subsidy. The SHG has a President and Secretary. The members have received training from the Agricultural and Horticultural officers and even otherwise since betel nut farming has been done for a long time in the village the villagers have a fair idea about this. The members have high hopes from the plantation and the Block officials are also of the opinion that it would be successful. In the village, community structure is strong and programmes like this have a fair change of succeeding. The other scheme, is for a piggery farm, to be developed by an individual.

Besides all this, the villagers also get money under Grants in Aid. The money under this programme can be used for both community benefits as well as for creating individuals assets. All those things, which cannot be taken up in any other schemes but are important nevertheless, are done in this programme. The amount depends on the number of households a village has. And at times, it has been more than the other schemes. In 1995-96, besides construction of houses; things like plantation and construction of granary wall were taken up. In 1996-97 the rice mill in the village was repaired and some footsteps were constructed in the later years, a waiting shed and a youth hall have been made. Thus a variety of programmes have been taken up and most of them have been the long-standing need of the people.

A look at the things done in the village reveals that the works are being done and much of the credit should go to the Village Council. It is a powerful body and having representation from all the clans is quite democratic. It ensures that, things are done properly. However, it is felt that, many a time, the things, which should have been given the first priority, are not being taken up. Every fourth person in the village feels that much good would come, if the other streams in the village land were also dammed. The water would then be used to irrigate more land and thus develop the wet rice cultivation even further. However, the amount required is substantial, more than what is given in schemes. Of course, if the money of all the schemes are combined and with some more funds, it is quite possible. But then, the money under each scheme can only be spent under some guidelines. What is required in fact, is some more flexibility in utilizing the funds. The DRDA should be allowed to have some say in this matter and money should be provided for the most pressing thing.

VILLAGE LEVEL INSTITUTIONS (PRIs)

The provisions of 73rd Constitutional Amendments do not apply to the State of Nagaland. This is because the State already has village and area councils constituted under the corresponding Act of 1979. The village council of **Medziphema** village has 17 members including the chairman. It is elected after an interval of 5 years. The members have to be citizens of India and not less than 25 years of age. The village council meets every 3 months.

Functions

1. To formulate village development schemes and to supervise their implementation.
2. To help various government agencies in carrying out development works in the village.
3. To act as a guarantor for any villagers wanting to take loan from a bank or a financial institution.
4. To collect house tax for onward submission to the Administrative Officer.
5. To resolve disputes, the matter can be referred to the concerned Administrative Officer or to a joint sitting of the concerned village councils.
6. Maintenance of law and order within the jurisdiction of the village and report any case of unnatural death or other offence or presence of strangers, vagabonds or suspects or outbreak of epidemics to the area's Administrative Officer.

All members of the **Medziphema** village council are men. There is no woman member. They have 1 chairman and 1 secretary. The election of members and decisions taken by the council are totally democratic. As the society is more or less egalitarian in terms of socio-economic status, there is no influence of any kind while getting elected as a member of the village council or discharging their duties. The village council chairman is also a member of the village education committee, which has to run the village primary school.

It is important to note that the 73rd and 74th Amendments of the Constitution are not applicable to Nagaland. Nagaland has a unique system of local self government, where the villages are administered by the village councils which are formed as well as they function as per the traditional customs of the Nagas. **Longkhum** also has a village council which has around 50 members. The members are selected from the same age group, with each clan having proportional representation. The whole population of the village is basically divided into 5 *putus* (age groups) and the village council is formed from the members from the senior most *putu* or the age group. Presently, the ruling *putu* is Madamsanger for Mongsen and Kuchachanger for Chungli. A village council remains for 30 years. The equivalent of the Mukhiya of the Panchayat is the village council chairman. The village council has a meeting when there is a need. The council is responsible for the general maintenance of law and order in the village and it also dispenses justice according to the customary law. The chairman of the village council is Mr. Pongenchang and he is 75 years old. In this study, the produce of rice in the previous year has been regarded as a measure of the land owned by each household, since in the absence of proper land records and fixed fields, the land holding of each family is not known. Mr. Pongenchang got about 120 tins of rice, last year. A few other prominent members of the village council are :

Name	*M/F*	*Age*	*Religion*	*Tins of Rice*
Mr. Wati Imchen	M	63	Christian	200
Mr. Meya Nungsang	M	68	Christian	220
Mr. Kilen Zulu	M	69	Christian	220
Mr. Tali Sumaran	M	76	Christian	240
Mr. Imkong Nungsang	M	75	Christian	180
Mr. Meya Wati	M	68	Animist	230
Mr. Nokin Maithun	M	66	Christian	250

Christian Youth Endeavour (CYE) is an NGO that has its presence in each of the three *khels* of the village. It is basically concerned with involving the youth in activities related to the church. At the same time, it has a significant role to play in evolving youths and the students in cultural matters, music and sports.

Multi Purpose Cooperative Society, **Longkhum**: The multi purpose cooperative society in Longkhum was started with much fanfare in 1996. By definition, everyone is supposed to be a member of the MPCS. Each household was supposed to contribute a sum of Rs. 200. 224 households have paid this amount. The shareholding amount is Rs. 2,50,000 and the rest of the money is in the bank. The MPCS owns a minibus which they operate between Longkhum and Mokokchung. A retired army person is functioning as the secretary of the MPCS. The chairman of the MPCS is a mechanical engineer stationed at Dimapur. Incidentally he is the younger brother of the MLA who belongs to this village. The secretary of the MPCS was not very happy to talk about the functioning of the MPCS. Actually, the bus they are operating has run into a loss. The bus was bought by spending about Rs. 5,50,000 which the villagers had got for the work that they had done in the playground and for the approach road. They have one driver and one conductor. They spent Rs. 13,000 on insurance. The returns from the bus is Rs. 1500 daily. The expenses are around 50 litres of diesel for every 2 days. The driver is paid Rs. 2000 and the conductor is paid Rs. 1200. But the problem lies in the fact that of Rs. 60,000 on the repairs. The villagers generally feel that they did not get a good bus and they were cheated. Incidentally, the bus was purchased through the chairman of the MPCS. A rough financial accounting of the operation of the bus is given below for the period from August to January (6 months). Proceeds from ticket sales:

Monthly returns from ticket sales = 1,500 × 25 = Rs. 37,500
Expenses on fuel = 50 × 8 × 12.5 = Rs. 5,000
Payment to driver and conductor = Rs. 3,200
Expenses on repair = Rs. 10,000
Incidentals = Rs. 5,000
Total expenses = Rs. 23,200
Income-Rs. 14,300

This is quite less for a bus operator. Thus it has been difficult to sustain the bus. Moreover, some private bus operators are making much more money. However, the MPCS has planned a lot of things. They plan to start the following schemes :

1. Tea plantation—with a turnover of Rs. 4-5 lakh, and
2. A co-operative shop—to provide villager quality goods at reasonable rates.

In Nagaland there are village councils which are similar to the panchayats elsewhere. The development aspect is looked after by the Village Development Boards (VDB), which are a very vital institution in Nagaland. In **Tsiese Basa** also there is a well functioning Village Council and Village Development Board. There are 7 members of the Village Council with no lady member in the council. Elections are being held regularly and the VDB is playing an important role in the development activities in the village.

The main persons involved in **Nerhema** village politics are the village council chairman and members, the GBs and the church leaders. Ex-UGs who held some substantial post in the UG army set up (say, Colonel and above rank) are also involved in the political decisions making in the village as also are the present UG groups the NSCN (K) group is the prominent one in the village though the NSCN (I-M) also has cadres from the village.

The politics in the village revolves around the village council. The village council, which can be equated with the panchayats in the rest of the country is a body given legal sanction *vide* the Nagaland Village and Area Councils Act, 1978. The Village Council is not an idea imposed from above but is the case of giving legal sanction to an institution which has been existing over the ages in the villages of the Naga tribes. Thus, this has not resulted in something alien being experimented out with the simple tribal villagers. As the village councils were operational since ages, meeting out justice to offenders and practicing the traditional law, an oral tradition, of the village and maintaining order in the village. There has been no problems of acceptability and it is a functioning customary practice.

The village council chairman is elected by the villagers in a general meeting from amongst the candidates who are up for election. The general meeting is attended by all the villagers and anybody—man or woman—can speak at these villages (but usually its is the man who takes the lead. However, if a woman speaks, she is not ignored). The chairman, then has to overlook the functioning of the village council. He can be removed if he displeases the villagers at another general meeting. The villagers are usually very enthusiastic and serious about the functioning of the village council.

The **Nerhema** village council is supposed to look after the development activities (formulation of schemes, etc. through the VDB), administration of traditional justice within the village boundaries, maintenance of law and order within the village. The GBs, who have been appointed in the villages since British times are also members of the village council usually and are supposed to look after the law and order in the village and report any incident to the nearest administrative officer.

The equivalent to Village Panchayats in Naga villages are Village Councils. These Councils, whose existence are from the inception of the village itself, are much more powerful and important bodies than the Panchayat as we understand. They deal in almost all aspects and in the eyes of the villagers enjoy quite an exalted status. In 1978 an Act known as the Nagaland Village and Area Council was passed, in which the powers of the traditional village councils, their tenures, functions and other such things were laid down, but it was also mentioned that wherever Councils had been running based on traditional customs and practices for long, these rules were not to apply *in toto* but modified according to he things in practice.

The customs and practices are not the same everywhere. It varies from one village to another village. Thus in the whole of Mokokchung district, one has Councils having a tenure of 30 years as well as Councils having a life of 10 years. However the business of council is to be run, is a matter to be decided by the villagers themselves.

Longjemdang village has a Council consisting of ten members. Each of the four clans selects two members from the clan, to be a part of the Council. The remaining two members of the Village Council are the two Gaon Buras of the village. In each village, some people are appointed by the administration to be Gaon Buras. The Gaon Buras act as a link between the administration and the villagers. If anything occurs in the village or if anything is there which should come to the knowledge of the administration, it is the duty of the Gaon Buras to convey the matter to the administration. When something is required to be conveyed to the villagers the help of the Gaon Buras may be taken. The tradition of Gaon Buras dates back to the time when the British first came into contact with the Nagas. In Longjemdang, the two Gaon Buras are L. Supong and K. Supong. It is to be noted that though the appointment is done by the administration, who is to be a Gaon Bura, but it is decided by the villagers themselves. The Gaon Bura should enjoy the confidence of the people. He can be removed too, if the people so desire.

The Chiarman of the **Longjemdang** village is Mr. L. Supong. He is an important figure of the village by dint of his post. He has been in the present post for the last 8 years. The Council does not have any fixed tenure as such. As long as members enjoy the confidence of the villagers they continue. The members are chosen by the whole village. Whenever there is a vacancy in the Council in respect of a particular clan; the clan members of that Council in an open meeting forward the names of the people they want in the Council and if others do not have any objection they are selected. After this process is over, the selected names are sent to the Deputy

Commissioner for approval. Approval is always given unless some people of the village have objections. If there are objections then the concerned administrative officer goes to the village or calls the villagers and along with the Gaon Bura try to find out the real situation. Approval is given only when everything is sorted out. Such things are however not very common and in most of the cases, selection of members pass off smoothly.

In **Longjemdang** Village Council some members are four years old, others two years and some others just completing one year. The work of the Council at times gets a bit hectic and members who feel that they cannot cope up with the work load drop out and new members are selected. The Village Council members are as follows :

1. L. Subong
2. K.Supong
3. I. Nukcha
4. R. Tinu
5. T. Nungsang
6. Yinli
7. Tali Moa
8. Lanu Wathi
9. S. Supong
10. Tushi Meren

It is to be noted that there are no woman members. In fact, according to Ao customary law women are excluded from the Councils. Since, according to the 1978 Act, customary practices are to be followed; one cannot direct the villagers to have woman members.

Twice in a year, in the months of June and December, there is an open meeting where all the villagers assemble and discuss all the matters relevant to the Village Council. Attendance in this meeting is compulsory. The matters normally taken up are: the things which should be done in the village, how much the wage rates should be, during what months the villagers should pluck the betel leaves and fines imposed for not following this, and besides all these any other issue which is important enough to be discussed.

The Village Council is a Court too. All the disputes in the village are first brought before it for settlement. The Village Council can try any type of cases, even as grave as a murder case. The whole Council sits and the judgment is by a majority. Fines are imposed on the guilty person. The fine is mostly in the form of pigs, fowls and in some other cases in the form of money. If the crime is a big one, it may also lead to banishment from the village and the property and land may be confiscated by the Council. If the parties to the dispute are satisfied with the judgement, the case or dispute does not go any further. However, if it is not so, then case comes to the Direct Court. More often than not, the case gets settled at the village level. People have faith in their Councils and these bodies too, try their best to be unbiased.

In **Longjemdang** village, the disputes coming to the Council for settlement have been mostly land disputes. The boundaries between the lands of the villagers are not marked out very properly and sometimes it becomes difficult to exactly know the extent of one's land. Besides this, there are disputes arising due to acts of misbehaviour.

The Village Council for its functioning requires money. Besides, many a time the Council members have to go to other village or towns in connection with some village work and for this too, they need money. Hence all the households in the village contribute an amount to the Village Council. All the money coming to the Council are accounted for, and every year a team consisting of some villagers who are not the members of the Council is formed to scrutinize the accounts. This way there is a check on the money under the disposal of the Village Council.

In 1980, the State Government for better management of development works in village established Village Development Board in every village. The members of the VDB, as it is popularly known, are chosen by the villagers. The number of members can be from five to twenty-five. In Longjemdang village the number of members is seven. One among them is chosen as VDB secretary. His main work is to act as the administrative head of the VDB and liaison with the government agencies. Government servants are normally not to be members of the VDB. However, if there are no literate members in the village then they may be part of the VDB. The tenure of the VDB members is three years unless decided otherwise by the Village

Council by a resolution. The VDB works under the overall supervision of the Village Council.

In **Longjemdang**, every year in an open meeting the VDB comes up with the schemes, which it thinks should be implemented in the village. The whole village deliberates on it and if the majority approves it is accepted by the village. These schemes are then put up to the BDO and if he finds them feasible and practicable he forwards to the Deputy Commissioner through District Rural Development Agency. Once approved the works are taken up. In case of individual benefits under some programme the persons are decided by the Village Council. In the village are giving benefits turnwise. One has to wait for his turn. However, one may be given out of turn benefit if the economic condition is too bad and the Council feels so. In the survey everybody mentioned this and it seems that the system is working fine.

Some members of the VDB, are members of the Village Council too. This is done to ensure that the Council can constantly look into the things of VDB. The VDB's accounts are constantly checked by the Council. Besides this, every year an independent team is set up by the villagers to check the accounts. This is effective because I am told by the villagers that some years back such a team while checking the accounts came across gross irregularities committed by the VDB secretary. This was reported to the Village Council and a decision was taken to confiscate the property of the VDB secretary, recoup the money from its sale and banish the culprit out of the village. That VDB secretary had to leave the village and lose all his property. Acts like this have made sure that the wo.kings of the bodies are above board.

Since in the Village Council woman members are not allowed, the government decided to have woman members in the VDB to let them also have a say in the development matters. If the village desires a separate women VDB can also be formed and some percentage of the development funds have to necessarily go to them. In **Longjemdang** village a woman VDB is working. Though one cannot say it to be as much active as the other one yet its view is respected. Some years back the women VDB utilized the developmental funds to set up a rice mill in the village. That rice mill is working quite fine.

The Village Council and VDB are in constant touch with the government functionaries. The Council members more with the administrative officers while the VDB with the Block officials. Every now and then, the members of these bodies come to the offices to bring forth the view of the villagers and the area administrative officer is also instructed to visit the villages and know the things. For the best results both the bodies of the village should work in tandem with the government functionaries.

SWOT ANALYSIS

The strengths of the village community in Nagaland are :

1. The preservation of village social and administrative structure and excellent organizational skills of the villagers. The VDBs were formulated in 1980 and are looking after the implementation of various rural development schemes in the village.
2. Another strength is the retention of rights over land and very low population density.
3. Knowledge of weaving clothes, making furnitures and other handicrafts with local forest produce and rearing of poultry, piggery, cattle comes to the Nagas as a part of the rearing process.

Weaknesses

1. Lack of manpower : As the population density is low and all the children go to schools. Nuclear family is the norm. Only available persons for work in the fields are husband and wife. Most of the time the wife goes into giving birth to children and looking after them as on an average, each Naga family has 5-6 children.
2. Lack of use of modern technology for agriculture.
3. No habit of saving and lack of business acumen.
4. Lack of planning especially regarding land use.

Opportunities

There is a huge market for consumable goods in Nagaland especially in nearby town of Dimapur and the products can be sent across the border into Assam also.

SWOT analysis of the **Nerhema** village for development :

Strengths

1. The relative honesty of the people.
2. The egalitarian nature of the tribal people.
3. The hard working nature of the people.
4. Closeness to the district road, subdivision headquarters and also to the Kohima town.
5. The vast land resources at the disposal of the village.
6. The large educated/literate population and the enthusiasm to educate themselves.
7. The village council and the VDB system.
8. The easy accessibility to the politicians and hence the pressure that can be put on them for allotting something to the village.

Weaknesses

1. Absence of saving skills, the propensity to spend and lack of experience in handling large money.
2. Lack of proper infrastructure.
3. Lack of any industrial setup in the State.
4. High level of corruption in the State.
5. Lack of systems and too much reliance on arbitrariness.

Opportunities

1. The funds available to VDBs and through the district plan.
2. The vast land available. A portion can be regeneratively used for commercial plantations.
3. The closeness to Kohima and the district road and the township of Chiephobozou gives a great opportunity for trading, catering to passengers of the Wokha, Mokokchung bound buses.
4. There is a great potential for tourism. The place is ideal for adventure sports like hand-gliding.

Threats

1. Insurgency.
2. The church (although beneficial to a large extent, the frowning upon of the traditional customs can lead to a rootless, fundamentalist society which is totally alien to the nature of the Nagas).
3. The migration of educated people to the towns.
4. The aimless wanderings of the educated unemployed youth.
5. AIDS.

CONCLUSION AND POLICY SUGGESTIONS

The government has undertaken a number of programmes in the State. The only programmes, however, which the villagers have heard of and which have really been implemented to some extent, resulting at least in some flow of money to the villages are the ones implemented through the VDBs. Thus, the only programmes which can be said to be implemented in Nerhema village, to whatever extent are the grant-in-aid, matching cash grant scheme, JRY, IRDP, district plan and to a certain extent the EAS scheme. The environment programmes have not been taken independently in the village by any department. However, as part of the VDB schemes and the district plan schemes social forestry can be taken up and has been quite popular, though may be for the wrong reasons (easier to divert funds from this scheme).

The public distribution system in the whole of the State is in shambles. There is high leakage at the top most levels. In fact, the amount of quota allotted to Nagaland if sincerely distributed will require at least 200 trucks moving continuously throughout the State. In the village there is no fair price shop, the nearest place where PDS supply is available is at Chiephobozou. There, the CPO store stocks rice which is fit for consumption for pigs and is being bought for such purposes. Sugar is not available at all. Kerosene is available once in a while at least at Rs. 6 per litre. This situation, however, does not seem to concern the villagers and they keep on suffering without complaining and buying from Kohima. In election time, they will also collect money from the politician who is up for election and the process continues.

The programmes like the AWRSP, etc. are hardly implemented as the PHE is hardly operational in the region. Of whatever programmes which are taken up, the schemes under them are also hardly undertaken. Most of the programmes involve only distribution of money—mostly at the top levels, with some trickling down. The infrastructural facilities are stressed to the maximum because of lack of any maintenance and repairs and improper construction. The condition of the Kohima-Wokha district road is an apt example of the condition of the PWD (and other departments as well) in the State.

The impact on the villager's life is there in the greater spending power with them and better infrastructural facilities. However, this must not be confused. The infrastructural facilities though are there are of very poor quality and could have been constructed at half the costs shown on paper, in some cases even at one-fourth the cost—the rest money going out in various forms, in some cases as equitable cash distribution amongst all. When asked as to what will be the effect of the withdrawal of the government supported programmes from their village, after some ruminations the reply got was that it would not effect them much, they will go back to their old life (may be they were referring to the old insurgent days) and will manage. This, I believe is very much true. It would not make much difference to the level of lifestyle led by them. The only ones who will be affected will be the ones at the top—the ministers, MLAs, the bureaucrats, the engineers, etc.

Poorest person: There is not much of difference in the level of the villagers in the village—the only difference being in the condition of the house and the furniture inside. The poorest person in each *khel* is usually some widow/widower or mentally infirm person, a person whose children has left for greener pastures. The person is looked after by the *khel* people. Usually the house has a thatched roof and a room/kitchen, a storage room (for paddy) and a makeshift bed inside. The house possesses minimal utensils, and the day time of the old person is spent in looking after himself, cooking for himself, etc. In one *khel*, the poorest person was a person with a family, but still he had around 0.5 ha of land which was tilled by himself. The rest he managed to get by working here and there, getting land from the community for cultivation. The *khel* people were very supportive.

Inferences

1. No family planning is practiced. The size of the family varies from 6 to 13.
2. The need for educating the children is felt and the children are given education without regard to the sex. However, the dropout rate is high and continuing of education beyond class 10 is rare.
3. Most of the houses have CGI sheets for roofs and unplastered bamboo walls. Some have mud plastered bamboo walls. RCC buildings are rare (4-5 in the village).
4. Each household is keeping some form of livestock—poultry, pigs or cattle. Pigs are the most popular.
5. Both terraced and *jhum* cultivation is undertaken and produce ranging from 30 bags to 80 bags are produced (each bag contains 80 kg of paddy).
6. Almost all the families interviewed supplemented their agricultural produce by working for cash/kind on other's fields, etc. as labour.
7. Nobody relies on the Chiephobozou civil dispensary. For medical facilities the reliance is either on the army compounder or on the facilities available in Kohima.

With 102 households, **Longjemdang** can be said to be a medium sized village when it is compared to the other villages in Mokokchung. However, the amount of land that the village has, is greater than money, and when the number of households is taken into account, per capita land holding comes to a very high figure. Besides being fortunate in that, the village lies in an area where the betel leaves grow very well. A lot of households have betel leaf farms which provide a steady source of income. Finally, about 800 acres of the village land is even, fit for permanent cultivator; a thing not to be found in 80 per cent of the Mokokchung villages. With so many things going for the village and with access to this many resources, one would have expected the village to be one of the most prosperous ones, but surprisingly, it is not so. **Longjemdang** can be considered to be one of the moderately well-off villages if not a poor village.

One reason why the village has not really taken off is the underutilization of the resources that it has. With the coming of wet rice cultivation the villagers have started to totally ignore the land where they were earlier doing *jhum* cultivation. Of course, *jhum* cultivation is bad and weaning away people from it has been one of the policies of the government. However, rather than doing *jhum* cultivation the land could have been used in some other way, say raising some plantations or planting timber trees. This the villagers have not done. They have put up farms, no doubt, but these are very small when compared to the amount of land they have. To increase their economic status even more the households should be encouraged to go for more plantation crops. A beginning is being made in the common village land where the households besides the betel leaf farm, are also going for orange plantation, tapioca plantation and betel nut farms. The Horticulture Department could come to the help of the villagers by making them aware of the type of plantations they can take up and by providing them with the technical know-how. Actually plantation crops can be taken up in every village of Mokokchung but in most of the other villages land is not so much, and the villagers have to use them for growing food crops. In Longjemdang, since the food crops are being grown in the wet rice fields a lot of *jhum* lands can be devoted entirely for the plantations.

Most of the energy of the households is now spent in wet rice cultivation known as *Paani Kheti*. The yield of rice that the villagers are getting is mostly below 60 quintals per acre. This much yield, the villagers are getting without using any fertilizer of manure whatsoever. It is not that the villagers do not know about this thing, they know, but they cite economic compulsions for not using them. Of course, there are some villagers too, who feel that using fertilizers would harm the taste of the rice. To bring about a change in this, what can be done is that the Village Council should advance some money on loan to those desirous of using fertilizers. The technical know-how and other things can be obtained from the Agricultural Department. The increased yield and the crop should be then brought to the notice of the others, thus generating awareness about fertilizers and removing misconceptions about them. Besides all this something can be done about the seeds too. The villagers are using a variety of seed for rice cultivation known as Pankaj given to them a long time ago by the Agricultural Department. Since then a lot of better varieties have come up, but due to ignorance none of the farmers are using them.

Something has to be done regarding this so that the villagers use the latest varieties.

A study of the development schemes makes one feel that many of the community projects, which are being taken up, should have been substituted for some other schemes. A look at the wet rice cultivation brings this out clearly. For Longjemdang, wet rice cultivation is the most important thing. Yield is more and it has the advantage of being carried out at a permanent place unlike *Jhum*. However, it is seen that the villagers are unable to use some 300 acres of even land because of irrigation problem. There are streams running nearby but it has to be dammed so that water collects and canals are taken out. Wet rice cultivation in the village could start only when one of the streams was dammed some thirty years ago. All the land towards that side has been put to use but those far away from it has not been. To bring this into use, the streams on this side have to be utilized. However damming requires quite good amount, which the villagers are unable to get. Of course, if all the money obtained in all the development schemes are put together something can be done, but then money granted under some scheme can be only used for that purpose, not for any other purpose. This system is fine but in the village, extension of wet rice cultivation is the most important issue, and doing something for this would do a lot of good to everybody. It is difficult to say what can be done to get such an amount. All I can say is that at the District level the DRDA should be given the flexibility in utilizing the funds in a way which suits a particular village the most.

SUGGESTIONS

1. Villagers should start by making self help groups to start the habit of saving money and to organize themselves on the economic front. Later, 2-3 self help groups should merge to form a cluster for taking up self employment ventures. Once the villagers show their saving skills, financial institutions will not hesitate to extend them monetary help. The making of clusters shall not only give economic strength but also numbers in terms of manpower. Through these clusters, the villagers should take up self employment ventures like piggery, poultry, fishery, etc. at a larger than household scale.

This shall make it easy for them to tap far off markets as well.

2. On the land management front, they should carry on paddy, maize and vegetable cultivation in *paani khetis* but *jhuming* should be totally abandoned. The villagers should take the help of Agriculture University at Medziphema and get their soil tested to find out what kind of crops are suitable for growing on the *jhum* lands and these should preferably be horticultural crops.
3. From the money available for rural development programmes, the villagers should make pucca roads and marketing sheds. Self-employment ventures should be got funded by the financial institutions like rural, cooperative and nationalized banks, KVIC and the State industry department, etc.
4. After building rural roads and marketing sheds, the village should try to exploit the non conventional energy sources to make up for the power and LPG scarcity. For drinking water supply to all the villagers rain water should be harvested and used as rainy season is for as long as 7 months in a year in the State.
5. Marketing facilities should be provided by either making a separate marketing cooperative society or through the clusters of self help groups arranging for marketing of their own produce. The planning for all these activities can be done at the local level and the local Administrative Officer can take the help of NGOs to guide the villagers and can request the banks to organize loan *melas* in the village.

REFERENCES

Ashokvardhan, C. *Socio Economic Profile of Rural India,* Volume 2 (North East India), Concept Publishing Company, New Delhi, 2004.

Ashokvardhan, C. *Tribal Land Rights in India*, Centre for Rural Studies, LBSNAA, Mussoorie, 2006.

BPL Census, Assam 1998.

Burman, B.K. Roy, *Towards Poverty Alleviation Programmes in Nagaland and Manipur*. Mittal Publishers Distributors, Delhi, 1984.

Census of India, 1991.

Census of India, 2001.

Census of Nagaland 1991.

Census of Nagaland 2001.

http://rural.nic.in (official website of Ministry of Rural Development, Government of India)

http://www.nagaland.nic.in/profile/history/about.htm official webportal of Government of Nagaland.

Kumar, B.B., *Modernization in Naga Society*, Omsons Publications, New Delhi, 1993.

State Human Development Report, 2004, Department of Planning and Coordination, Government of Nagaland, 2004.

3

Manipur and Tripura

C. ASHOKVARDHAN

PART 1

MANIPUR

This study is based upon the socio-economic village assignment reports prepared by the following IAS probationers in Manipur as given in Table 3.1.

Table 3.1 : IAS Probationers Village Assignment

Sl. No.	*Name of the Probationer*	*Village*	*District*	*Year of submission of the Report*
1.	Prashant Kumar Singh	Thingra	Tamenglong	1995
2.	Vivek Kumar Dewangan	Chawainamei Khunous	Senapati	1995
3.	Rajesh Agrawal	Kachai	Ukhrul	1996
4.	Sushil Kumar	Monsang Pantha	Chandel	1997
5.	Tinku Biswal	Sekmai	Imphal	1999
6.	Arun Kumar Sinha	Bhalok	Tamenglong	2001
7.	Prem Singh	Lambung	Chandel	2002
8.	R. Dinesh Singh	Kahulong	Tamenglong	2002

THE STUDY AREA : AN INTRODUCTION

The universe, under study, is tribal dominated. The society is egalitarian and labour is dignified. It is a free society and is guided by traditional laws and customs. Traditional laws do not prescribe inequality. Everyone is equal and has equal access to all the community resources. Everybody can go to a water resource in the village and anyone can go to the community forest land and collect forest produce. All the tribals are converted Christians and have equal access to the Church. The Khulakpa (headman) and the Church Pastor are respected by all and yet it is more of a tradition or a custom than of any social hierarchy.

Traditionally, the office of the chieftainship in a Kuki village is called Haosapa who is assisted by a council of ministers, the representatives of all the clans called Semang Upa or Pachong. This council of the Kuki village resembles the village council of the Naga tribes. However, the Chief of a Kuki village is the overall authority over the villagers. The Village administration is, therefore, in the hands of the village chiefs among the Kuki-Chin group of tribes.

On the other hand, republican type of village polity exists among the Nagas where the village administration is run by the village council constituted by the elderly representatives of the clans or households in the village. The village council performs both administrative and judicial functions. Usually, the eldest son or any responsible person of the family represents the village council. Yet, monarchical system of chieftainship is not absent among the Naga tribes, e.g. the Mao, the Zeliangrongs etc. Among the Zeliangrongs, the first settler of the village automatically becomes the head/chief of the village called Nampou, i.e. the village chief is only a nominal head in the village. The administrative powers lie in the hands of the village council headed by Khulak/Chairman elected by the villagers. Despite the presence of democratic elements, there will be a village chief called as Awunga by the Tangkhuls in every Naga village.

The status of women is remarkably high among the tribals. They enjoy the same status as men and suffer no gender discrimination. They are more hard working and enterprising than the males. Majority of the household works are carried out by the women. In addition, they contribute in *jhuming* land for cultivation, digging the paddy fields, transplanting paddy and protecting growing crops from birds and animals. The elderly girls assist their mothers in pounding and dehusking rice, weaving, chopping wood and the like. The women, therefore, play a vital role in the family, rendering great service and also indirectly helping the alleviation of poverty and raising the standard of living.

In spite of this elevated position enjoyed by the women, there are a few traditions carrying a gender bias. Females have no right of inheritance in immovable property. Further, they find no place in the village authority.

The Village Authority is a full-fledged village panchayat. The village panchayat is basically a blend of the traditional panchayat and the modern democratic institutions in the sense that the Chief or the Khulakpa of the village is the ex-officio chairman of the Village Authority of the village and other executive members are elected on the basis of adult suffrage, who generally represent various clans. The Village Authority is recognized by the Manipur (Village Authorities in Hill Area) Act, 1956. The Authority also administers the traditional laws and customs of the society.

The village Panchayat is also a development agency. In fact, the scheme of the Jawahar Rojgar Yojana is carried out at the village level by the panchayat only. The preparation of muster rolls, selection of work etc. is done by the panchayat. The panchayat contributes a lot to the Integrated Rural Development Programme as well in the identification of the beneficiaries etc.

Nonetheless, the new generation in the villages has grown materialistic and its consumer need parameters are altogether different. The new generation does not feel inclined to learn weaving. Other crafts like pottery, basket making etc. may also vanish with the passage of time. Wood-work and bamboo-work is also becoming rare. There is a perceptible swing towards non-conformity especially among the youths. The educated younger lot has started moving away from land and is seeking white collared jobs elsewhere. Since such jobs are scarce, frustration and alienation are bound to set in, which may, in turn, lead to insurgency.

The study universe has limited resources. The villagers are mainly engaged in the agricultural and horticultural activities. Large areas are still under the *jhum* cultivation. The need of the hour is to switch over to terrace cultivation because of the advantage it has over *jhum*. Terracing is a difficult and costly affair but once it is done, the benefits are manifold. The output of a terrace field is twice than that of a *jhum* field for the same area. The input required is also less in case of terrace cultivation. But this is only possible if the villagers realize the importance of terrace cultivation and the damage caused by *jhum* cultivation.

The damage being caused to the climate of the region due to the practice of *jhum* is immense. There is a perceptible rise in the average daily temperature of the region and the soil cover is also fast depleting. But *jhum* is not the sole culprit as there is large scale deforestation due to the commercial value of wood. The illegal cutting of trees has to be stopped if this area has to develop. Forestry and horticulture are the only viable resource. Secondly, *jhuming* is the traditional heritage of these people. So to think of abolishing and stopping *jhuming* overnight is not proper. The people should be asked to change over to terracing gradually. This change will require not only technical change but also social change. Technical change means shifting to terrace cultivation and going in for horticulture plantation. Social change means change in the lifestyle and values. The people should feel that the change is not going to finish their identity. The technical change can be brought about by official help and expertise but for bringing about social change, we need the help of the village authority, headman, church leaders and the village organization. A positive thing about the villages is that there are a large number of village organizations which can play a constructive role in this. They should be taken into confidence first. They in turn, can definitely convince the villagers, about the need for change.

In the present deteriorating condition of law and order, and increasing insurgency, private investment is ruled out. The villagers themselves will have to take over income generating activities. Some of the suggested income generating activities are rearing of pigs and poultry, fruit plantations, cooperative weaving societies, basket making etc. Rearing of pigs and poultry is quite a common activity in the villages but it is consumption oriented. The need is to organize it on a commercial basis and start earning. The people in the North-East are meat loving. A readymade market exists for the same. Rearing pigs does not require very special skills. This can be taken up very effectively. Rearing poultry is also an easy job but care is to be taken when chicken are small.

Presently traditional tribal heritage of weaving and basket making is gradually disappearing. The reason for this is that there are no marketing facilities and demand is also limited in Manipur because every tribe makes its shawl and basket, but these shawls and other handicraft items have demand in big cities like Delhi, Kolkata etc. The villagers can supply their produce through some cooperative society in the villages to the Manipur Development Society (MDS), Imphal which can make arrangements to market the same through the State showrooms in the Metros. This will require a concerted effort on the side of the Government also.

In order to fulfil the declared objective of the Government to impart free and compulsory education to all the children of 5-11 age group, there has been special emphasis on primary education in the Five Year Plans. As a result of the concerted efforts of the authorities we find that there is at least one school, pre-primary or primary in almost every village. In the hills of Manipur there is hardly any village, even in the remotest areas without a school. Before Independence, people, especially in hills, maintained aloofness from education to a large extent. This was also due to the non-availability of schools. This attitude was discarded later on. There are two most important reasons for this. These are: (1) urban influence and (2) conversion to Christianity. A new way of life was introduced in which education was a must.

It is necessary to mention that the decisions about the creation of assets under the employment generating schemes are taken by the villagers themselves. The village authority decides on what is required on a priority basis. No contractor system prevails in the villages under study.

Saving habits among the big cultivators is present but it is not very much. They save only that much which is sufficient for their children studying outside. But some of them do not have even this habit. They would sell the paddy as and when required and earn the money. But one thing worth mentioning is that they invariably save paddy without realizing the potential of selling the same in the lean season to earn more money. They save the paddy basically to consume it later and to sell it whenever they require money. Similarly, they keep bundles of firewood with them to be sold whenever required. Besides these, there is not much of saving by the cultivators in the study area.

Agricultural labourers work in the fields of others and most of the time they get their labour repaid in terms of kind. All they save is for the next few days and is basically to feed themselves. This saving is not productive. Moreover, instead of saving they are invariably indebted to meet their daily needs and to perform festivals and feast. Thus we see that in general, saving as a habit, is absent.

The agricultural labourers do not have any terrace or *jhum* fields. Incidentally the females working in the fields get at Rs. 25 per day while males at Rs. 30 per day. The workers get 10 per cent of the total produce of the fields. For example, if a field gives 150 tins of paddy the worker will be paid 15 tins as his labour. For those who work on the *jhum* field they get daily vegetables so that they can meet their daily needs. For example, everyday they will get one cabbage, some chilly and some rice. The labourers are happy with what they get and there is no sense of exploitation. This is mainly because of self-contained tendency of the villagers and low level of expectations.

The present wage rate for different types of agricultural work is as follows :

(a) Ploughing: at Rs. 35 per day or at Rs. 600 per acre.
(b) Harvesting: at Rs. 35-40 per day.
(c) Sowing: at Rs. 35 per day.

The minimum wage for unskilled labour as per the guidelines issued by the Government of Manipur is Rs. 47.65 for hilly region. In actual practice, the wage rate is less than this. But at the same time working hours are also less in the present situation.

The tribals in this region are totally dependent on nature. As the economy is predominantly agriculture based, land is the most productive asset of the villagers. Being a hilly region with undulating terrain, there is scarcity of plain paddy fields and the villagers have to resort to *jhuming* which is not so productive. All the families own the required agricultural implements and except for tractors, they do not have to hire anything from others.

The villagers' dependence on forest is complete. *Jhuming* is done on the forest land. They collect firewood from the forest which is the only source of fuel for the villagers. Most of the families covered under the surveys are collecting firewood for selling which supplements their income in a significant manner. They collect forest produce like bamboo, timber and minor forest produce for their own use as well as for selling. Forest land is also used for the grazing of the cattle. Some families are also involved in horticulture activities like growing of fruits and vegetables which provide them some income.

Most of the families covered under the socio-economic survey are owning some form of livestock. Buffaloes, cows, hens, dogs, pigs, etc. are the most significant of them. These are used mainly for their own consumption. When in need of money, they also sell them in the market fetching them a good price. Buffalo is used for ploughing of fields.

Almost all the families are in possession of handlooms. Womenfolk in the families in leisure work with the loom to make shawls, phaneks, mufflers, etc. which can be sold in the market to earn profit.

The selection of beneficiaries under the IRDP in the universe area is generally done on the basis of the decision taken in the General Body meeting of the village. As per the information gathered from the surveys conducted, most of the beneficiaries covered under the scheme were genuine and deserving candidates. The schemes undertaken in a village include piggery, poultry, sugarcane plantation, carpentry, banana and potato plantation etc. However, the maintenance of assets was found to be very poor. The number of pigs, poultry were found to be less than the stipulated requirement. The IRDP has hardly succeeded in any asset creation. This is mainly because of the non-availability of any forward or backward linkages. Further, the amount sanctioned per beneficiary is so small that hardly any durable asset creation is possible. There is a lack of entrepreneurship among the villagers. Sometimes the amount sanctioned for taking up any scheme was utilized in purchasing rice or for medical treatment of one of the family members. For the IRDP to make any impact, the beneficiaries should be consulted before hand. The schemes should be decided in consultation with the beneficiary. None of the beneficiaries covered under the surveys repaid the loan component of the scheme. They were never pressurized to pay the loan. One reason for this is that since they do not have the *patta* of the land, it was not possible to mortgage the land against the loan.

In a nutshell, the performance of the IRDP in the villages has been pathetic. It has hardly helped to improve the poverty situation in a substantial way. If the selection process is followed as per the guidelines of the IRDP manual, the benefit would reach the targeted people. But many a time, due to pressure from the influential people, politicians and underground organizations, wrong selection of beneficiary takes place. The cluster approach for the selection of beneficiaries and training under the TRYSEM for taking up works with the locally available raw material may help in improving the poverty situation in the villages under study and elsewhere.

Hilly districts in Manipur have vast potential for growing horticulture crops, such as fruits, vegetables, tuber crops, spices, medicinal plants, floriculture plantation crops, etc. The moderately warm climate and regular rainfall in the Tamenglong district, for example, are conducive for growing many kinds of fruits. The potential area for horticulture crops in Tamenglong is about 47,876 ha which is 17.3 per cent of the State figure out of which only 3,353 ha is already covered by horticulture fruit crops, 323 ha by vegetables and 640 ha by spices. The remaining vast area can be taken up by new horticulture massive plantation in a phase-wise manner. It will help soil conservation, increase income of the hilly population through increase in high value produce, create more employment opportunities, improve the nutritional status of the poor and protect environment.

An integrated development approach is required, in which crop production, transfer of latest technology, post-harvest management and marketing facilities should be dovetailed together by keeping the following objectives as per the Government of India guidelines:

(i) Production of quality planting materials of improved variety.

(ii) Improving productivity through the adoption of improved cultivation technology, plant protection chemicals, nutrients and water management.

(iii) Transfer of technology through farmers' participatory demonstrations, training/visits of farmers by exchange of views with successful farmers, media support, extension work literature etc.

(iv) Creation of on-farm and post-harvest infrastructure such as, collection centres, packing, transport, storage and marketing facilities.

For convenience of condensed presentation the village assignment reports prepared by the IAS probationers are being studied under the following principal heads :

1. Demography
2. Land
3. Irrigation
4. Agriculture and Allied Activities

5. Rural Industries
6. Poverty Alleviation Programmes

Demography

The total population of village Kahulong (Tamenglong: Manipur) as per the 2001 census is 746, out of which 370 are males and 376 females. The positive sex-ratio of 1.02 females per male is a good indicator of the social set-up. The rate of population growth is also quite high. A perusal of the death and birth register at the church revealed that the relative growth in population over the last decade has been quite high. However, this steep increase in population has been offset to some extent by the migration of villagers especially the younger 15-40 age group to other places with more opportunities and facilities for employment and studies.

As per the Hill House Tax Register maintained in the office of the SDO Ukhrul, the following data could be obtained regarding village Kachai (Ukhrul : Manipur) as given in Table 3.2.

Table 3.2 : Population of Village Kachai

Year	House	Population	Male	Female
1971	92	438	232	206
1981	124	598	318	280
1991	178	904	484	420
1994	221	1385	739	646
1995	240	1514	804	710

Age Group: The break up of the population according to the age group is given in Table 3.3 (as per the 1995 house counting register) :

Table 3.3 : Percentage to Total Population according to Age Groups

Age Group	Total	Per cent
0-6	316	21
6-16	152	10
16-30	667	44
30-50	227	15
Above 50	150	10
Total	**1514**	**100**

Most of them in this age group are married. They have to do their regular household work. The unmarried girls help their mothers in household works like fetching water etc. and they also go to the fields.

As per the 1991 census, the total population of village Sekmai (Imphal West : Manipur) was 4,796 with the male population being 2,386 and the female population being 2,410 indicating a sex ratio in favour of the females. However, as of now, this sex ratio has turned in favour of the males. This was indicated in the survey.

The total population of the village on the date of the survey was 6,786 with the male population being 3,946 and the female population being 2,840. As is indicated by the figures, we see a drastic reduction in the sex ratio in favour of the females.

The growth rate of the population in the region over a period of seven years has shown the following trend as given in Table 3.4.

Table 3.4 : Growth Rate of Population in Seven Years

Category	*%age increase in 7 years*	*%age increase per year*
Male	65	9.3
Female	18	2.5
Total	**42**	**6**

The figures indicate an extremely high rate of growth of population per year. This by itself is very alarming and needs to be checked. But an even more alarming feature is the huge variation in the growth rates of the male and female populations. This trend, if allowed to continue, might alter the population dynamics drastically which could cause problems of various kinds in the village society.

Sekmai is a predominantly scheduled caste village with more than 95 per cent of the population belonging to this caste. The total SC population as on the date of the survey was 6,146. This constitutes nearly 96 per cent of the total population. The rest are a few higher caste Hindus and there are no scheduled tribes in the village.

The village Thingra (Tamenglong : Manipur) has 88 households supporting a population of 570 as recorded in 1995. In the previous year it stood at 561. As per the census records available the population in 1981 stood at 440 and in 1991 at 520 (decadal growth rate of about 18%). A classification of the present population according to age is given in Table 3.5.

Table 3.5 : Classification of Population of Village Thingra

Age	*Total*	*Male*	*Female*
0-10	123	63	60
10-20	114	59	55
20-35	137	71	66
35-50	126	66	60
Above 50	70	37	33
Total	**570**	**296**	**274**

The majority of the people (95%) are engaged in agriculture over the fields owned by them. Only 1 percent (6 people) work as agricultural labourers in the fields of fellow villagers. The remaining 4 percent are engaged in other works like trade and services. Of the latter, 8 are in government service (4 working as Grade IV in the district headquarters, 2 as Grade III in the forest department and one each in the district council and the district veterinary department).

The important demographic figures for village Monsang Pantha (Chandel : Manipur) are given in Table 3.6.

Table 3.6 : Demographic Figures of Village Monsang Pantha

Indicators	*As per 1991 census*	*As per village authority survey of 1996*
Total population	387	451
Male population	194	222
Female population	193	229
Number of households	78	77

Population Classification (as per 1991 Census)

Table 3.7: Religion-wise and Caste-wise Population of Village Monsang Pantha

(a) Religion-wise

Sl. No.	*Religion*	*Number*	*Percent*
1.	Christian	387	100

(b) Caste-wise

Sl. No.	Caste	Number	Percent
1.	S.T.	387	100

Rate of Growth of Population

From Table 3.8 it is clear that there is no variation either on the basis of caste or religion in the population as the entire village is inhabited by Monsangs. All of them are practicing Christianity. There are few Meiteis also who have married Monsang girls and settled in the village adopting their religion and culture.

Table 3.8 : Variation of Population on the basis of Caste or Religion

Sl. No.	Year	No. of Families	Population	% Annual Growth Rate
1.	1990	65	384	—
2.	1991	78	387	0.8
3.	1996	77	437	2.6
4.	1997	77	451	3.2

Table 3.9 explains the distribution of population by age and sex in village Monsang Pantha (Chandel: Manipur):

Distribution of Population by Age and Sex

Table 3.9 : Population with age group

Sl. No.	Age Group (Years)	Male	%	Female	%	Total	%
1.	1	1	0.9	5	3.9	6	2.4
2.	1-4	9	7.7	16	12.5	25	10.2
3.	5-9	15	12.8	18	14.1	33	13.4
4.	10-14	12	10.2	18	14.1	30	12.0
5.	15-19	14	12.0	7	5.4	21	8.4
6.	20-24	5	4.3	9	7.0	14	5.6
7.	25-29	10	8.5	9	7.0	19	7.8
8.	30-34	10	8.5	9	7.0	19	7.8
9.	35-39	15	12.8	15	11.7	30	12.0
10.	40-44	8	6.8	6	4.7	14	5.6
11.	45-49	3	2.6	3	2.4	6	2.4
12.	50-54	4	3.4	1	0.8	5	2.0
13.	55-59	4	3.4	0	0	4	3.6
14.	60	7	6.0	2	9.4	19	7.8
	Total	**117**	**47.8**	**128**	**52.2**	**245**	**100.0**
	Sex Ratio	NA	NA	NA	NA	1.094	NA

The percentage distribution of the population against educational levels in village Monsang Pantha (Chandel: Manipur) can be explained as Table 3.10.

Table 3.10 : Percentage to Educational Level of Village Monsang Pantha

Age (Years)	*Males*								
	Illiterates	*Literate Primary*	*Upto V*	*Upto VIII*	*Upto X*	*Upto XII*	*Upto Graduation*	*Above Graduation*	*Total*
6-12	4.6	18.5	0	0	0	0	0	0	23.1
13-14	0	0.9	0	0	0	0	0	0	0.9
15-19	0	0	4.6	4.6	3.7	0	0	0	13.0
20-24	0	0	0	2.8	1.9	0	0	0	4.6
25-29	0	0.9	2.8	1.9	1.9	2.8	0	0	10.2
30-34	2.8	0	0	2.8	1.9	0	0.9	0.9	9.3
35-39	0.9	0	7.4	5.6	0	0	0	0	13.9
40-44	0.9	0	0.9	3.7	2.8	0	0	0	8.3
45-49	0	0.9	0.9	0	0	0.9	0	0	2.8
50+	1.9	0.9	6.5	1.9	0.9	0.9	0	0.9	13.9
Total	**11.5**	**22.1**	**23.0**	**23.1**	**13.0**	**4.6**	**0.9**	**1.9**	**100.0**

Age (Years)	*Females*								
	Illiterates	*Literate Primary*	*Upto V*	*Upto VIII*	*Upto X*	*Upto XII*	*Upto Graduation*	*Above Graduation*	*Total*
6-12	3.9	22.5	0	0	0	0	0	0	26.5
13-14	0	2.9	0	0	0	0	0	0	3.9
15-19	0	0	4.9	0	3.9	0	0	0	8.8
20-24	0	0	0	2.9	3.9	2.0	0	0	8.8
25-29	2.9	0	1.0	0	1.0	2.0	0	0	6.9
30-34	2.9	1.9	2.9	0	1.0	0	0	0	8.8
35-39	2.9	1.9	6.9	0	0	1.0	1.0	1.0	8.8
40-44	1.0	1.9	1.0	1.9	0	0	0	0	14.2
45-49	0	0	1.9	1.0	0	0	0	0	2.9
50+	8.8	2.9	1.0	0	0	0	0	0	12.7
Total	**22.4**	**34.0**	**19.0**	**5.9**	**9.8**	**4.9**	**1.0**	**1.0**	**100.0**

The village Lambung (Chandel : Manipur) has a total population of 748 as per the 2001 census. It is important to note that the sex ratio is favourable to women. The male population is 368 whereas the female population is 390. The growth in population from the 1991 census is phenomenal. According to the census figures of 1991, the population of the village was 502. The decadal increase in the population is about 50 per cent. This increase in much less compared to the overall increase of the district which is about 70 per cent. The rapid increase in population is caused by a large migration of people from the neighbouring areas after the Naga-Kuki clashes in the late 90. Most of the Nagas who fled during the ethnic clashes came to reside in this area because of proximity to the district headquarters. The favourable gender ratio for women is caused by peculiar socio-economic conditions. Tribal ethos and Christian values lead to balancing of the gender ratio. On the day of the survey the population was 770 with 362 males and 408 females. The increase in population has increased the demand for shifting cultivation. *Jhuming* is widely practiced in the area and of late an increased demand for foodgrains and lack of alternate opportunities has led to an increase in the shifting cultivation so much so that even around the district headquarters shifting cultivation is being practiced.

None of the families in the productive age group uses any contraceptive in village Bhalok (Tamenglong: Manipur). There is ignorance about the use of contraceptives. Even if people want to use contraceptives the same is not available at their door step. Even the Government hospital is not having contraceptives in its stores. There is a lack of awareness about family planning.

There is a need to create awareness about family planning through medical camp and NGOs.

Land

A study of the land-use patterns in village Thingra (Tamenglong: Manipur) has yielded the following information :

In some parts, the soil is lateritic whereas in others it is of the brown forest soil type. The soil is acidic and generally contains very little soluble salts. The village occupies an area of about 70 square km out of which 1/3rd is under cultivation and the rest is under thick forest cover. Cultivation is carried on *jhum* lands though wet paddy fields are also available. There are 6 clans in the village and the land is divided amongst them. The head of a clan further distributes land to the other clan members for cultivation. Some of the land is earmarked as community land. All the clan members have full-fledged rights over the community land of the clan subject to the permission of the head of the clan. Even though there are separate community lands for separate clans but no serious problem arises if a member of a particular clan collects forest produce or uses the community land of any other clan for grazing etc. The tribals, by nature, have a very strong community feeling and they are ever willing to help any member from the same tribe. Fruit and other trees are adjacent to every household. The presence of fruit trees in the backyard not only provides fruits but also adds to the aesthetic beauty of the village. Orange, lemon, parkia, goose berries are some of the trees present in most of the households. Fruit trees are also planted in the forests in a random manner. The community lands also support quite a lot of these trees. Banana trees are found in abundance in the *jhum* fields. On steeper slopes of the *jhum* land one generally finds pineapples. The fruit trees give a good yield but the consumption is generally restricted to the village. If developed properly and adequate marketing arrangements are made, the fruits can influence the village economy to a great extent. Tremendous potential was observed in this particular field.

Forests are facing considerable danger from the *jhumias*. Every year large tracts of forests are cut and burnt down to enable the villagers to have new *jhum* land.

The area under double cropping is approximately 30 acres. These areas are in the vicinity of the water sources or by the sides of streams. The yield obtained from the second crop is quite dependent on the availability of water. Hence, large fluctuations are observed in the yield from the second crop.

Majority of the landholdings in village Sekmai (Imphal West: Manipur) are less than a hectare. A few households have landholdings of area between 1-2 hectares. Though an exact figure was not available, land records show that as many as 50 households have land in this range. Very few, about 8-10 households, have landholdings with an area in the range of 4-10 hectares. No household has more than 10 hectares of land under its possession.

Kahulong (Tamenglong : Manipur) has nearly 12 sq. km of land. Of this, however, only a small fraction is utilized for agricultural purposes. *Jhuming* (or 'palm' in the local dialect) is the main agricultural practice here. The crops grown in this village are rice, maize, banana, orange, tree-bean or parkia, jackfruit, lemon, tea, etc.

The soil is wholly red hilly soil, which has very weak capacity to retain moisture. The soil fertility is also very low. About 0.1 per cent of the total land is homestead land. The major portion of the land (about 90%) is covered by thick forest vegetation. There is no common grazing ground for cattle and livestock. The rest area is cultivated once a year.

The land in village Kachai (Ukhrul : Manipur) is being used only for agriculture, horticulture and household purposes. The area of homestead land being 5 per cent of the total area, the agricultural and horticultural land accounts for the rest 95 per cent. All the families in the village have got houses to live in except 2 Nepali families. Every household has got a small kitchen garden adjacent to the house from where it meets the daily requirements of vegetables. Vegetables like cabbage, potato, chilly, beans, cucumber, etc. are grown here.

The agricultural land is further classified into three categories:

Jhum Field	:	45 per cent
Terrace Field	:	35 per cent
Forest Field	:	20 per cent

As we see from the above data, the *jhum* field accounts for approximately half of the area of the village. In this village, the *jhum* field is also owned by the individuals. If one person has to do *jhuming* in other's field he has to take permission from the owner and has to pay a token rent of one tin of paddy. Terrace field accounts for 35 per cent of the total agricultural area. These fields are inherited. So every household does not own such field. Since these fields are not productive, the poor people do not have such fields or they have fields of small area. These terraced fields are only in the low lying areas of the village where the slope is gentle and water for irrigation is available.

Forest occupies 20 per cent of the total agricultural land in the village. The forest field is invariably owned by every tribal house. The size varies from one household to another. It is mainly used for firewood collection. Sometimes it is being used for the cultivation of vegetables like cabbage, potato, beans, cucumber, paddy, etc.

In addition to the agricultural land in Kachai, a large area of land has been brought under horticultural crops. The main crop grown is lime or lemon. Some amount of pineapple is also grown in the village. The exact area under the horticultural crops cannot be ascertained but the villagers said that they sold about 200 metric tonnes of lemon in Imphal and Ukhrul every year. This includes the quantity utilized by a pickle producing unit set up in Kachai itself. The pineapple, banana, etc. grown are generally used for household consumption only and very little is sold in the market.

This is mainly because of *jhum* cultivation and high rainfall in this area. The soils have about 1.3 per cent of organic carbon and are suitable for paddy cultivation and plantation crops after terracing, contour bunding etc.

In the Zeliangrong landholding system in village Bhalok (Tamenglong : Manipur) there are eight classes of land. They are as follows :

1. Kailong ram (village land where houses of villagers are constructed)
2. Pih or Pihkon ram (garden)
3. Lao ram (cultivating land)
4. Ngouhor thingjok ram (forest)
5. Rambou (a belt of land around the village)
6. Ranggaan (a portion of land which is very close to the village)
7. Duikhum (village water point)
8. Khouringh impahmei ram (grazing ground)

In village Monsang Pantha (Chandel : Manipur) there are three major types of land: homestead, wet paddy land and *jhum* land. On the basis of ownership, the land may be classified into three types—individual land, clan land and community land. No land records are maintained for *jhum* land or homestead land. *Jhum* land as such belongs to the village as a whole and the Village Authority every year distributes this among various clans residing in the village. Every clan, in turn, distributes land to the individual household. Any dispute arising out of the distribution of land or the demarcation of boundaries is settled amicably by the Village Authority, whose decision in most of the cases is acceptable to the villagers.

There is some community land also in the village. If a particular clan migrates out of the village permanently, the land belonging to that clan forms a part of the community land. The Village Authority distributes land to any landless family in the village out of that community land. The collection of firewood, other minor forest produce and cutting of trees for the construction of houses or furniture etc. is done from the forests available over the land demarcated as community land. Apart from this any kind of construction for community use or for Governmental purposes etc. is done over this community land.

Monsang Pantha has approximately 5 acres of homestead land, 50 acres of wet paddy cultivation land and approximately 150 acres of *jhum* land. For wet land, the land ownership right is with the individual persons and the Village Authority has no jurisdiction over that land. This is a surveyed land and land patta is available with the owner which is transferable to anybody irrespective of his place of residence.

The forest cover in the village mainly consists of ordinary pine and bamboo interspersed with other hardwood trees. There are some other trees also. The villagers collect the firewood and other minor forest produce like twigs, branches, etc. for own use.

Irrigation

The village Kachai (Ukhrul : Manipur) has got irrigation facility from the following sources: (a) Canals/other streams; (b) Tanks/ponds; and (c) rain. In fact the village is rather lucky to have a large number of small streams originating from the hill top and Iril river and Ihang river touching its western and south-eastern boundary respectively. Paddy is the only crop which is irrigated because paddy alone is grown on the terrace fields which have got water supply. Other crops grown on the *jhum* field do not have any assured supply of water. The *jhum* crops have to depend upon the rain for good yield. The area under different types of irrigation for paddy is as follows :

(*Area in hectares*)

Canal/Streams	*Tank/Pond*	*Total Irrigated*	*Not Irrigated*	*Total*
183	0.5	183.5	114.8	296.3

The rest of the agricultural and horticultural land which consist of *jhum* land and agricultural land is totally unirrigated and heavily dependent on rain water. Due to heavy rainfall the fields do not face any irrigation problem. One basic thing to notice was that the village does not employ any pump sets to pump out the water from the river. The reason for this could be that in any case they do mono-cropping only for which canal/stream/tank/pond/rain water is always sufficient. Also the cost of pump sets is high which cannot be afforded by the villagers.

Almost all the families in village Monsang Pantha (Chandel: Manipur) are practicing shifting (*jhum*) cultivation due to the non-availability of plain cultivable land. The land for cultivation is available only on the hill slopes where there is no water source. Only 23 families in the village are in possession of wet land. The mode of irrigation is mostly rain water. There are four nallas passing through these wet lands.

There are no irrigation schemes operational in village Thingra (Tamenglong : Manipur). The only irrigation is through canals from the water sources. The cultivation is mainly rainfed. In some cases, the villagers have to carry water to the field. It was observed that proper watershed management could help solve some of these problems. Small earth dams could be built at proper sites near the water sources from which canals could be taken out.

Soil erosion poses a great threat to the village. The area has heavy showers during the rainy season and because of the practice of *jhuming* most of the hill slopes are without forest cover. This results in tremendous loss of top soil making the land unfit for cultivation. This, in turn, prompts the villagers to look for newer *jhum* fields.

The cultivable land in village Sekmai (Imphal West : Manipur) is made up of rich alluvial soil, which supports agriculture. The Government should have taken adequate steps to provide assured irrigation in the region. Unfortunately, it has not done so, the result of which is seen in the extremely poor output of crops as agriculture is completely dependent on rains for irrigation. There are a few tube wells provided here and there, but these are hardly sufficient for irrigation. Further, the villagers have dug a few ponds, which are used more for cultivating fish than for irrigating fields.

Agriculture and Allied Activities

In village Kahulong (Tamenglong : Manipur), crops are grown once in a year. The whole cropping cycle is governed by the arrival and departure of rains. Irrigation is done through small canals which are fed by the rain water. Till date no Government scheme for developing irrigation facilities has been implemented. Agricultural productivity is low due to the low fertility of the soil, non-usage of pesticides, fertilizers, high yielding varieties of seeds, modern implements like the tractor etc. The agricultural technology employed is rather primitive. More stress is given to the 'slash and burn' technique instead of using other methods like terrace farming which is done at present near Kangpokpi, in Senapati District in Manipur. HYV seeds and tractors are not used here. Instead, the seeds of the last crop are reserved for use. Bulls and pure manual labour are used to till the land. There is no storage facility either in the village or nearby to store the agricultural produce. There is also no market nearby. Coupled with the lack of proper means of transport and communication, the incentive to the villagers to produce more is not high. Whatever produce they sell after carrying them on back to the market provides just enough money for their daily needs. The price at which they sell (especially the perishable items like fruits and vegetables) is dictated by the buyers since they have to return home the same day (the market is open every alternate day and not everyday).

No agricultural labourers are utilized in this village. Hence, the question of wages does not arise. The land is tilled by the entire joint family. In those cases where the land is not owned by the family, a token amount of two baskets of rice, irrespective of the size of the land or the productivity of the land, is given annually to the actual owner of the land as a sign that the land still belongs to the owner.

In so far as village Sekmai (Imphal West : Manipur) is concerned, agriculture plays only a secondary role in the village economy, which is surprising, considering that almost every household owns a plot of cultivable land. This is because the brewing and sale of local liquor has brought in enormous revenue into the village and is a much more lucrative job than agriculture. Further, many young people are pursuing jobs in Imphal and are more interested in white-collar jobs than in agriculture. Many have found jobs in the Government sector, while a few others have begun enterprises on their own.

The main crop grown here is paddy, which is sown in the Rabi season and harvested in the Kharif season. Almost the entire sown area of 1129.85 hectares is devoted to the paddy cultivation. The net production figures around 4,680 quintals per year. Wheat and pulses are not grown and only a very small area is devoted to producing maize. Horticultural plants like fruits and vegetables are grown in plenty. Vegetables include tomatoes, cauliflower, cabbage, squash, carrots and spinach.

However, the potential of the region for the production of rice, maize and vegetables has not been fully exploited. There are no forward and backward linkages that would make this sector a viable and alternative means of earning revenue. There are no proper inputs. There are no primary agricultural cooperative credit societies to provide credit at reasonable rates of interest. There are no farmer service centres that could take up orientation courses for the farmers to educate them about the modern methods and techniques or about the better quality inputs that may be used. The lack of PACs has meant that there are no backward linkages for getting better quality inputs and no forward linkages for better marketing. The crops produced are generally marketed locally and at times produced by the designated Government procurement agencies. The nearest market for the purchase of inputs is the district headquarters in Imphal.

Animal husbandry is another major activity. The village has a veterinary dispensary that caters to the local needs. All animal products are sold locally, be it milk, pork or other pig products.

In village Thingra (Tamenglong : Manipur), about 95 per cent of the work force of the village is engaged in agriculture. The main food crop grown in the village is rice. It forms their staple diet throughout the year. Rice is grown in the wet paddy fields as well as in the *jhum* fields. The *jhum* rice is somewhat inferior in quality but many claim that it is more tasty. The labour is contributed by the family members with the womenfolk playing a major role. There is also a system of working in groups where all the members of a clan work on common fields, one by one. There is a great sense of community participation.

The yield of rice in the hills is not very high as compared to the yield in the plains. The main reason is the absence of water in the initial period. For a good yield, the paddy field must be full of water in the initial period. Since paddy is planted on slopes, water cannot be stored in the field. Terracing is almost absent. The problem of requirement of water in the initial stages could be solved if the slopes are properly terraced. The villagers are being encouraged to develop terrace fields instead of resorting to *jhuming*.

Whatever is produced in the village is meant for local consumption. If some surplus is there, it is stored for future use as a lot of uncertainty exists regarding a good yield.

The bazaar has had an influence on the cultivation practices of the villagers. These days the farmers are being encouraged to use better quality of seeds as well as some of the fertilizers. Previously, the green manure used to be the main source of manure to add to the soil fertility. Better farm implements are also being used. It is noteworthy to mention that by burning down the forests the *jhum* land acquires increased fertility. Recently, a seed farm has come up at Noney Bazaar from where the villagers can get better quality seeds.

There is a good balance between food and non-food crops. The forests also serve as an important reserve for many fruit bearing trees like orange, papaya, banana, lemon, plum, pineapple, yongchak, umorok, etc. The fruit trees are also planted in the courtyard or backyard of almost every household. The fruits form a reliable source of money for the villagers. On an average, every household manages to sell rupees two to three thousand worth fruits every year in the local market.

Unfortunately, no cooperative is functioning in the village. Cooperatives could prove to be extremely beneficial, especially in the case of horticulture and poultry.

Cattle are not used for milk. The only work in which they are engaged is ploughing fields. They also serve as a source of meat to the villagers. The villagers take very little care of these animals. The animals are simply left to graze in the forests. Buffaloes and Mithuns are also a very common sight. The buffalo is used in the fields during the ploughing season. The Mithun is of great importance in a Naga society. It has a very special place as a Mithun sacrifice is imperative on any festival.

The following is the distribution of livestock in Thingra :

(i)	Mithun, Buffalo, Cow	120
(ii)	Pigs	205
(iii)	Chicken	1120
(iv)	Dogs	131
(v)	Goats	50
(vi)	Horses	2

Other Allied Activities

For the cultivators of Thingra village, horticulture is a reliable source of money. They utilize land in their courtyard or backyard for growing a few plants or trees like papaya, orange, banana, pineapple, lemon, plum, yongchak, etc. The trees with their presence add to the aesthetic beauty of the surroundings. Papaya, banana, pineapple, plum and lemon give fruits. Papaya, banana and lemon can also be used for vegetables. The 'yongchak' grows to the size of a moderate tree. It yields very long and moderately broad, approximately 30 cm. long and 5 cm. broad beans. It is very popular in Manipur and is used in vegetable preparation. It is always in great demand. The plants and trees mentioned above are a source of seasonal or intermittent income because they mature or ripen at different times of the year. Part of the produce is consumed at home and part of it is sold for cash at Noney Bazaar. Banana, yongchak, lemon and plum are the main horticulture crops. Both banana fruits and leaves are sold. It is to be noted that such fruit trees are not grown in every household. They are mainly grown on the *jhum* fields. Horticulture has not been experimented in this village in an organized manner and no household has come for such an enterprise so far. However, marketing is a big problem as the nearest market available is at a distance of 25 km. (on foot). Furthermore, the entire area is hilly, making the whole exercise extremely tiring. Market exists in Imphal and the fruits can be transported easily to Imphal. Pineapple is in great demand. It can be made use of for making juice and the same can be sent outside Manipur. For this purpose a juice extracting unit can be established at the village. At present 1 pineapple is costing Rs. 2 while outside it is costing Rs. 10. Hence, there is a great scope for pineapple development. Similarly lemon is also found in plenty. Presently, some of it is consumed, some is sold and some just rots. If proper planning is done by the villagers they can sell the same in the market at Imphal which is hardly 65 km away from the bazaar.

There are fish farms in the villages. The villagers having wet paddy field practice pisciculture in the fields. When paddy is harvested, with the onset of winter rains, fresh fingerlings are dropped into the fields and within 3-4 months they get a good yield. This is mainly confined to own consumption. This is practiced by the villagers who own terraced paddy fields.

Poultry farming besides having high potential for income is also a source of self-employment, but it has to be managed on a scientific line. It is necessary to undergo a short period of training to start the venture.

People are not engaged in any industrial activity in village Bhalok (Tamenglong : Manipur) but they are engaged in plantations like pineapple, orange, lemons, umorok, passion fruits, etc. There is also some handicraft work like shawl making, basket making, etc. in which women are engaged. But this is not done on a commercial scale. It is just to cater to their needs. Oranges are grown on a large scale in the village but because of poor communication they do not fetch a good price.

The following is the Status of Agriculture and Allied Activities in Village Monsang Pantha (Chandel: Manipur) :

Agriculture is the main source of livelihood for majority of the families in the village.

Almost 70 per cent of the workforce is engaged in this. Women form the backbone of agriculture and other allied activities. Single cropping pattern is being followed in the agricultural activities. Almost 90 per cent of the families practice *jhuming*. 40 per cent of the families surveyed in the village were also possessing wet paddy fields. The main crops are paddy and maize. Paddy is grown on both types of land whereas maize is grown only on *jhum* land. Other products are moom, potato, ginger and many other types of vegetables like pumpkin, beans, cabbage, squash, plum, etc. For wet paddy cultivation, the field is prepared by ploughing in the month of February-March. Sowing is done during pre-monsoon rains in the month of May or June. The crops mature by the month of November and harvesting is done in December. Fur *jhum* cultivation, burning of forests, also called *jhuming*, is done in the month of March or April. The cleaning of fields is done after that. Sowing is done in May or June and harvesting in November or December.

100 per cent families surveyed were growing paddy. 60 per cent of them were also growing maize in their *jhum* land. 20 per cent of those surveyed were growing moom also which is a local variety of coarse grain used for preparing beverages after fermentation for a period of one month. Ginger is also being produced by about 10 per

cent of the families. Almost 60 per cent of those surveyed were growing some kind of vegetables for their own consumption.

None of the families covered under the survey was found using HYV seeds. They cited the reasons like unsuitability of HYV seeds for the local soil leading to low production. Moreover, there is preference for traditional seeds amongst the population.

The details regarding various inputs used by the families surveyed and the average input cost is given in Table 3.11.

For wet paddy fields, fertilizers are being used. Some of the important fertilizers are diamond and urea. The price of one bag of 50 kg of diamond (a potash fertilizer) is Rs. 500 and for one bag of urea it is Rs. 250. Due to the high cost of fertilizers the farmers are not able to use it extensively. Cow-dung is used only in the case of vegetables etc.

Table 3.11 : Inputs and its Average Input Cost

Sl. No.	*Inputs*	*% of Households using it*	*Average cost per family (Rs.)*
1.	Ploughing (tractor or labour hiring)	48.0	880
2.	Seed	12.0	250
3.	Fertilizer	45.0	740
4.	Irrigation	0	0
5.	Pesticide	15.0	200
6.	Harvesting (labour charge)	66.0	500

Except for one family, all the other households are in possession of a certain type of livestock. The popular livestock is buffaloes, hens, dogs, pigs, cats, cows and ducks. The number and types of livestock possessed by a particular family has direct correlation with the occupation of the family members.

Buffalo is generally used for ploughing of wet land and eating purpose during some feasts etc. in the family. When in urgent need of money, it can be sold in the market.

Although each household is keeping some poultry, they are using chickens and eggs for their own consumption. The poultry farming has a good potential in the village as it is easy to maintain a few chickens in each households.

Yongchak is very popular in this region and is used for making chutney and vegetable preparation called '*Iromba*'. The tree is of moderate size. Other vegetables are also grown but mostly for self-consumption. It also provides intermittent incomes as they mature at different times of the year. Among the fruits, pineapple, banana and plum have very good economic viability if processing facilities are established nearby. At present, different kinds of fruits are being grown for own consumption only.

The pisciculture has not been developed in the village. There is no fish farm, only one person in the village has a small fish pond. Sometimes, villagers do fishing in the wet paddy field when there is some water-logging in case of heavy rains.

There is enough of possibility for taking up horticultural activity in village Oinamlong (Tamenglong : Manipur). Necessary initiative on the part of the Government/NGOs in this direction will definitely lead to economic prosperity in this area.

In village Chawainamei Khunou (Senapati : Manipur) maize and horticultural crops are grown in the rainfed pockets or in the dry fields where no irrigation facilities are available. The seeds for paddy, maize and potato are taken by the farmers from their previous production. For cabbage, the seeds are procured from outside. The farmers use the traditional implements for sowing and harvesting. The average number of buffaloes in each household is one, therefore, the farmers borrow buffaloes from one another. For wet paddy fields, cow dung is used as fertilizers. But in the rainfed areas, chemical fertilizers are used.

Rural Industries

The inhabitants of village Thingra (Tamenglong : Manipur) are peasant cultivators and depend greatly on agriculture for their living, and industry as such does not occupy any significant place in their economy. In their leisure when the two major works related to agriculture, that is sowing or transplantation and harvesting are over, the ladies take up weaving. There is a handloom or loin loom kept in each household. The workers are mainly women and young girls. Each girl has received her training from the elderly ladies.

The usual items of cloth prepared are ladies' lower garment called '*phanek*' and upper garment the shawl. Women's cloths have exquisite design on the border. Small pieces of cloth for children are prepared in the loin looms. Men's lower garments of '*dhoti*' type are also made. They do not prepare cloth comparable to those of the Meitei villages. It is due to the limitation of back-pressure loom in which only the cloth of very limited width can be woven. The other point worth mentioning is that they have not taken to modernization, as has been done in the Meitei villages of Manipur plains. They should switch to the use of improved looms for weaving fine cloth.

Rural arts and crafts are minimal in village Oinamlong (Tamenglong : Manipur). Bamboo and forest wood could provide the principal raw material for woodcraft.

Poverty Alleviation Programmes

In Kachai (Ukhrul : Manipur), out of 40 households surveyed, there were 7 IRDP beneficiaries. 6 of them were males, 1 female. In all the cases, the beneficiary was selected through the Village Authority and trade was chosen in all cases by mutual consultation between the BDO and the beneficiary. In none of the cases any loan has been returning and everyone felt the scheme to be good as it helped them to tide over temporary financial crisis.

The following assets have been created under the JRY from the year 1989 onwards in village Thingra (Tamenglong: Manipur) are shown in Table 3.12.

Table 3.12 : Work done and Cost incurred

Year	*Work*	*Amount*
1989-90	Construction of Jeepable road (2 km)	17905
1990-91	Improvement of road from Kabul Khullen to Thingra	12528
1991-92	Improvement of road	8616
1992-93	Improvement of road from Old Thingra to New Thingra	5930
1993-94	Improvement of road from Thingra to Nagaching	11920
1994-95	Land development around Church area	16500

The assets created under the JRY are mainly the inter-village roads and footpaths. They are being frequently used by the villagers. The money provided under the JRY was spent in paying wages to the workers employed in cutting the earth. The work has been done properly and as such the asset can be called a good quality one.

The following schemes have been taken up under the IRDP in village Thingra (Tamenglong : Manipur) as given in Table 3.13.

Table 3.13 : Schemes undertaken under IRDP

Sl. No.	*Name of Scheme*	*Number*
1.	Beekeeping	2
2.	Heifer	2
3.	Goatery	4
4.	Piggery	1
5.	Umorok	4

Of all the government sponsored schemes the IRDP appears to be doing the worst. There is no consultation with the beneficiary and the schemes are allotted at random to those short-listed for being the beneficiaries. At times, the people have to offer bribe in the form of chicken, liquor, etc. to the lower staff to get their names included.

The amount sanctioned per beneficiary is so small that hardly any durable asset creation is possible. There is also a lack of drive among the villagers for income generation. Most of the assets bought are sold out within a year. To have some impact, at least, the beneficiaries have to be properly counselled. This selection procedure should also be such that only the poorest of the poor is selected.

The inter-village roads and footpaths constructed under the JRY and the EAS in village Monsang Pantha (Chandel : Manipur) are in good shape. The ring road requires some repair. These assets are being used by the villagers. The construction of community hall has been done properly.

The minimum wage rate is Rs. 47.65. As per the information gathered from the survey, the prevalent wage rate in the village is between Rs. 40-45 per manday. Normally, there is no difference between the wages paid to a male and a female worker.

Under the JRY, some durable community assets have been created in the village like inter-village roads, footpaths, ring roads, wooden bridges, etc. These roads have improved the transport and communication network inside as well as outside the village, connecting the village to the nearby villages as well as the district headquarters.

Coverage of the IRDP

Table 3.14 : Type of Beneficiary and Percentage under IRDP

Sl. No.	Type of Beneficiary	Number	%
1.	S.T.	13	87.2
2.	Handicapped	2	12.7
	Total	**15**	**100.0**

Credit Disbursement under the IRDP

Table 3.15 : Amount and Percentage to Credit Disbursement under IRDP

Sl. No.	Type of Beneficiary	Amount (Rs.)	%
1.	S.T.	29500	78.7
2.	Handicapped	8000	21.3
	Total	**37500**	**100.0**

Distribution of the IRDP Beneficiaries Sector-wise

Table 3.16 : IRDP Beneficiaries Sector-wise

Sl. No.	Schemes	Number of Units
1.	Piggery	3
2.	Sugarcane Plantation	2
3.	Banana Plantation	2
4.	Potato Plantation	1
5.	Sewing Machine	1
6.	Carpentry	1

Under the IRDP, the number of beneficiaries assisted during 1997 in village Sekmai (Imphal West : Manipur) is as follows :

(i) Total number of beneficiaries 18

(ii) Number of SCs 18

(iii) Number of women 06

The beneficiaries were selected as per norms after placing the list in the Gram Sabha.

Beneficiaries came from the following occupations

Agricultural labourers	8
Non-agricultural labourers	4
Rural artisan	6
Total	18

Sector-wise details of beneficiaries

Primary (Agriculture and Animal Husbandry)	10
Secondary (Handloom, Handicraft and Village Industry)	8

An analysis of the past and present figures shows that more emphasis is being laid on the secondary now than in the past.

The following figures pertain to the status of TRYSEM in village Sekmai (Imphal West : Manipur) :

Trainees in Sekmai (1997-98)

Total number of trainees	4
Total number of the Scheduled Castes	3
Total number of Women	1

Assistance to trainees under IRDP

Number of trainees wage employed	2
Number of trainees self-employed	2

Number of trainees trade-wise

Electronics	2
Welding Units	1
Weaving	1

Works completed under the JRY (1997-98)

Roads	3
Houses	5

Latrines	5
House wiring	10

One DWCRA unit started functioning in the Sekmai Panchayat with 10 women, all of whom belonged to the Scheduled Castes. The group was provided with a revolving fund of Rs. 25,000 and is engaged in weaving

The overall poverty situation is not quite alarming in village Chawainamei Khunou (Senapati : Manipur). At least everyone has sufficient to eat. The incidence of the educated unemployed youth is quite noteworthy. There is a flight of youth from the village to bigger towns in search of jobs. They do not seem to be interested in self-employment or in developing entrepreneurial skills.

PART 2

TRIPURA

This study is based upon the socio-economic village assignment reports prepared by the following IAS probationers in Tripura Table 3.17.

Table 3.17 : Assignment Report of IAS Probationers

Sl. No.	*Name of the Probationer*	*Village*	*District*	*Year of submission of the Report*
1.	Atish Chandra	Radhanagar	North Tripura	1994
2.	Shikhar Agrawal	Uttar Takmachara	South Tripura	1995
3.	M.V. Subha Reddy	Raghna	North Tripura	1995
4.	Anil Garg	Baishyamani Revenue Para	South Tripura	1996
5.	Nitin Kulkarni	Deoracherra	North Tripura	1997
6.	Sanjeev Kumar	Satchand	South Tripura	2000
7.	Puneet Agrawal	Jalai	North Tripura	2000
8.	Syed Sabahat Azim	Rajiv Nagar	South Tripura	2001
9.	Ashutosh Jindal	East Manikya Diwan	South Tripura	—
10.	Niharika Barik	Garjeecherra	South Tripura	—
11.	Sheo Shankar Shukla	East Champa CHerra	West Tripura	—
12.	—	Purba Singhi Cherra	West Tripura	—

THE STUDY AREA : AN INTRODUCTION

As far as the social profile of the villages under study is concerned, there has not been any communal or caste feeling among the villages. In some of the villages, the Muslims and the Christians are in a minority but other people respect their religious customs and traditions. Even the migrants from Bangladesh have been allowed to become a part of the village life.

The female enjoy equal status *vis-à-vis* the males. They bear the brunt of the housework. They look after the household needs, take care of the young ones and also work as agricultural labourers.

The wage rate for the men and women was found to be same. The elderly females are engaged in weaving the loin cloth which is used by the members of the family. The traditional craft is still alive in the village and the expertise of these women has to be appreciated. The literacy rate among the females is very poor. Also, the number of school-going girls was less than the school-going boys.

A particular type of male discrimination was seen in the vaccination of the children and their treatment. The male children were getting the vaccination on time and also they were receiving complete doses, while the vaccination coverage among the female children was seen to be poor. The general health of the women was not satisfactory. This was mainly due to the large size of the families. The women were ignorant about the family planning methods and the practice of family planning was almost non-existent.

People's participation in the JRY scheme was found satisfactory and people wanted to work in the Government schemes. Earlier, the participation of the people in the selection of the schemes used to be nominal as the Panchayat members themselves were making all the decisions regarding the selection of works and their beneficiaries. With the three-tier set up, the people's participation has increased significantly. But, reports have been received that the attendance in the Gram Sabha meetings used to be very low because of its timing not suiting many villagers. As a result, there are not many people to raise their voice against the wishes of the Panchayat members. This practice can be corrected only by holding Gram Sabha meetings at a time, which is suited to most of the villagers, so that the schemes could be discussed in reality in the open Gaon Sabha meetings and appropriate decisions could be taken.

Still, people are involved in the process of development right from the stage of the selection of the beneficiaries to the selection of the site and the work to be taken up. For any work taken up under the Panchayat Development Fund (funds placed with the Panchayat Samiti and the Gram Panchayat), the resolution of the Panchayat Samiti and the Gram Panchayat is a must. This ensures that the fund placed for the villages is utilized with the consent of the villagers.

The Assignments Reports reveal that normally, the list of the selected IRDP beneficiaries was being kept for discussion in the Gaon-Sabha meetings. But, it was noticed that the Panchayat members were selecting their own relatives. It was the Gram Pradhan and few other influential persons of the village who used to select the IRDP beneficiaries. Despite all this, it was strange to see that there was not much opposition. No family was supplied with any of the input required for the IRDP schemes. All the beneficiaries were given only the cash amount in instalments as per the loan sanctioned to them against various schemes.

There was also no marketing support of any kind made available to the IRDP beneficiaries. Most of the beneficiaries were marketing the produce to the middlemen, as they could not carry the produce to the market themselves. It was noted that the middlemen were making profits in the process and the actual cultivator was not getting any advantage.

It was found in the surveys that the beneficiary families received loan from the DRDA but there has been no repayment of loan. The beneficiaries are of the view that the Government may waive the loans at any future point of time. It is also observed that the beneficiaries have not used the loan amount for the purpose for which they got it sanctioned, rather they used this amount for domestic consumption.

The failure of the cooperative movement in the areas under study is due to the following reasons :

(i) The staff members managing the affairs of the cooperatives get salary from the cooperative only. They do not get salary from the Directorate of Cooperative Societies (DRCs).

(ii) The loans given by the cooperatives are not being repaid by its members.

(iii) The margin in giving loans and buying and re-selling of agricultural products from the growers is smaller. PAC takes funds from the bank at 11 per cent interest and disburse it as loan to the villagers at 12 per cent. As long as the cooperative is not run on a totally professional basis and the repayment of loans is not ensured by its members, the PACs is going to remain a loss making society. The cooperative members need to take more interest in the PACs so that the purpose of constituting the cooperative to play an important role in improving the economic conditions of the members could be fulfilled.

The villages under study do not have any NGO working there. In fact, the culture of NGOs and the Government doing some work or the NGOs helping the scheme has not yet developed in the State as a whole and only a few NGOs are doing some work related to health issues in the district. Due to the lack of any such initiative, the much needed thrust for the implementation of the schemes is not there and the entire burden of getting the scheme properly implemented falls only on the Government.

There are very few common property resources available in the villages studied. There is no designated grazing land in the villages and the livestock moves around in the forests for fodder. The cattle grazing is generally done in the Government *khas* land adjacent to the roads or in the forest land. As it is not possible for the forest department to stop this, the grazing goes on uninhibited resulting in a lot of damage to the young plants. However, since the number of animals is limited in the villages, the problem has not yet taken any acute shape. Since most of the flat area is either put to use as homestead land or the paddy land, the availability of the common property resources is very less. The terrain of the villages is such that *lunga* land is interspersed in between the *tilla* land. Most of the *tilla* land, which is used by the tribals for plantation, belongs to the forest department. Many villagers possess the Government land without proper allotment and the homestead land without proper *parcha*. There has been shrinkage in the common property resources due to the pressure of the increased population on the land. There are cases in the villages where forest reserve land is brought under individual plantations thus reducing the common property resource area for the villagers as a whole.

The main occupation of the villagers in the study area is agriculture. There are two categories of people engaged in it, one the landowners who cultivate their own lands and the other the landless labourers. As there is only one cropping season, almost all the people get the employment during the period. All these remain unemployed after the harvest of the kharif crop.

The people who work as farm labourers usually get Rs. 40 to Rs. 50 per day as wages. The payments are made in cash weekly. Some people are engaged in the non-farm sector like the brick kiln. They get the weekly payment and get assured employment for about 7-8 months in a year, barring the rainy season, when the kiln is not operational.

Unemployment in the villages is both disguised and seasonal as agriculture is the only subsistence activity in the area. Due to increasing population pressure, the hands requiring work and the mouths to be fed are increasing. But due to the scarcity of land in the State of Tripura it is very difficult to provide employment and food to all only from the produce of the land. Different employment generation schemes like the JRY and the EAS are implemented in the areas and different works were taken up for employment generation under various schemes. But, these schemes are not able to ensure the wage employment to the registered labourers for the prescribed number of mandays in a year. Even this small share comes only for 2-3 months as very few works are being taken up in the area. Hence, the promise of the schemes to provide employment of 100 days for one member of the family remains a mirage. With such a poor employment generation, these schemes have not been able to make any significant dent in the poverty and unemployment situation of the village. Still, many villagers are interested in taking wherever small amount of employment is available from the Government. The revised rate of Rs. 40 per day as wages is a positive measure but it has to be matched by the increasing number of mandays per family per year. Lack of any industrial activity in and around the villages studied has resulted in lack of employment for the villagers. So, special efforts are required for providing assured employment to the people of the area.

Concerted efforts in soil conservation are the need of the hour in selected pockets in the study area. Most of the villages are raised on hillocks of soft soil. The rapidly declining vegetative cover in the area has resulted in soil erosion. The top layer of the tilla has been washed away resulting in the reduction of fertility to a certain extent. This has been reflected in the reduced yield and has retarded the growth of the banana and arecanut plantations. During the rainy season, the water run-off is very fast from the hill slopes and carries with it the top layers of the soil. Due to the looseness of the soil, the run-off is more.

In areas where watershed development projects have been taken up, some water conservation tanks have been created. Such tanks are used by the people for fishery as well as for domestic purposes. Compared to cultivators operating in the non-watershed areas, there has been definite improvement in the income of the beneficiaries of the watershed projects. People who have started fishery in the tanks are particularly well off. Still, there is a vast scope for the improvement of the irrigation facilities in the area under study and elsewhere. A planned and pragmatic use of the stream water, which is available round the year, may help in improving the yield of the cultivators.

For convenience of condensed presentation, the village assignment reports prepared by the IAS probationers are being studied under the following principal heads :

1. Demography
2. Land
3. Irrigation
4. Agriculture and Allied Activities
5. Rural Industries
6. Poverty Alleviation Programmes

Demography

The total population of the village East Manikya Dewan (South Tripura : Tripura), according to the 1991 census is 1947 (Males—964: Females—983). The rate of growth of the population over different censuses is given in Table 3.18.

East Champacherra (West Tripura : Tripura) is a village of 526 households with a population of 3,043. It is a small village having an area of 3588.88 acres. It is situated in the *tillas* (small hillocks).

There are 4 hamlets in Baishyamani Revenue Para village (South Tripura : Tripura), namely Baishyamani Para, Ramkanta Para, Bangshi

Para and Halua Para. The village retains its totally tribal character. It can be partly attributed to its being a haven for the dreaded insurgents—thereby deterring the non-tribals. At the para level, Ramkanta Para has 35 families. Baishyamani Para has 112 families, Bangshi Para has 31 families and Halua Para has 30 families.

Table 3.18 : Year-wise Population and Rate of Growth of East Manikya Dewan

Year	*Population*	*Rate of Growth*
1961	—	—
1971	—	—
1981	1633	—
1991	1947	19.2%

The total population of village Raghna was 2,647 as on 1=7=1994. The village has a mix of the Scheduled Castes, Backward Castes, other castes of the Hindus and the Muslims. Classification of the population in terms of caste and sex are given below. The other castes of the village includes two families of Brahmins, 63 families of Manipuris and 384 families of Pals. The major activity of the village is agriculture. Apart from agriculture, major occupation is carpentry. The village has about 50 landless families (Table 3.19).

Table 3.19 : Classification of Population of Village Raghna

Backward Castes (14 families)		*Scheduled Castes (14 families)*		*Muslims (14 families)*		*Others (14 families)*		*Total (14 families)*	
Male	*Female*	*Male*	*Female*	*Male*	*Female*	*Male*	*Female*	*Male*	*Female*
48	35	77	87	140	138	1090	1021	1355	1292

Some of the sections of the society have made conscious effort towards family planning. Muslim community has, in general, more number of children per family. Average number of children per family is three (alive) and dead (none). The average number of children per family is high, might be due to the Muslim population, as the Muslims have about 5 children per family.

The statistics of births and deaths for the last six years is given in Table 3.20.

Table 3.20 : Births and Deaths Year-wise in terms of Sex

Year	*Births*			*Deaths*		
	Male	*Female*	*Total*	*Male*	*Female*	*Total*
1989	39	47	86	16	2	18
1990	14	34	48	10	2	12
1991	41	32	73	12	5	17
1992	59	41	100	4	3	7
1993	49	34	83	2	7	9
1994	55	61	106	5	7	12

The Uttar Takmachara revenue village falls in the Takmachara Gaon Panchayat of the Bagafa Block in the Belonia sub-division (South Tripura : Tripura). There are as many as six hamlets or *paras* in the village, namely:

1. Mishti Chand Noatia Para
2. Bishun Chand Noatia Para
3. Chatra Muni Debbarma Para
4. Kani Chandra Tripura Para
5. Jatindra Debbarma Para
6. Kupilung

Kupilung is the interior-most hamlet of the village, whereas Mishti Chand Noatia Para is on the road side. There are people of only one tribe i.e. Noatia residing in Kupilung, whereas in Mishti Chand Para, there are people of other tribes like Debbarma, Murasing also, apart from the non-tribals.

These two paras namely Mishti Chand Noatia Para and Kupilung, both having around 50 families each, have been selected for the purpose of this study to get an overall picture of the village.

Dearth of reliable records at para level, poses a definite problem in analyzing the change in the demographic composition of the village, over a period of time. But there are definite evidences which show that the village has gone through a significant demographic change, over a period of time. For example, the Kupilung, which is an interior para, has only tribal population whereas the road side Mishti Chand Noatia Para, has a significant non-tribal population in it. Further, the name of the Para also indicates that at some point of time it would have been a Para of only the Noatia people.

The demography of the village is slowly changing in favour of the non-tribals. Further, the tribal character starts losing as one moves from an interior Para of the village to a road side one. The latest reliable record with respect to the population is available in the BPL survey conducted in the year 1993-94. At the Para level, Kupilung has 62 families, all belonging to the Noatia tribe, Mishti Chand Noatia Para has 51 families residing in it. 50 per cent belong to the Noatia tribe and the rest half consist of a mixture of Bengali and other tribal families.

While the tribals of Kupilong are basically dependent on *jhum* or some paddy cultivation in whatever lunga available, the people of Mishti Chand Noatia Para have taken up other activities like fishery, *chana chur* making etc. as well. The economy is basically subsistence based and most of the people in the village find it difficult to get the two ends meet. A large percentage of the population earns its bread by way of wage employment over a significant period of the year. Although there is not much of conscious effort towards family planning among the people of the village, the people especially the literate ones have started paying due attention in this direction. The tribals speak mainly the Kakborak whereas the non-tribals speak Bengali. Most of the tribals especially the younger generation is able to converse both in Kakborak as well as in Bengali.

Radhanagar Gaon Panchayat is a part of Kumarghat R.D. Block, which falls in the Kailashahar sub-division (Tripura). There are four paras (villages) in Radhanagar: New Radhanagar, Radhanagar East, Radhanagar West and Chaunag Para. The name of the Mouza is Radhanagar. The total population of the Gaon Panchayat is 3,438 out of which there are 660 SC, 246 ST, 1200 OBC and 1339 General. In terms of families there are 151 SC, 87 ST, 190 OBC and 204 General.

Purba Singhi Cherra is a small village having an area of 3588.88 acres in the Khowai sub-division of the West Tripura district (Tripura). This is a village of 375 households with a population of 1843. This village is predominantly tribal in composition.

Household Details

Table 3.21 : Caste-wise Household Distribution

No. of Households	*Population*	*Community*	*% in total population*	*Average size of family*
197	987	ST	53.56	5
134	570	General	30.93	4
44	286	SC	15.51	6
Total: 375	**1843**		**100**	

Table 3.21 gives the caste-wise household distribution.

The population of village Satchand (South Tripura : Tripura) in 1991 was 2,499. The composition of the population was as follows :

Number of families: 362

Total population: 1569

(i) *Sex Distribution*

Male : 789

Female : 780

(ii) *Caste-wise Distribution*

ST : 511

SC : 460

OBC : 248

General : 350

(iii) *Religion-wise Distribution*

Hindu : 764

Muslim : 452

Christian : 353

(iv) *The Rate of the Growth of Population*

The comparative population of the village during different censuses operations is given in Table 3.22.

Table 3.22 : Comparative Population of Village Satchand (South Tripura) per census Year

Year	*Population*
1961	NA
1971	856
1981	1074
1991	1415
1999	1569

It can be seen that the rate of growth of population during the decades is as high as 25.46 during 1971 to 1981 and 31.75 during the decade 1981-91. This was mainly due to the fact that many families have settled in the area from nearby places particularly from the Bangladesh who settled here.

The population of village Deoracherra (North Tripura : Tripura) in 1991 was 2499. The composition of the population was as follows:

Number of families: 553

(i) *Sex Distribution*

Male	:	1,147
Female	:	1,152

(ii) *Caste-wise Distribution*

ST	:	1,677
SC	:	7
General	:	815
OBC	:	The OBC as a caste was not mentioned at the time

(iii) *Religion-wise Distribution*

Hindu	:	764

Muslim : 452
Christian : 1283

(iv) *The Rate of Growth of Population*

The comparative population of the village during different census operations is given in Table 3.23:

Table 3.23 : Comparative Population of Village Deoracherra Year-wise (North Tripura)

Year	*Population*
1961	NA
1971	1356
1981	1874
1991	2499
1996	2807

It can be seen that the rate of growth of the population during the decades is as high as 51.8 during 1971 to 1981 and 62.5 during the decade 1981-91. This was mainly due to fact that many families have settled in the area from the nearby places particularly from the Karimganj district of Assam. Also due to the presence of a Tea estate, most of the labourers working there are from outside and have now become the residents of this village. Some of the Muslim families have come from Bangladesh and settled here.

Land

Radhanagar (North Tripura : Tripura) the distribution of land area family-wise (in acres) is given in Table 3.24.

Table 3.24 : Land Area Family-wise of Radhanagar (North Tripura)

ST				*SC*				*ST*				*SC*			
0-2	2-4	4-10	10	0-2	2-4	4-10	10	0-2	2-4	4-10	10	0-2.	2-4	4-10	10
36	32	14	Nil	43	67	20	Nil	81	82	20	2	79	102	19	4

It can be seen that maximum families fall between 0-4 acres and very few families have land more than 10 acres. The holdings are small and uneconomical. Therefore, there is, in general, poverty in the area. People are mostly dependent on mandays generation work undertaken by the Government during the lean agriculture period for their livelihood. People having very small holdings are engaged in tenancy in lands of those who have slightly bigger holdings.

The total area of village Garjeecherra (South Tripura : Tripura) is 1761.42 hectares. Around 30 per cent of the land, that is, 275 hectares is under cultivation. Most of the land is under forest cover. It measures around 1150.40 hectares. Land under miscellaneous trees and groves is around 5 hectares. There is a huge amount of cultivable wasteland, which measures around 220 hectares. The village has around 5 hectares of fallow land. There is no facility of canal irrigation in the village. Only 30 hectares of land is irrigated under watershed and area irrigated by tanks and wells is 5 hectares. Only a small portion of the households who are a little well off can afford private pump sets. The total area of land under such usage is only 6 hectares. Those who hire the pump set pay Rs. 40 per hour.

The average land holding in the village is very small. 275 landholders hold an average of less than 1 hectare. Only 25 persons have 1 to 2 hectares and 10 persons have 2 to 4 hectares. No one has an operational holding of more than 4 hectares. The average rainfall in this area is around 175.55 mm. The soil type is red soil. Even though the conditions are very favourable for good agriculture, the small size of holdings makes use of pump sets or modern techniques of agriculture uneconomical. Agriculture remains as sustenance agriculture.

The area under self-cultivation of the landholders is 227.28 hectares. The area owned by the absentee landholders is 55.54 hectares. It is interesting to note that though there are a large number of tenants in the village only four of them are registered tenants whose names are recorded in the record of rights as *bargadar*. In Tripura, the Bargadar System is prevalent in which the tenant is a *barga* who gives a fixed share of the produce to the landowner annually. The other system is the Korfadar system in which the tenant or Korfa pays the landowner in cash.

As regards the Government land, in 1971 the extent of such land was 1142.28 hectares which is reduced to 1305.21 hectares as of now. Out of this 13.05 hectares are lying as wasteland, 143.53 hectares are used as homestead land, 11.48 hectares are under cultivation. The rest is under forest cover or used for other purposes. A total of

137.06 hectares of land has been allotted to 113 persons of which 50 are tribals, 14 SCs and 49 others. Apart from that a lot of such land has been encroached.

The last survey was conducted in 1997. The final publication has been done and the new record of rights is operational. The *patta* pas book or the *khatian* is not yet distributed fully.

The land details of village East Manikya Dewan (South Tripura: Tripura) are as follows (in acres) :

Types of Land

(a) Land for cultivation	667
(b) Land under forest cover	2085.82
(c) Fallow land	—
(d) Pasture and grazing land	123.13
(e) Wasteland	—
(f) Land for homestead	24.53
(g) Net sown area	580
(h) Community land	1.67
(i) Miscellaneous (Departmental land) river, streams, roads	15.35

Land Area under

(a) Ownership cultivation	517.51
(b) Tenancy	—
(c) Other (sharecropping)	6.18

Distribution of Landownership (household-wise)

(a) Landless	69
(b) <1 acres	103
(c) 1-3 acres	124
(d) 3-5 acres	37
(e) 5-10 acres	24
(f) 10-20 acres	—
(g) 20 acres +	—

Distribution of Operational Holdings

(a) 1 acre	45.10
(b) 1-3 acres	224.62
(c) 3-5 acres	150.13
(d) 5-10 acres	135.77
(e) 10-20 acres	—
(f) 20 acres +	—

The details of different classes of lands allotted to the people of village Baishyamani Revenue Para (South Tripura : Tripura) are as follows:

ST: 83 families and 159.06 acres

Bastu	:	18.87 acres
Nal	:	21.09 acres
Chara	:	6.79 acres
Doba	:	1.54 acres
Viti	:	18.30 acres
Lunga	:	10.13 acres
Bagan	:	6.46 acres
Tilla	:	74.85 acres
Pukurpar	:	0.31 acres
Pukur	:	0.92 acres
Total	:	159.06 acres

Out of the different classes of lands Nal and Lunga are most suited for purposes of cultivation and provide maximum returns.

Total Land allotted	:	159.06 acres
Nal and Lunga allotted	:	31.22 acres
Per cent of Nal and Lunga to the total	:	19.63 per cent

This figure is abnormally low. Statistical analysis of land allotted in district South Tripura over the past few years reveals that per cent of Nal and Lunga land to total land allotted is 26.15 per cent in case of tribals, 81.75 per cent in case of SCs and 47.23 per cent in case of others.

It is clear from the figures above, that significant percentage of land allotted to people belonging to the Scheduled Castes and others is either Nal or Lunga. The corresponding figures for the tribals who are the original inhabitants of the place is comparatively too much low.

This is a clear manifestation of how non-tribals who have immigrated over the past few decades, have taken lead by getting better quality of land allotted to them. The phenomenon of tribals losing their say is constantly on the rise all over the State and consequently, majority of benefits being given by the Government are being pocketed by the non-tribals.

The details of land-use pattern in village Raghna (North Triupra: Tripura) are as follows :

(a)	Land for cultivation	:	910 acres
(b)	Forests	:	Nil
(c)	Fallows	:	49.5 acres
(d)	Grazing lands	:	22.5 acres
(e)	Wastelands (cultivable)	:	24.9 acres
(f)	Community lands	:	2.0 acres
(g)	Fruit trees/plantations	:	12.0 acres
(h)	Land not available for cultivation (homestead etc.)	:	18.45 acres
(i)	Water tanks area	:	71.28 acres
	Total	:	**1110.63 acres**

In this village, the size of the holdings is very small. There is no surplus land available which is over and above the ceiling limits. The *khas* land (Government land) was allotted to the eligible homeless and landless people.

Major portion of the land is with the *raiyats*. The allottee holdings, too, comprise considerable portion of land. Regarding sharecropper holdings the number of holdings and the area is only approximate. The sharecroppers' names are not entered in the *khatians*.

The land reforms are very effective in Tripura. In Raghna village, there was nobody having land over and above the ceiling limit before the commencement of the TLR and LR Act, 1960. At present also, all the holdings in the village are of less than six acres, i.e. much below the ceiling limit. Nonetheless, it is not possible to give a clear picture about whether there is any socio-economic impact on the people who are receiving ceiling surplus land.

Area-wise Distribution of Holdings among Various Categories

Table 3.25 : Category and Area-wise Distribution

Sl. No.	*Category*	*No. of families*			*Area in acres*		
		SC	*Others*	*Total*	*SC*	*Others*	*Total*
1.	Upto one acre	9	162	171	8.00	160.00	168.00
2.	From one to two acres	25	320	345	40.00	569.53	609.53
3.	From two to three acres	1	41	42	2.50	114.00	116.50
4.	From three to six acres	Nil	3	3	Nil	15.97	15.97
	Total	**35**	**526**	**561**	**50.50**	**859.50**	**910.00**

The revenue records show the total area of village Uttar Takmachara (South Tripura : Tripura) as 2561.65 acres, out of which 444.12 acres is under the Reserve Forest. The detailed break up of different categories of lands is given below :

1.	Jote	: 997.30 acres
2.	Reserve Forests	: 444.12 acres
3.	Khas (under unauthorized occupation)	: 161.77 acres
4.	Protected Forests	
	(a) Under forest cover	: 548.29 acres
	(b) Vacant	: 259.91 acres
	(c) Allotted (prior to 1978)	: 142.58 acres
5.	Under BSF	: 7.78 acres
	Total	**: 2561.65 acres**

As many as 310 families have been allotted 623.36 acres of land. Moreover, the major share of the allotted land has gone to the tribals. The category-wise details of the allotted land are given in Table 3.26.

Table 3.26: Land Allotment Category-wise

Category	*No. of families*	*Areas*
ST	276	573.67 acres
SC	10	11.15 acres
Others	24	38.54 acres
Total	**310**	**623.36 acres**

It is true that the major share of the allotted land has gone to the tribals, but to see how much impact it has had on the lives of these people, it is essential to look at the class of land allotted. The land is undoubtedly the most important economic asset in a rural setting. Moreover, out of the different classes of lands, *Nal* and *Lunga* are most suited for the purpose of cultivation and provide maximum returns. The details of *Nal* and *Lunga* lands allotted to different sections of the population in the village have been given in Table 3.27.

Table 3.27 : Percentage of Nal and Lunga Lands in terms of Categories

Categories	*Total land allotted*	*Nal & Lunga allotted*			*% of Nal and Lunga to the total*
		Nal	*Lunga*	*Total*	
SC	573.67 acres	103.07	75.14	178.21	31.06%
ST	11.15 acres	7.64	2.33	9.97	89.42%
Others	38.54 acres	20.35	2.88	23.23	60.28%

It is clear from the above figures, that although a significant percentage of land allotted to the people belonging to the Scheduled Castes and others is either *Nal* or *Lunga*, the corresponding figures for the tribals, who are the original inhabitants of the place is comparatively very low. This shows how the non-tribals who have come in the last few decades and have taken over the hold of a lot of area by way of unauthorized occupation, have also succeeded in getting the better quality of land allotted. This phenomenon of tribals losing their say is constantly on the rise all over the State and consequently a majority of the benefits flowing from the Government are being pocketed by the non-tribals.

The landholding pattern in village Purba Singhi Cherra (West Tripura : Tripura) is given in Table 3.28.

Table 3.28 : The Landholding Pattern of Purba Singhi Cherra (West Tripura)

Size of holding (in acres)	*No. of people possessing Nal*	*% in the total land*	*No. of people possessing Tilla*	*% in the total land*
Below 1	10	9	9	23.68
1	5	11	11	28.94
2	8	10	10	26.31
3	1	2.63	3	7.89
4	1	2.63	5	13.15
5	1	2.63	—	—
6	1	2.63	1	2.63
7	1	2.63	—	—
8	—	—	—	—
9	1	2.63	—	—

Nal land is possessed by only 29 villagers (households) but *Tilla* is possessed by many. *Khas* land is the Government land given to the people. This is almost always *Tilla* land. As we can observe from the Table 3.28, the average size of the holding is very small, i.e. below one acre to 2 acres. 23 of the 29 who possess Nal land own below 2 acres (79.31%) and 30 of the 38 Tilla land owners fall into this size (78.94%). During the study it was found that the villagers possess as less as 0.20 acres.

Among the 7 landless respondents, 4 belonged to the Scheduled Castes and 3 to the Scheduled Tribes. In the study, only 10 per cent of the tribals do not possess the land whereas 50 per cent of the Scheduled Castes do not possess the land.

The uneconomic size of the landholding results in more costs in the cultivation. As stated earlier, it was almost rainfed agriculture till recently but of late, the villagers have started digging wells. But this is not due to the assistance of the million wells scheme, rather due to the own initiative of the villagers. Anyhow, in the *tilla* land it is single crop agriculture and the principal crop is rice. After the harvest of the rice, few vegetables are grown on this. The inputs for the cultivation like seeds and manures are available locally. The manures are the organic manures as they do not have the resources to opt for chemical fertilizers. These organic manures are bought from among the villagers or are home-made. The credit taken for these activities is generally from the relatives or the moneylender or as in many instances *dukandar* (shopkeeper). They do no prefer the formal credit institutions.

The landholding patterns in village Satchand (South Tripura: Tripura) are as follows :

The land under ownership cultivation	: 279.72 acres
Land under tenancy occupation	: Nil
Land with the Tea estate	: 84 acres

Distribution of the Landownership (Household-wise)

Table 3.29 : Land and Number of Families

Sl. No.	*Category*	*No. of families*
1.	Landless	98
2.	<1 acre	174
3.	1-3 acres	43
4.	3-5 acres	46
5.	5-10 acres	01
6.	>10 acres	Nil

From the distribution of the holdings it is clear that most of the households are having lands less than 3 acres. In all 98 families are landless. The fact that only one cultivator has more than 5 acres of land is a noteworthy feature.

Distribution of the Operational Holdings

Table 3.30 : Operational Holdings and its Distribution

Sl. No.	*Category*	*No. of Families*
1.	<1 acre	192
2.	1-3 acres	113
3.	3-5 acres	19
4.	>5 acres	Nil

The landholding patterns in village Deoracherra (North Tripura: Tripura) are given in Table 3.31.

Table 3.31: Village Deoracherra (North Tripura) and its Landholding Petterns

Sl. No.	Types of Land	Area (in acres)
1.	Land for cultivation	1117.47
2.	Land under forest cover	697.56
3.	Fallow land	6.40
4.	Pasture and grazing land	No such demarcated land for the purpose
5.	Wasteland	8.31
6.	Land for homestead	51.93
7.	Net sown area	448.14
8.	Community land	1.4
9.	Departmental land	33.72 (land with different Government Departments)
10.	Land with Tea estate	484
11.	Barga land	Nil

Distribution of the Landownership (Household-wise)

Table 3.32 : Land ownership Distributioner

Sl. No.	Category	No. of families
1.	Landless	63
2.	<1 acre	174
3.	1-3 acres	143
4.	3-5 acres	46
5.	5-10 acres	01
6.	>10 acres	Nil

From the distribution of the holdings it is clear that most of the households are having lands less than 3 acres. 63 families are landless. The fact that only one cultivator has more than 5 acres of land is a noteworthy feature.

Distribution of the Operational Holdings

Table 3.33 : Operational Holdings Distribution

Sl. No.	Category	No. of Families
1.	<1 acre	192
2.	1-3 acres	153
3.	3-5 acres	19
4.	>5 acres	Nil

Area under cultivation yielding

One crop	:	190.27 acres
Two crops	:	123.79 acres
Multi crops	:	134.18 acres

Here the only crop which is grown is paddy. Whatever land is mentioned as under two or multi crops means paddy plus vegetables or some plantations like banana and arecanut. As there are no irrigation facilities the question of taking the second crop during the rabi season does not arise. Most of the people grow vegetables like potato, brinjal and beans by using the water from the stream. Some cultivation of tomatoes and chillies was also seen. Two farmers were seen to be growing mustard and were getting average to good yield. Also, most of the farmers had grown plantations on the available *tilla* lands or had encroached upon the nearby forest lands. Some people were using the bed of the stream during dry season and growing vegetables. The plantations were mostly of mixed types having pineapple, banana and arecanut. At Muruibari, betel leaf (Pan) plantations were also seen.

The following landholding pattern has emerged from a study of village East Champacherra (West Tripura: Tripura) is given in Table 3.34.

Table 3.34 : Landholding Pattern

Size of holding (in acres)	*No. of people possessing Nal*	*No. of people possessing Tilla*
Below 1	5	4
1	3	6
2	1	5
3	1	2
4	1	1
5	0	0
6	0	0
7	0	0

The output of these crops has to be sold in the nearby Khowai market. Villagers carry the harvest on particular Bazar (market) days and sell it there. The income from the land is varied in nature. Average amount of the income ranges from Rs. 2,000-5,000 per annum.

Irrigation

The village Raghna (North Tripura: Tripura), is almost dependent on rainfall for the cultivation of crops. One tributary of a river is passing nearby the village. But there is no mini barrage to facilitate the irrigation of crops. It has also no lift irrigation system to pump water from the river. In the rainy season MIFC (Minor Irrigation and Flood Control) Department constructs seasonal bunds to divert rain water into the fields. As there is abundant rainfall, the entire kharif season does not need even a single supplementary irrigation. That is why there is no proper canal network for water distribution. During rabi season farmers use water from their own ponds located in the fields or from the nearby river to irrigate vegetable crops. The total area under irrigation for the year round is only 25 acres, which is due to a deep tube well owned by the government.

Sometimes, the villagers hire pump sets to pump water from the river. The hiring charges of a pump set per day is about Rs. 60-75.

There is a lot of scope for sustainability of the irrigation projects. The government can provide lift irrigation facilities to the village, which will irrigate about 200 acres of land. The construction of one or two sluice gates will also help in irrigating about 60 acres of land. Installation of private irrigation projects may not be possible, since the farmers are not economically sound enough.

There are no irrigation facilities in village Satchand (South Tripura: Tripura) and entire agriculture and horticulture is rainfed. Even for drinking purposes there is shortage during the dry months of January to April. The only source of water for the village is the stream Deoracherra, which has water round the year. Some cultivators have diverted the stream water into their fields but the impact is very less and there is practically no irrigation in the area.

The State Agriculture Department has launched a Watershed Development Project in the area. The hamlet colony Bari and Satchand para are having the beneficiaries of the project. The programme consists of mainly constructing the water harvesting structures and water tanks. Till date, 5 small tanks have been constructed under the project on the individual beneficiary land. As the size of landholding is very small there is very less land available for making a water tank. Hence, the project has not made any significant impact on the agriculture of the area.

The project also includes the Sloping Agriculture Land Technology (SALT) promoted by the Agriculture Department for making cultivation possible on the sloping *tilla* lands. The technique used is mainly the creation of graded bunds on the hill slopes so as to prevent the direct water and soil run off from the tops. This is mainly suitable for the pineapple plantations. This area does not have much pineapple plantations. Now the department is promoting the plantations.

The project also includes giving of free pineapple and banana suckers and some fertilizers to the cultivators. But there was no follow up of the action and also no technical guidance was given for the purpose. Only one VLW was looking after the project and hence the actual benefits were not being realized.

There was also no proposal to use the Feni stream water for irrigation purposes by making a check dam or the storage tank. The concept of putting bunds on the hill slopes to reduce the erosion of the soil was not known.

There was definite improvement in the income of the beneficiaries, particularly people who have started fishery in the tanks. Still there is a vast scope for the improvement of the irrigation facilities in the area and the use of the stream water, which is available round the year, may help in improving the yield of the cultivators.

The village Deoracherra (North Tripura : Tripura) is made up of hillocks of soft soil. The rapidly declining vegetative cover in the area has resulted in soil erosion to a great extent. The top layers of the *tilla* have been washed away resulting in the reduction of fertility. This has been reflected in the reduced yield and delayed growth of the banana and arecanut plantation. During the rainy season the water run off is very fast from the hill slopes and carries with it top layers of the soil. Due to the looseness of the soil the run off is more. The changing course of the Deora stream and high speed flow during the rainy season has resulted in the erosion of the banks of the stream. The ground water level has also gone down in the area and the ring wells and the sanitary wells go dry in January and February. According to the village elders, the flow of the water in the stream has also been reduced since the last 10-15 years.

In village Uttar Takmachara (South Tripura: Tripura), there is no irrigation facility or water harvesting structure. The private means of irrigation are negligible, as the economy is basically subsistence based and most of the people are not left with any surplus for investment in this direction.

Recently, under the new area based approach of planning, watersheds consisting of 4-5 Gram Panchayats have been identified, all over the State. The village falls in watershed No. 2 of the Bagafa Block. But the whole thing is still in very initial stages and it is likely to take very long before anything substantial materializes in the field out of it. An immediate government intervention to provide irrigation facility in the village is definitely the need of the hour. With a lot of money pouring in under the Employment Generation Schemes, few water harvesting structures at the right locations may go a long way in changing the pathetic irrigation scenario of the village.

Agriculture & Allied Activities

The soil in village Uttar Takmachara (South Tripura : Tripura) is laterite with low water absorption capacity. The lungas are alluvial and *tillas* have loamy sand devoid of humous. Moreover, the soil which is grossly deficient in nitrates, phosphorus, potash, organic matters and trace minerals is acidic in nature. Consequently, it cannot be treated with the usual fertilizers. The combination of tropical sun and torrential rains has leached out most of the minerals from the soil, over a period of time. Further, the reduced *jhum* cycle has also had an adverse impact over the fertility of the land. Consequently, the health of the plant, animals and human beings has been affected severely. The main rainy season in the area starts around June and lasts upto the month of August. In addition, there are occasional rains in the month of April-May and September-October as well.

Paddy is the principal crop of the village. There are three cultivation seasons, namely *Aush, Aman* and *Boro* in the State. But in the absence of irrigation facilities, most of the people in the village are able to take only one crop, i.e. *Aman*. In *Aman*, sowing is done around May-June and plantation in July. The crop is harvested around November. Some people are able to take the second crop, locally called *Boro*, as well. In *Boro*, the plantation is done in January and the crop is harvested around April. The yield from the first crop is on the average around 10 maunds per *pant* in the village. Whereas the yield from the second one is generally half of the first crop, mainly because of uncertainty of the rains and the absence of irrigation facilities. The most common variety of the rice being used by the people is paizom and IR8. Very few people are able to use inputs like fertilizers and pesticides.

The subsistence economy of the village leaves no scope to market the produce outside the village. Most of the produce is being consumed within the village itself. There is no institutional marketing arrangement and whatever little is sold out of the village is totally dependent on the prevailing market forces in the area.

There has not been much change in the cropping pattern of the village over the years. Paddy continues to occupy the prime slot. Only some non-tribals have recently shifted to potato, which fetches a slightly better return.

All the cows available in the villages are of the local variety, with a yield of around half to one litre of milk per day. The people use cow-dung for home apart from using it as manure. The cattle feed is not available in the area. Cows generally graze in the jungle or during the post-harvest period, in the fields. The nearest veterinary dispensary at Birchandra is around 10 km away from the village. Goats are reared for meat and not for milk. Piggery is popular among the tribals. There are not many waterbodies in the village at present, otherwise fishery is a profitable economic activity. Poultry is limited mainly due to shortage of birds, feeds and veterinary facilities in the area.

In general, the Animal Resource Development Department has failed to make any impact in the area. The upgradation of the quality of animals and arrangement for suitable linkages are the need of the hour, which if provided are bound to bring a substantial change in the lives of the people of the village.

As mentioned earlier, the villagers in East Champacherra (West Tripura : Tripura) possess two types of land—*Nal* and *Tila. Nal* is the land which is located down the hills with irrigation facilities. *Tilla* land is mainly rainfed. The nature of the soil is hilly and loamy. The productivity of the land is less and even among these lands *tilla* is more unproductive. In the village, total *khas* land is about 2602.5 acres out of which various government departments hold ownership rights over 750.02 acres. The government has allotted 179.80 acres to 490 landless people according to the provisions of the TLR and LR Act, 1960. In the village, there are 8 *bargadars* and 10 *kurfadars* (a form of tenancy). The concept of double cropping did not enter this village. The obvious reasons are lack of irrigation, less fertility, small holdings, lack of advanced technology, traditional methods of farming etc. The small size of holdings makes agriculture an expensive affair. Among the 25 households, 19 possess land which forms around 76 per cent of the respondents and the rest are landless. But possessing land does not imply that they have regular income from the land. Out of 19 land holders, 8 do not have any income from the land.

Livestock consists of the pigs, goats and cows. These are bought by the respondents from their meagre savings or with the help of the loans (not just the government loans). The cattle are put to different uses like milching, using in cultivation, to obtain manure, to supply meat etc. But only around 50 per cent have cattle, the other half do not possess cattle. Most of the households have one or two cattle, there are very few who possessed cattle around five or six. The highest number of cattle is possessed by a single exceptional case. From the economic point of view, the livestock rearing does not result in much positive income. The remaining households do not possess livestock as they cannot bear the cost of purchasing and maintaining the cattle. But of late, the people are showing interest in rearing the livestock on commercial lines through the government aided piggery, cattle rearing schemes. But the allied activities like fisheries, horticulture and poultry are not remarkable in this village.

The following is the status of the production of main crops in village Raghna (North Tripura : Tripura). The main crop of this village is paddy. During kharif, vegetables are grown on the field bunds. Due to continuous rains and flooding in kharif, it is not feasible to grow vegetables. During rabi, because of water shortage, generally paddy is not grown and the farmers prefer to grow vegetables. Vegetables fetch good profits on account of a neighbouring town. The production figures in the kharif and rabi seasons are given in Table 3.35.

The other crops like tea, coffee, rubber, sugarcane, betel leaves and spices which are grown in some parts or other of Tripura are not seen in this village. The area under crops like wheat, beans, peas, bottle gourd, palak, mustard and banana is very less in this village.

Paddy is the principal crop of village Baishyamani Revenue Para (South Tripura : Tripura). There are three cultivation seasons, namely *Aush, Aman* and *Boro* in the State. But in the absence of irrigation facilities, most of the people in the village are able to take only one crop, i.e. Aman. Sowing is done around May-June and plantation in July. The crop is harvested around November. Some people are able to take the second crop, locally called *Boro*, as well.

Table 3.35 : The Production Figures of Kharif and Rabi

Name of the crop	*Season*	*Area (ha)*	*Annual yield (tonnes)*	*Value per hectare (in Rs.)*	*Cost of inputs (in Rs.)*	*Family labour value (Rs.)*
Paddy	Kharif	364.0	2.3	10350	7266	4255
Paddy	Rabi	32.0	2.2	9675	8401	5405
Cabbage	Rabi	16.0	12.0	36000	15000	7000
Cauliflower	Rabi	8.0	10.0	23000	12000	6500
Reddish	Rabi	12.0	7.0	17000	11500	6500
Brinjal	Rabi	8.0	20.0	20000	13000	7500
Tomato	Rabi	8.0	15.0	30000	12000	5200
Potato	Rabi	8.0	20.0	40000	23950	5405
Chillies	Rabi	4.0	10.0	15000	9000	5200
Arecanut	—	3.0	5.0	15000	4000	2000
Pineapple	—	2.0	40.0	40000	12400	4250

Most of the people in the village are not aware of the crop rotation techniques. The access to different inputs required for agriculture is difficult for most of the people in the area. Most of the people preserve a part of the produce as seed for the next crop. The lack of surplus and improper coverage of institutional credit makes it difficult for the people to go for improved quality of seeds, fertilizers, pesticides and private means of irrigation. The cooperatives have also failed miserably in this direction.

The cow yields around half to one litre of milk per day. The people use cow dung for house apart from using it as manure. The cattle feed is not available in the area. Cows generally graze in the jungle or during the post-harvest period in the fields. The nearest veterinary dispensary is around 10 km away from the village. Goats are reared for meat and not for milk. Piggery is popular among the tribals. There are not many waterbodies in the village at present otherwise fishery is a sustainable economic activity. Poultry is limited mainly due to shortage of bird's feeds and veterinary facilities in the area.

The upgradation of the quality of animals and arrangements for suitable linkages are the need of the hour, which if provided are bound to bring a substantial change in the lives of the people of the village.

In village Radhanagar (North Tripura: Tripura) more than 80 per cent of the families are engaged in cultivation. Other activities like handicrafts, trade etc. are generally done as side activities which gain prominence during the lean agricultural season. Paddy is the main crop and generally two crops are grown—*Aush* Paddy and *Aman* Paddy. But mostly land remains fallow as many farmers are engaged in growing only one crop. The attitude is stocking rice for the year through one crop after rains between June and October. People are not enterprising.

Crops are grown mostly for personal consumption and only if there is something extra after stocking for the year, it is sold in the local market.

Vegetables like potato, brinjals, chillies, cabbage etc. are grown for personal consumption as well as for selling in the local market. Generally 70 per cent is kept for personal consumption and only 30 per cent is sold in the local market. The fair price shops are very well distributed in Tripura, and meet the additional requirement of the rural areas, as far as food requirements are concerned.

The primary agriculture cooperative society extends loan for agricultural activities and out of the 48 people who filled the questionnaires, 25 families had taken loan ranging from Rs. 3,000 to Rs. 5,000 for agricultural activities. However, most of the farmers were unable to repay the loan. The percentage of repayment around was 55 per cent only.

Under the allied activities, fishery, poultry and piggery are also undertaken. But they are always in addition to cultivation. Most of the inputs are extended by the government whether it is a fishery pond or fishery bandh. Poultry and piggery inputs are either provided under the IRDP or under the tribal welfare schemes.

The cropping pattern of major crops in village Jalai (North Tripura: Tripura) is given in Table 3.36 and Table 3.37 for Kharif and Rabi season respectively.

Table 3.36 : The Cropping Pattern of Kharif Season

Sl. No.	*Kharif Crops*	*Area under cultivation (in ha)*	*Area under irrigation (in ha)*	*Source of irrigation*
1.	General crops (paddy)	180	—	Rainfed
2.	Summer vegetables	20	—	Rainfed

Table 3.37 : The Cropping Pattern of Rabi Season

Sl. No.	*Kharif Crops*	*Area under cultivation (in ha)*	*Area under irrigation (in ha)*	*Source of irrigation*
1.	Paddy (Boro)	20	—	Private Pump Set
2.	Wheat	21	—	Private Pump Set
3.	Pulses	15	—	Private Pump Set
4.	Oil seeds	10	—	Private Pump Set
5.	Winter vegetables	33	10	Private Pump Set
6.	Potato (including) TPS	15	15	Private Pump Set

The non-farm activities taken up by the villagers are quite limited. In the village, there is a unit which collects wood from the forest and makes *agarbatti* sticks out of it. The unit itself does not have the capacity to make *agarbatti* out of them by putting incense material on these sticks. Therefore, it has to supply these sticks to the industrial units of other areas. Because of the limited role of this unit, its profit margin is low. There is one brick kiln industry in middle Jalai which is providing employment opportunities to the people. However, majority of its labourers, is from outside the village.

Fishery is a good profit giving activity in the area. Fishermen catch fish from the river Manu. Different cherras flow through the village and in the fishery tanks. The market price of the fish is about Rs. 80-100 per kg. whereas the villagers are selling at Rs. 40-60 per kg. Still, there is a lot of earning in this business and the income of the people engaged in the business has improved substantially. Poultry has not developed very nicely as most of the birds are being sold in the market at the time of the need and eggs are used for family consumption. Milch animals are also very less and the yield of milk is poor. Mainly due to poor feeding and poor care, the health of the animals is not very good.

There is a huge Tea Plantation in Sonaimukhi which is providing employment to several families. The plantation has got its labourers from Bihar and it also engages the tribals of the nearby areas. But, the wage structure that is prevailing in the tea garden is very low and it is not adequate to meet the basic necessities of a family. Hence, labour work in the tea garden is not attracting people any more.

The non-farm sector is not very rewarding in the area and not many people are engaged in it.

The phenomenon of both out-migration and in-migration from village Jalai (North Tripura: Tripura) was seen. People go to work in the brick kiln area and also go to the town for work. The village itself does not have enough employment generation activities, and hence people have to migrate to other areas for employment. The people who go to the town area for employment mostly work as daily wage workers in the area and earn something like Rs. 50-60 per day. Some people also work in the brick kilns in the nearby areas. Though the kilns were not being maintained hygienically and the workers were seen to be having health problems due to working for longer duration, the wages were good and many people were interested in getting the job there. The number of people migrating outside is quite low.

People also migrate from the nearby areas and come to Jalai village to work in the brick kiln of the village and to work as tea-garden labourers in the Sonaimukhi tea estate. In fact, most of the labourers working in the tea estate had migrated from Bihar quite long time back and they have, by now, got almost settled in Jalai for their livelihood.

The total area of the village Rajibnagar (South Tripura : Tripura) is 641 standard acres out of which cultivable land is 248 acres, i.e. 38.68 per cent of the total land. The irrigation is primarily rainfed though a lift irrigation project from Manu river has been proposed. The village Rajibnagar has 50 acres of land categorized as community and Panchayat land. The net sown area is 248 acres and 17 acres of land has been left fallow. The land is very fertile and productive and has the provision of assured irrigation. Out of the total cultivable area, 98 acres, i.e. 39.51 per cent of the cultivable land is yielding two crops whereas 150 acres yield single crop. These figures imply that in general single cropping pattern is followed in cultivation.

The average landholding in the area is 1 acre that is much below the land ceiling limit and hence there was no surplus land declared in the village after the Land Ceiling Act came into force. The village is also located in the most fertile and irrigated area of the river bed where traditionally agriculture has been the mainstay of the economy.

The average rainfall in the village is about 2,000 mm each year. There are 190 acres of land under ownership cultivation and 58 acres under tenancy.

The land is highly fertile and can yield multiple crops. However, due to lack of money for fertilizers etc. most of the cultivators stick to one crop a year, which is paddy. Some of them also grow pulses and vegetables. Piggery, poultry and fishery are the other important sources of income.

Kharif Crop

It is sown in the month of April and harvested in the month of October. Since the area has high rainfall, the farmers can afford to go for crops with very high water requirement. Most common crops in kharif season are that of paddy and pulses. The normal source of irrigation is rainfall. Watertable is not a problem in the area.

Kharif crop which is widely cultivated in the village is paddy. It is sown in the month of July and is harvested in the month of September and October. Paddy cultivation has been the traditional crop of the place being close to the river bed. The district *per se* is the largest producer of rice in the State. Generally, the rice produced is the common boiled rice variety. There are also some farmers who produce Basmati rice which fetches good prices in the market though they also require heavy investments.

Rabi Crop

During the rabi season also the entire cultivable land is sown either for paddy or vegetables. Paddy is the major crop of the rabi season and it is sown in the month of October or November and is harvested in the month of April generally after the festival of Baisakhi. The average yield of wheat is nearly 1,600 quintals per hectare.

For the activities like sowing and harvesting the farmers engage labourers and they are generally paid in cash at the wage rates fixed by the Government of Tripura. None of the respondents complained of underpayment. During the off season, landless labourers go to South Tripura as daily wagers and most of them said that they got 15 to 20 days of work in a month either in the village or at the district headquarters. Most of the landless people in the village are employed as agricultural labourers and since there is a general lack of labourers their rates are on the higher side. The local labourers were given wage rate of about Rs. 75 per day, while the minimum wages were Rs. 45 per day. The wage rate actually changes with the season. From April to May and from October to December it remains high at Rs. 75 per day but during other times it remains more or less equal to the official rate.

The majority of the farmers get credit from their respective private traders in the village or nearby village called *Arhati*. Although a rural bank is available within 7 km from the village many times farmers take credit from *Arhati* because of many reasons. First of all, it is not always easy to get loan from banks as and when required. Getting loan from a bank is not an easy task for the poor and illiterate villagers and the lower staff of banks keep on harassing them.

The farmers have flexibility in getting loan from the private moneylenders. Surplus agricultural produce, i.e. paddy, is marketed in the cooperatives. Other agricultural produce like vegetables are marketed in open markets.

Rural Industries

There is no rural industry in village Radhanagar (North Tripura: Tripura). However, around 73 families are engaged in small time artisan activities like making of *Agarbatti* sticks, bamboo handicrafts, loin loom and fish net. These are all small activities and are generally consumed in the local markets of Sripur, Fatikroy or Kumarghat. But in terms of finances, they do not bring enough cash for the family. The raw material for bamboo related handicrafts are locally procured from the nearby forest area. For raw material no payment is made and it is just picked from the forest as bamboo grows wild in the forest area.

Among the OBC community, the Vishnupriya Manipuris are generally running handloom, but their production is only for local consumption or for exchange among the family members. Very few items are actually sold in the market.

In village Baishyamani Revenue Para (South Tripura : Tripura), there is no industrial activity worth mentioning, except household spinning and weaving by the tribal ladies—for domestic consumption. The looms used are traditional and of low efficiency.

The following is the status of village industries in village Raghna (North Tripura : Tripura). There are two rice mills in the village. The other cottage industries are pottery, water filter making and carpentry. The following are the details of the people engaged in the rural industry as given in Table 3.38.

Rice mills are running in profits, because the main crop of the village is paddy. Villagers consume parboiled rice. As water available

Table 3.38 : Engagement of Poeple in Rural Industry

Sl. No.	*Name of the rural industry*	*No. of people engaged*	*Main or supplementary income*
1.	Rice mill (First)	12	Main
	Rice mill (Second)	14	Main
2.	Carpentry	16	Main
	Pottery	7	Main
3.	Water filter making	6	Main

in this area has very high content of iron, one has to take filtered water only. To meet the requirements of the village and also to sell in the nearby town, one family is engaged in water filter making. Tripura water filters are in demand in other North Eastern States, as these filters are good in quality and available at very cheap rates i.e. Rs. 450 per filter of 40 litres capacity. The Ministry of Rural Development, Government of India has also recommended to other States to use Tripura filters in problematic areas. Every month, this unit is producing about 35-40 filters.

In village East Champacherra (West Tripura : Tripura) the tribals weave the tribal cloth/garments. They do not buy any of their garments but they make the same themselves. The same is the case with the present village. The weaving is done for household consumption not on commercial lines. In other parts of the West District, the non-governmental agencies are taking keen interest in giving a commercial shape to tribal weaving by giving them the yarn and receiving the final product and marketing them. The beneficiaries are given suitable prices for their work. The industrial scene needs great boost.

In Mishti Chand Noatia para in village Uttar Takmachara (South Tripura : Tripura) some non-tribals are gradually shifting to non-farm activities. One family is involved in chana-chur making and earning a hefty sum out of it. Whatever is produced is sold out without any problem.

Poverty Alleviation Programmes

IRDP

The IRDP is a failure not only in village Uttar Takmachara (South Tripura : Tripura) but also all over the State. Basically, it is a vicious circle. The bankers do not disburse full amount timely as the recovery in the past has been very low. The beneficiaries, in turn, treat whatever little amount is disbursed in part, as consumption loan.

With almost all the Blocks being cash disbursement Blocks and everybody busy in chasing targets, nothing better can be hoped out of the existing situation. The survey reveals that the selection of the beneficiaries in the village is a highly political affair. Some 'nominated member', who himself does not know, which committee's member he is, is the single most important person in selecting beneficiaries.

In view of a large percentage of population already covered under the IRDP and a sharp political polarization of the population, it is becoming very difficult now-a-days to find beneficiaries for the IRDP. All types of innovations are in practice to find the beneficiaries. One such example is the DWCRA groups. The DWCRA groups are coming up consisting of women whose husbands are defaulters. The members of these groups are, in turn, being given 'priority' in a bid to help these women to take up some income generation activities.

There is another important feature related to the IRDP beneficiaries. It was found that the families, close to the poverty line, i.e. of relatively higher income group are being selected under the programme instead of the lowest group. This tendency has set in the system, mainly because of the bankers who hope that by selecting better placed families, they have a better chance of recovery.

A sex-wise distribution of the families indicates that the female headed families get very low preference in comparison to the male headed ones. The sector-wise distribution indicates that the primary sector continues to occupy the prime position.

The practice of part disbursement is widespread. There is no consciousness regarding insurance and, in general, it is highly irregular. Asset verification is scanty and does not even serve the academic purpose.

The linkages for most of the schemes are absent in the area. Not even a single rupee has been invested from the IRDP infrastructural fund so far in the area.

In totality, the programme instead of making people independent and better off has made them defaulters and in the process has blocked their way to get other assistance being extended by the financial institutions and the Government.

The assets created under the JRY in Uttar Takmachara (South Tripura : Tripura) are in general satisfactory, in nature. It was found during the survey that one family has been provided an amount of Rs. 3,700 under the land development for the mulberry plantation.

Moreover, it was found that the assets related more to the requirements of the non-tribals and most of the time, the choice and location of the works leaves the tribals high and dry. The reasons for this are not difficult to find, as the numerically growing non-tribals have acquired an upper edge *vis-à-vis* tribals in all the spheres of life.

The EAS is in operation in village Uttar Takmachara (South Tripura : Tripura) right from the beginning when the scheme was launched. The persons willing to work have been registered and the family cards have been issued to them. The wage rate being paid is Rs. 23.65 per day.

During the survey, it was found that a huge water storage tank above the surface has been constructed in the village under the EAS. Needless to say, it is situated next to the house of the 'nominated' Pradhan and will cater mainly to the needs of the non-tribals who are pocketing most of the benefits coming to the village and have a major say in deciding what work to take up where.

There have been problems in the past regarding supply of the foodgrain part of the wage under different Employment Generation schemes.

As far as the contractor system is concerned, it is not evident in its direct form. But the 'work committee' tries its best to get its 'preference' exercised regarding the source of the procurement of materials etc. In general, the assets created have not provided adequate returns to the village *vis-à-vis* the official money spent.

In village Deoracherra (North Tripura : Tripura) normally the list of the selected beneficiaries was being kept for discussion in the Gaon Sabha meeting. But in this village as the Gaon Sabha does not exist, the nominated Panchayat members are taking the decision of selecting the beneficiaries. As there is no formal Panchayat, there is no formal meeting of the Panchayat and the Gaon Sabha. It was noticed that the members were selecting their own relatives under the IRDP. Out of 11 members of the Panchayat, 4 had taken the IRDP loan themselves. The decision of the members in the matter of selecting the beneficiaries was seen to be accepted by all. As more than 70 per cent population is belonging to ST category, the question of the violation of the stipulated percentage for the backward classes is not very relevant here. Out of the total 40 beneficiaries in 1995-96 selected for the IRDP, 33 belonged to the ST category and 2 belonged to the SC category. In 14 cases, the beneficiaries were of the General category. No family was supplied with any of the inputs required for the schemes as all the beneficiaries were given the money for the banana plantation and in 4 cases milch cow. In addition, there was no need for any material inputs being supplied by the Government. There was also no marketing support of any kind made available to the beneficiaries. Most of the beneficiaries were marketing the produce to the middlemen, as they could not carry the produce to the market themselves. It was noted that the middlemen were making profits in the process and the actual cultivator was not getting any advantage. Most of the beneficiaries were not having own land for raising the plantations, they were using the Reserve Forest land for the purpose. In many cases, the beneficiaries had sown the plantation in their backyards.

Another surprising feature was the selection of the scheme. It was seen that in all the 49 cases disbursed last year the scheme was to raise the banana plantation. In only 4 cases the beneficiary was given the additional scheme of milch cattle and in other 4 cases the pineapple plantation.

In 1996-97, all the 34 beneficiaries had taken the scheme for banana plantation only. The question of viability of having so many beneficiaries with the same scheme has not been considered at all. With no assistance for the marketing of the produce, the chances of success appear very dim. None of the beneficiaries had started earning income from the garden or repaying the loan portion of the scheme.

DWCRA

There is no DWCRA group in the village. Also the village women are not aware of any such scheme being implemented by the Government.

The women of the beneficiaries of the tea project can be given the benefit of the DWCRA scheme.

Considering the fact that all these women folk belong to the same social group, the DWCRA group formation can be more easy in this case.

The opinion of the Panchayat members was different, and they were not very convinced about the idea of the formation of any sort of self-help group. The local Anganwadi worker was also not aware of the procedure for the formation of the women's groups and hence, the much required support for such activity was seen absent in this case.

The proposal for the formation of such a group has been initiated after discussion with the Gramsevika of the area and she has started counselling the women about the importance of the formation of such a group.

Under the JRY, mostly earth-works were taken up in year 1995-96. Mandays works were taken up under the SREP scheme also.

It was seen that the roads which were constructed under the JRY were not laid properly and also not maintained subsequently. Hence, the only link to the village connects only 6 hamlets and the rest of the 4 are left out as the road is not jeepable even in the dry season.

It was seen that 15 kutcha wells were taken up. The selection of the kutcha wells could not be understood. Many of these were already out of use and had become useless. The water quality in these wells is also not good and these wells mostly go dry in the dry season. The water is dirty and muddy in the rainy season. Instead, the ring well or the sanitary well could have been done. The 5 sanitary wells in the village are providing drinking water to the people for the last 3 years. The tribals are not very receptive to the Mark II tube well, and due to non-use, most of these have become useless. Also the area being hilly and the soil strata being rocky in most of the area, Mark II tube wells cannot succeed here. Hence, the only alternative is to go for the sanitary well or the ring well.

It was seen that no activity was undertaken in the Social Forestry sector or the water harvesting structures under the JRY. The area is strongly in need of the irrigation facilities, but no such scheme was undertaken. The schemes like the construction of bund across Deoracherra, which can provide irrigation, or making graded bunds to bring the *tillas* under cultivation were not considered at all.

The mandays generated in the village, having more than 800 families scattered in 10 hamlets, was very less. In 1995-96, the total mandays generated under the various employment generation schemes were 2600. Most of the families who got the works got only 4-6 days of work in the whole year. This forces the people to go out of the village for work. As the area falls in the category of the distress pockets more emphasis should be given on generating the mandays in the area.

People's participation in the scheme was good and people wanted work in the Government schemes. But they were not getting it. The participation of the people in the selection of the works was not seen as the formal Panchayat does not exist. The villagers should be consulted in the execution of the works so that their aspirations are fulfilled. This can be achieved only by discussing the schemes in the open Gaon Sabha meetings.

The representative sample in village East Champacherra (West Tripura : Tripura) reveals that the beneficiaries in the village had taken up schemes of the IRDP like piggery, fishery, etc. These beneficiaries were given loans depending on the necessity and the scale of the project. But none of these beneficiaries was serious about the repayment of the loan. In fact some did not know even the rate of interest. The current status of the assets created under the IRDP is discouraging.

If the scheme is piggery, most of the pigs are dead after the purchase and in the case of fisheries, no yield was obtained because the area was flood affected. So, this condition left the beneficiaries in no better position and all are again back to work as agriculture labourers. Here, the insurance of the assets comes to one's mind. Out of the three only two piggery projects were insured. But the insurance was not paid.

There is absence of forward and backward linkages in the maintenance of the assets. The beneficiaries, too, do not have linkage with each other. Though institutional help was supposed to be extended it was so in only one case. In the piggery scheme, no institutional help seemed to have come out.

The consultation with the officers at the time of creating the assets was quite rigorous. But the aspect of consultation with the officials at the time of marketing did not arise because there was no yield practically to sell.

Two of these beneficiaries are beneficiaries under the JRY and EAS. This picturises the economic status of the IRDP beneficiaries. Out of the 25 households only 24 per cent are covered under the IRDP scheme.

The Jawahar Rozgar Yojana is implemented in the village of Purba Champacherra. Out of the 25 households, 15 are beneficiaries under the JRY scheme. Another five are said to be the beneficiaries of the scheme but so far they have stated that they do not have employment. The utility of the JRY scheme is doubted compared to other places outside Tripura. This village does not have any employment opportunities as it is situated in the interior *tolla* and also there is no industrial activity in and around the village. The plight of the landless workers is pathetic in the absence of such programmes.

The JRY beneficiaries are engaged in the general assets creation. In Purba Champacherra under the JRY scheme the villagers/ beneficiaries laid an approach road to the village. They have also constructed a Panchayat bhawan (office), higher secondary school building and a community centre. The water conservation works like the construction of a village tank was done by the beneficiaries of the village. No work was undertaken under the million wells scheme or the Indira Awas Yojana.

Under the Employment Assurance Scheme, all the 15 persons are given employment cards. This scheme proved to be fairly successful as all the 15 beneficiaries are getting employment definitely for five days in a month. The wage rate paid to all the 15 beneficiaries is the same. It is Rs. 23.70 per day. It is nearer the market wage rate which is around Rs. 25. This wage has two components—food wage and money wage. The division of the amount into these two is not specified. It is done according to the local demands and convenience. In Purba Champacherra, for these beneficiaries, there are two rates, one is 1 kg. rice and Rs. 17 as money wage and other one is two kg. rice and Rs. 9 as money wage. Either of the two is offered from time-to-time. But the wages are paid to these 15 beneficiaries regularly and the quality of the rice supplied is good.

The beneficiaries themselves have expressed the view that they are willing to work anywhere (with only one or two exceptional cases). Among the 25 households, around 45-50 per cent of the beneficiaries are covered under the JRY schemes. This shows the wider scope of the JRY in the village. However, the EAS which is intended to provide 100 mandays during the year to at least one person from each household failed in its objective in the village.

The report on village East Manikya Dewan (South Tripura: Tripura) comes out with the following findings on the working of the IRDP/JRY:

On paper, everything seems to be fine but in practice, the situation is different. All the five of the beneficiaries chosen randomly told that they were sanctioned a scheme with a loan component of Rs. 7,000 and a subsidy component of Rs. 6,000, i.e. with a project cost of Rs. 13,000. The beneficiaries do not even know about the actual schemes they have been sanctioned and the total money they are supposed to get.

A glance at the list of projects taken up in the JRY will reveal that some of the projects have individuals as beneficiaries. As per the Guidelines of the scheme, the objective is clearly to create community assets. But here the lands of some individuals—who might be politically suited for the Panchayat—have been chosen for development. Otherwise, the progress is very good. Beneficiaries do not complain of any under payments or over recording in the muster rolls. When asked whether they are satisfied with the working of the programme, they wanted more money to be spent on the generation of mandays, especially during the lean season. This indicates their faith in these schemes.

Under the IRDP, in village Radhanagar (North Tripura : Tripura), all the selections were made through the Gaon Panchayats. The schemes are generally selected after consultation with the beneficiary and direct cash is extended to the beneficiary, since the Government is not able to provide them good quality assets and hybrid varieties in the case of animals. However, payment is made to the beneficiary in phases and only after asset verification, the second instalment is given to him. In most cases, the financial help has been properly utilized and it has definitely brought about some improvement in the quality of the life of the beneficiary but they are unable to sustain the initial profits and more cash is required from time to time for their betterment.

In one or two cases, the loan has been completely utilized for personal consumption or for social obligations. Animals received under piggery, poultry or duckery have also been consumed by the beneficiary. However, the Government approach in this regard is quite clear from the data collected during the survey. Preference is given to the SCs and STs in all the development schemes and extensive efforts are on to alleviate them from poverty. In 1995-96, the Panchayat of Radhanagar has approved the names of 50 beneficiaries under the IRDP. They would probably be covered in 1996-97.

The quality of the assets created under the JRY in village Jalai (North Tripura : Tripura) was found to be, by and large, satisfactory. The IAY houses are being used by the beneficiary satisfactorily, the fishery ponds created by the Block under various schemes are also existing physically and being used for the production of fish etc. The drinking water sources are serviceable with some exceptions. The *rasta* cutting works are also done satisfactorily. By and large, the works done in the village through the different Block schemes are satisfactory and one draws an impression that the Government is reaching the poor. But despite all this, the following points need to be considered :

1. It was seen that the roads which were constructed under the JRY were not laid properly and also not maintained subsequently. Hence, the only connecting link to the village from the 5 hamlets is not jeepable even in the dry season.
2. It was seen that two kutcha wells were taken up. One was already out of use and had become useless. The water quality in the other well is also not good and the wells mostly go dry in the dry season and the water is dirty and muddy in the rainy season.
3. It was seen that no activity was undertaken in the Social Forestry sector or on the water harvesting structure under the JRY. The area is strongly in need of irrigation facilities, but no such scheme was undertaken. The schemes like the construction of bund across the Bhutucherra Dhatucherra, which can provide irrigation, or making the graded bunds to bring the *tillas* under cultivation were not considered at all.
4. The mandays generated in the village having more than 612 for families scattered in 5 hamlets was very less. In 1998-99, the total mandays generated under the various employment generation schemes were about 4,600. Most of the families who got the works get only 4-6 days of work in the whole year. This forces the people to go out of the village for work. As the area has a large number of people without regular employment, more emphasis should be given on generating the mandays in the area.

Bibliography

NORTH-EAST

Adiseshiah, Malcolm S. (ed.), *Planning Perspectives for the North-Eastern and Eastern Zone,* Lancer Publishers Pvt. Ltd., New Delhi, 1992.

A Study of the Land System of Meghalaya. Law Research Institute, Eastern Region, Guwahati High Court, Guwahati, 1990.

A Study of the Land System of Mizoram. Law Research Institute, Eastern Region, Guwahati High Court, Guwahati, 1990.

Bhattacharjee, J.B., *Sequences of Development in North-East India.* Omsons Publications: Guwahati, New Delhi, 1989.

Chib, S.S. *North Eastern India,* ESS ESS Publications: New Delhi, 1984.

Constantine, R. "Manipur Marches Ahead" in *Yojana* (New Delhi: 16-31 August, 1982), pp. 75-83.

Das Gupta, Malabika; Arun Kumar Gangopadhyaya; Tanmay Bhattacharya; Mahadeb Chakraborti, (eds.). *Forestry Development in North-East India,* Omsons Publications: Guwahati, New Delhi, 1986.

Datta Ray, B. *The Emergence and Role of Middle Class in North-East India,* Uppal Publishing House, New Delhi, 1983.

Deka, Dinesh. "Tripura—The Land of Romance" in *Yojana* (*op. cit.*), pp. 104-106.

Development of Horticulture, Plantations and Forests in North-Eastern Region, Agriculture Refinance and Development Corporation, Bombay, 1975.

Dutta, B.B. *Land Use Pattern in North-East India,* Gagan Publishers, Ludhiana, 1986.

Goswami, Atul (ed.). *Land Reforms and Peasant Movement: A Study of North-East India,* Omsons Publications, Guwahati, New Delhi, 1986.

Horam, M., *North-East India: A Profile,* Cosmo Publications, New Delhi, 1990.

Mahajan, V.S. (ed.). *Emerging Patterns of North-Eastern Economy,* Deep and Deep Publications, New Delhi, 1987.

Mali, D.D. and P. Deka. *Industrial Development in North-East India,* Omsons Publications, Guwahati, New Delhi, 1987.

Saikia, P.D.; U. Phukan. *Rural Development in North-East India,* B.R. Publishing Corporation, Delhi, 1989.

Samanta, R. K. *Rural Development in North-East India: Perspectives, Issues and Experiences,* Uppal Publishing House, New Delhi, 1991.

Shukla, S.P. and A. K. Agarwal. *Agriculture in North-Eastern Region,* National Publishing House, New Delhi, 1986.

Singh, J.P. *Human Resources of North-Eastern India,* Inter-India Publications, New Delhi, 1982.

Thakur, Pankaj. *Profile of a Development Strategy for India's North-East,* Span Publications Pvt. Ltd., 1998.

Yogi, Anand Kumar. *Development of North-East Region: Problems and Prospects,* Spectrum Publications, Guwahati, Delhi, 1991.

MANIPUR

A Study of the Land System of Manipur, Law Research Institute, Eastern Region, Gauhati High Court, Guwahati, 1985.

Brown, R., *Statistical Account of the Native State of Manipur,* Sanskaran Prakashak, Delhi, 1975.

Chaki-Sircar, Manjusri, *Feminism in a Traditional Society: Women of the Manipur Valley,* Shakti Books/Vikas Publishing House, New Delhi, 1984.

Chakravartti, Rama. *People of Manipur: Anthropogenetic Study of Four Manipur Groups,* B.R. Publishing Corporation, Delhi, 1986.

Constantine, R. *Manipur: Maid of the Mountains,* Lancers Publishers, New Delhi, 1981.

Das, Rajat Kanti. *Tribal Social Structure,* Inter-India Publications, New Delhi, 1988.

Dena, Lal. *British Policy Towards Manipur: 1891-1919* (Publishers not mentioned), 1984.

Dev, Bimal J. and Lahiri, Dilip K. *Manipur: Culture and Politics,* Mittal Publications, Delhi, 1987.

Dun, Captain E.W. *Gazetteer of Manipur,* Vivek Publishing Company, Delhi, 1981.

Economic Review 1981-82, Directorate of Economics and Statistics, Government of Manipur, Imphal.

Gangte, T.S. *The Kukis of Manipur: A Historical Analysis,* Gyan Publishing House, New Delhi, 1993.

Ghosh, G.K. *Tribals and their Culture in Manipur and Nagaland,* Vol. 3, Ashish Publishing House, New Delhi, 1992.

Goswami, Atul. *Land Reforms and Peasant Movement,* Omsons Publications, New Delhi, 1986.

Gougin, T. *History of Zomi,* Published by the Author, 1986.

Gougin, T. *Discovery of Zoland,* Published by the Author, 1980.

Government of Manipur Revised Tribal Sub Plan: 1986-87, Department for Development of Tribals and Backward Classes, Manipur.

Government of Manipur Draft Special Component Plan for Scheduled Castes 1990-91, Department for Development of Tribals and Backward Classes, Manipur.

Grimwood, Ethel St. Clair. *My Three Years in Manipur,* Vivek Publishing House: Delhi, 1975.

Hodson, T.C. *The Meiteis,* B.R. Publishing Corporation, Delhi, 1975.

Hodson, T.C. *The Naga Tribes of Manipur,* Low Price Publications, Delhi-52, 1989.

Johnstone, Sir James. *Manipur and the Naga Hills,* Vivek Publishing House, Delhi, 1971.

Kabui, Gangmumei. *Anal: A Transborder Tribe of Manipur,* Mittal Publications, Delhi, 1985.

Kirti Singh, M. *Religion and Culture of Manipur,* Manas Publications: Delhi, 1988.

Mahajan, V.S. *Emerging Pattern of North-Eastern Economy,* Deep and Deep Publications, New Delhi, 1987.

Meitei Villages: Imphal, East Block, Manipur Rural Development Plan, Research and Development Unit: Association of Voluntary Agencies for Rural Development, New Delhi, 1976.

Panchani, Chander Sheikher. *Manipur: Religion, Culture and Society,* Konark Publishers Pvt. Ltd., 1987.

Pandey, S.N. (ed.). *Sources of the History of Manipur and the Adjoining Areas,* National Publishing House, New Delhi, 1985.

Roy Burman, B.K. *Towards Poverty Alleviation Programmes in Nagaland and Manipur,* Mittal Publications, Delhi, 1984.

Roy, Nilima. *Art of Manipur,* Agam Kala Prakashan, Delhi, 1979.

Sanajaoba, Naorem (ed.). *Manipur: Past and Present: The Heritage and Ordeals of a Civilization,* Vol. 1, Mittal Publications: Delhi, 1988.

Seventh Five Year Plan 1985-90 and Annual Plan 1985-86, Manipur.

Singh, K.M. *History of Christian Missions in Manipur and Other Neighbouring States,* Mittal Publications, New Delhi, 1991.

Singh, K.M., Hijab Irabot Singh. *Political Movement in Manipur,* B.R. Publishing Corporation, Delhi, 1989.

Singh, Ravindra Pratap. *Electoral Politics in Manipur: A Spatio-Temporal Study,* Concept Publishing Company, New Delhi, 1981.

Singh, Lairenmayum, Iboongohal, *Introduction to Manipur,* Published by S. Ibochaoba Singh, Imphal, 1987.

Singh, N. Tombi. *Manipour—A Study,* Publishers not mentioned, 1972.

Soppitt, C.A. *A Short Account of the Kuki-Lushai Tribes on the North-East Frontier.* Firma K.L.M. Ltd. on behalf of Tribal Research Institute, Aizawl, 1976.

Thakur, Pankaj (ed.). *Profile of a Development Strategy for India's North-East,* Span Publications Pvt. Ltd., Guwahati, 1988.

Techno-Economic Survey of Manipur: Economic Report (Report of the National Council of Applied Economic Research), Manipur Administration, Imphal, 1961.

TRIPURA

Adhikari, O.S., *The Problem of Indebtedness among the Tribals in Sadar Sub-division of Tripura,* Directorate of Research, Department of Welfare for Scheduled Tribes and Scheduled Castes, Government of Tripura, Agartala, 1982.

A Guide for the Entrepreneurs, Directorate of Industries, Government of Tripura, Agartala, May 1989.

A Study of the Land System of Tripura, Law Research Institute, Eastern Region, Guwahati High Court, Guwahati, 1990.

Barman, Debapriya Deb. *Treatise on Traditional Social Institutions of the Tripuri Community,* Directorate of Research, Development, Department of Welfare for Scheduled Tribes and Scheduled Castes, Government of Tripura, 1983.

Bhattacharya, A.C. *Progressive Tripura,* Inter-India Publications, New Delhi, 1985.

Bhattacharya, Gayatri. *Refugee Rehabilitation and its Impact on Tripura's Economy,* Omsons Publications, New Delhi, Guwahati, 1988.

Bhattacharjee, Pradip Nath. *The Jamatiyas of Tripura,* Department of Welfare for Scheduled Tribes and Scheduled Castes, Government of Tripura, 1983.

Bhattacharjee, Pradip Nath. *Lokabritter Aloke Koloi Sampraday,* Directorate of Research, Department of Welfare for Scheduled Tribes and Scheduled Castes, Government of Tripura, 1983.

Bhattacharya, Banikantha, *Tripura Administration: The Era of Modernization (1870-1972)*, Mittal Publications, Delhi, 1986.

Biswas, A.B.; A. K. Saha; S.P. Das Gupta and C. Chakravarti, *State of Environment in Tripura,* Prepared by the Centre for Study of

Man and Environment, Presidency College, Calcutta for the Department of Science, Technology and Environment, Government of Tripura, Agartala, 1989.

Chakravarti, Mahadev (ed.). *Administration Report of Tripura State Since 1902,* Vol. 1-4, Gyan Publishing House, New Delhi, 1994.

Chatterjee, S.N. *Tripura: A Profile,* Inter-India Publications, New Delhi, 1984.

Chaudhuri, Saroj and Bikash Chaudhuri. *Glimpses of Tripura,* Tripura Darpan Prakashani : Agartala, 1983.

Chib, Sukhdev Singh, *This Beautiful India: Tripura*, ESS ESS Publications, New Delhi, 1988.

Deb, D.B. *The Flora of Tripura State*, Vol. II, Today and Tomorrow's Printers and Publishers, New Delhi, 1983.

Devvarman, S.B.K. *The Tribes of Tripura, A Dissertation,* Directorate of Research, Government of Tripura, Agartala, 1986.

Dutta, Dr. Jyotish Chandra. *An Introduction to the History of Tripura,* Book Home: Calcutta, 1984.

Gan-Chaudhuri, Jagadis. *A Political History of Tripura,* Inter-India Publications, New Delhi, 1985.

Gan-Chaudhuri, Jagadis. *An Anthology of Tripura,* Inter-India, Publications, New Delhi, 1985.

Gan-Chaudhuri, Jagadis. *Tripura: The Land and Its People,* Leeladevi Publications, Delhi, 1980.

Gan-Chaudhuri, Jagadis. *The Corpus of Tripura,* Inter-India Publications, New Delhi, 1990.

Gan-Chaudhuri, Jagadis. *The Riangs of Tripura,* Directorate of Research, Department of Welfare for Scheduled Tribes and Scheduled Castes, Government of Tripura, 1983.

Ganguli, J.B. *The Benign Hills: A Study in Tripura's Population Growth and Problems,* Tripura Darpan Prakashani, Agartala, 1983.

Ghosh, Kamalini. *Tribal Insurrection in Tripura: A Study in Relative Deprivation,* Booklinks Corporation, Hyderabad, 1984.

Menon, K.D. *Tripura District Gazetteers: Tripura,* Department of Education, Government of Tripura, Agartala, 1975.

Roychoudhury, Nalini Ranjan, *Tripura through the Ages,* Sterling Publishers Private Ltd., New Delhi, 1983.

Saigal, Omesh. *Tripura: Its History and Culture,* Concept Publishing Company, Delhi, 1978.

Singh, Ram Gopal. *The Kukis of Tripura: A Socio-Economic Survey,* Directorate of Research, Department of Welfare for Scheduled Tribes and Scheduled Castes, Government of Tripura, Year of publication not given.

Socio-Economic Survey of the Cobbler Communities of Agartala Municipality and its Adjacent Areas, Directorate of Research, Department of Welfare for Scheduled Tribes and Scheduled Castes, Government of Tripura, Agartala, 1980.

Strength of Achievement, Motivation and Personality of Two Cultural Groups in Tripura, Directorate of Research, Department of Welfare for Scheduled Tribes and Scheduled Castes, Government of Tripura, Agartala, 1982.

Thakurta, S.N. Guha. *Contract Labour in Construction Industry,* Firma KLM Pvt. Ltd., Calcutta, 1980.

The Kaipengs, Directorate of Research, Department of Welfare for Scheduled Tribes and Scheduled Castes, Government of Tripura, Agartala, 1980.

Varman, S.B.K. Dev, *A Study over the Jhum and Jhumia Rehabilitation in the Union Territory of Tripura,* Directorate of Research, Department of Welfare for Scheduled Tribes and Scheduled Castes, Government of Tripura, Agartala, 1971.

Index